NATURE AND HISTORICAL EXPERIENCE

NATURE AND HISTORICAL EXPERIENCE

Essays in Naturalism
and in
The Theory of History

JOHN HERMAN RANDALL, Jr.

FREDERICK J. E. WOODBRIDGE PROFESSOR OF PHILOSOPHY
COLUMBIA UNIVERSITY

COLUMBIA UNIVERSITY PRESS, NEW YORK

First printing 1958
Second printing 1959

PUBLISHED IN GREAT BRITAIN, CANADA, INDIA, AND PAKISTAN
BY THE OXFORD UNIVERSITY PRESS
LONDON, TORONTO, BOMBAY, AND KARACHI

LIBRARY OF CONGRESS CATALOG CARD NUMBER: 57-11694

MANUFACTURED IN THE UNITED STATES OF AMERICA

To

JAMES GUTMANN

Selig, wer sich vor der Welt
Ohne Hass verschliesst,
Einen Freund am Busen hält
Und mit dem geniesst,

Was, von Menschen nicht gewusst
Oder nicht bedacht,
Durch das Labyrinth der Brust
Wandelt in der Nacht.

FOREWORD

THIS VOLUME owes its existence to the suggestion and the persuasive insistence of my friend and colleague Justus Buchler, who urged me to collect various papers, printed and unprinted, written during the past twenty years. It was originally intended to include in a preliminary section on "Studies in the History of Ideas" six essays in intellectual history now scattered in various periodicals and books.

When the material was brought together, however, the unpublished papers dealing with "the theory of history" and "the theory of nature" bulked large enough to form a volume in themselves. To Professor Buchler's long editorial experience and judgment it seemed wiser to confine the book to these philosophical analyses not elsewhere accessible. Other colleagues consulted strongly advised the same course. Hence the volume appears without those historical studies, but with the essays in philosophic analysis of two themes that have for some years been central in my own interests.

Each of the two Parts deals with a unified theme, and the two together not only exhibit, it is hoped, a consistent philosophic attitude and approach, but also treat two different aspects of what is a common metaphysical inquiry. Aside from the prologue and the epilogue, none of these papers has appeared in this form before. Three of them embody some passages from articles previously published. But these, together with the unprinted papers, have been completely rewritten for the present volume.

The two Parts are offered tentatively: they are still definitely "work in progress." Should they be so fortunate as to meet with criticism and suggestions, it is hoped they may eventually bear fruit in a more systematic treatment. History and nature together offer the great challenge to the philosophic mind.

To Justus Buchler, from whom I have long derived so much philosophic inspiration, as well as repeated practical assistance, I owe one more debt which I can never hope to repay.

J. H. R., Jr.

Peacham, Vermont
September, 1957

CONTENTS

PROLOGUE

Historical Naturalism

I REMEMBER, as a college student, being asked by a friend the not unusual question, what did I intend to do? I can still recall the mood in which I realized I could not answer. Such a question had never seriously occurred to me. "Why," I replied, "I really do not know. But I think I do know clearly some of the things that must be done." This incident might be taken as a symbol of many things. It might be taken as the text of a discourse on the passing, for many of my generation, of the desire for romantic self-expression, and its replacement by the impersonality of participation in necessary work. It might be made the occasion for pointing out the compulsion in human affairs of the problems that are set before men and must be solved, whether they will or no. It is God who proposes, and though man disposes, he disposes with the tools God puts in his hands. This is true even if we prefer to view God somewhat narrowly as the forces of production. The incident might easily be pushed to a pragmatic insistence on the necessity of working in a concrete situation with the materials that are available, and to an end appropriate to that situation. Given a personal reference, it might well serve to illuminate the manifest shortcomings and blind spots of both the pragmatic temper and the person. Or it could be made to point to the determining character of subject-matter, forcing its facts, its structure, and its implications upon the mind in utter disregard of the preferences of the imagination.

All of these things that reply suggests. Surely they may be united

---

Originally published in *American Philosophy Today and Tomorrow,* ed. Horace M. Kallen and Sidney Hook (New York, 1935), pp. 411–32. Reprinted by permission of the Macaulay Company.

in a single mind, as they are obviously entangled in the same network of idea. And as such they would reflect the several teachings to which that mind had been exposed, at the hands of those who all unwitting played the part of instruments of God in its education. My teachers are no longer among the living. It would therefore be unfair to charge them with a more particular responsibility than they must assume through the mere fact of having been my teachers. What I have learned from them is presumably not what they intended to teach. Doubtless John Dewey did not set out to impress me with the overwhelming importance of tradition; nor did Felix Adler try to convince me, against all my natural intellectual sympathies, of the significance and perhaps necessity of that type of faith of which Communism is today the cardinal example. That such was the outcome, amongst many other things, of their teaching, is due, I think, to the fact that, being great teachers, they made me see the world, in spite of myself, perhaps in spite of themselves. The man who most consciously tried to show me what is inescapably there, F. J. E. Woodbridge, I can not speak of as a teacher. I can only attempt to illustrate his teaching. In the face of what he showed me, I forget the showing, although I realize that without him to show, I should not have seen. That I may not see just what he saw is of no consequence. To him is due the fact that I can see at all.

I must renounce, however, the pleasant task of pursuing further the education that is owed to teachers. Instead, I wish to return to that early symbolic reply. "To know what must be done"—there is a whole philosophy and a method implicit in the phrase. Many of the things that when I first used it I thought I knew clearly, I have since come to doubt; and much that I see now was then undreamed of. And yet I should like to think that what I have learned and unlearned I have come upon because of adherence to that philosophy and that method. For to know what our world presents, and to know that it presents not only the possibility of thought and action, but also a possibility of thought and action in very definite and limited channels which yet demands to be realized, still seems a fundamental wisdom. Our world may not achieve its natural end, but if it does, it will be only because men have studied the ends implicit in it, and have discovered the means to bring them to pass. If this sounds a little like Aristotle, and Marx, and Dewey, it is because it is intended to comprehend them all, and because they all saw the world. They all realized—at least that is what they have told me—that we must begin with what we find, and that we must find what is there in our world, not what we might wish were there. And what we are, what we can do, what must be done, and how we can do it, are all things that are there to be found. What is not already there is whether we shall do what must be done. That depends upon the finding, upon whether we know.

We must begin with what we find. And what we find, unless our eyes are closed, is an entire culture in course of fundamental change. In that culture are many revolutionaries working for revolutions they hope will come. It would be surprising did we not find such men. But more significant than the revolution that is to come is the revolution that is now taking place, and that has for some time been in progress. For that revolution is a fact, and it must be accepted as a fact. It is not something to be fought for or against, it is something to be respected and understood. It is not a revolution that men have worked for or now intend; it is a revolution that men have brought about in working for other things—the discovery of truth, the control of nature, the making of what men want, the achievement of power through the possession of money. That in pursuing these ends men have created a new heaven and a new earth is perhaps surprising; that the creation should have destroyed the old heaven and the old earth should occasion no wonder. Yet what is least surprising has caused the most surprise, and the incidental destruction has been harder to bear than the incidental creation. Men have been more concerned to defend what they have destroyed than to understand what they have created. Yet the destruction is irrevocable, while the creation is an opportunity. It is an opportunity for further creation. To God it is given to pronounce the results of his labors good, and to rest upon the seventh day, but not to man. Man is doomed to unremitting toil, and it is not human to create such good as will not demand further creation.

The fact of what man has brought about, and must bring about, need not, of course, be understood. Our culture will not cease to change because we fail to understand that change. It is not even certain that understanding would alter the main outlines of its course.

What men have done sets inescapable limits upon what they can do. But men who understood would be different, and within those limits they would act differently. A revolution understood is a revolution with less wastage, a more efficient and a speedier revolution. It is a revolution in which men can make the most of the possibilities resident in what they have created, instead of leaving that realization to chance.

The acceptance of this fundamental fact of revolution in our world implies, for a philosophy resolved to know what must be done, that cultural change must be taken as a basic subject-matter. If we are to hope to understand what we find in our world, and its possibilities of thought and action, we must understand a culture in process of changing into another culture. No philosophy which leaves that fact unintelligible, whatever the illuminating insights it may develop, can be for us an adequate philosophy: it will not tell us what must be done. That this involves relegating many philosophies of today, and many philosophic activities that have awakened wide interest—like a concern with mathematical logic—to a subordinate and subsidiary position, is obvious. It is accepted with full awareness of what it involves. Such concerns are facts in our changing culture; but they are facts to be understood, not instruments of understanding. Understanding must be in terms of the problems set by cultural change itself. How is such change to be understood? What is its general pattern and method? How is our particular changing culture to be grasped? What is the stock of ideas and values and institutions we have inherited, at once the material on which we must work and the tools we must use? What are the new conditions, intellectual and practical, we have created for ourselves, within which lie our opportunities for work? What must be done? Such questions are not so much questions we ask of our world, as questions our world asks of us.

To answer them, it is obvious we must inquire into our world in its temporal dimensions: we must understand our past, the past that made us what we are and still constitutes us, the past that is an essential part of our present world. Our culture that is changing is itself the precipitate of a long series of changes; and these our materials and our tools can only be understood in terms of the past changes that forced men to create them. To know what our ideas meant at their birth enables us to understand better what they have become; it helps us both to use them and, perchance, to free ourselves from them. And to realize the many episodes of change that have given us our culture aids us to know what must be done in the episode that is robbing us of it; it throws into relief the permanent elements of change.

In some such way it would be easy to show how inquiry into our present world leads us inevitably into our past. But the logic of circumstance is stronger than the logic of subject-matter; and a series of happy accidents, necessitating some acquaintance with the history of ideas, was the personal introduction to the understanding of the past. They were accidents because they forced the development of a philosophy of social change as the lesson of the whole sweep of Western culture, rather than of its present crisis; but they were happy, in that to the present they brought a knowledge which the present demands. It was another happy and prior accident that made possible an approach to the past at once detached and sympathetic, and quite without emotional bias. Fate had provided a father valiant enough to win liberation from tradition, yet wise enough to learn from it, a father able both to teach and to illustrate freedom from the tyranny of attachment and the tyranny of emancipation alike. His example made honest inquiry seem more natural than defense or rebellion.

And so the philosophy of social change was developed because circumstance dictated that what must be achieved was an understanding of a whole series of changes rather than a single one—the series that is both the intellectual record of the making of our civilization, and the basic substance of that civilization itself. It was developed out of the study of the history of ideas. Doubtless this fact both colors and limits the philosophy. Though it hardly tempts one to minimize the importance of economic forces, it does make one realize that ideas as well as economic forces are continuing to have a history, and that it is an entire culture, not merely an economic system, that is in process of change.

Yet what the history of ideas has to teach about cultural change is no less important than what it leaves unsaid. It teaches men to look upon history as the continual readaptation of materials in the light of changing needs and problems—as a human achievement, within the narrow limits set by what is inescapably there, like everything human, but nonetheless a construction the architects of which are men. The materials they shall employ, the needs and purposes for which they shall build, are beyond their control; but the structures they erect are original, and endure beyond their builders. Sometimes, like Greek thought, they last as impressive ruins, to be looted by those who stumble upon them. Sometimes, like much of the medieval world and more of the world of the eighteenth-century revolutionaries, they last as prisons, from which men struggle long to free themselves, and even in collapse their stones are obstacles. More normally in our Western tradition they have been the familiar homes from which pioneers went out to find new treasure, and to which they built additions as their wealth increased. The edifices of medieval thought have been rebuilt time and again, but their main outlines are still discernible today. We are still in a significant sense Augustinians or Aristotelians.

There is thus a genuine continuity in the materials of which a culture is built, which go on piling themselves up; there is an ever-new grappling with the unforeseen ideas and conditions which have emerged because of what men have done. It is these conflicts between traditional beliefs and novel experience which drive men to construct philosophies, to fit opposing or irrelevant ideas together into some not too chaotic scheme, to adjust warring values so as to give some direction to life without excluding too much. Somehow the novel idea or condition has to be seized and worked into the accustomed pattern of living and thinking; but ideas, like conditions, have a structure and implications of their own, and when the readjustment has been made men find they have created a new pattern.

The history of ideas thus points both to a cumulative continuity in the materials of thought, in the distinctions and concepts to be used, and to a bewildering variety in its problems, in the adjustments to change that must be made. The problems which give rise to philosophies emerge when the strife of ideas and experiences forces men back to basic assumptions in any field. They have varied from age to age, and are to be understood only as expressions of fundamental conflicts within a culture, leading men on to thoroughgoing criticism. Yet the great philosophies, though they start as the battle-cries of warriors or peacemakers in the strife, have been able to raise themselves above the battle to a comprehensive vision of life. And though they speak in differing languages, they seem, to an attentive ear, to be speaking of the same universal pattern of experience. And this recurrent pattern is due not only to the fact that they once spoke a common tongue, which was Greek; not only to the fact that amidst much that is colloquial and in the latest fashion they have preserved the archaisms that point to a common source; it is due to the fact that Greeks and moderns alike have beheld the same world, and each in his own dialect is expressing the same permanences of man's experience of that world. The enemy and the fight are ever new; but fighting is not, nor are the weapons by which men can conquer.

It is well to attempt to digest this lesson before going on. The problems of one age are irrelevant to those of another. But the fact that problems must be faced does not vary. And the facing of problems illustrates a recurrent pattern. The persistence of tradition, the impingement of fresh experience, intellectual and social, upon that tradition, generating new ideas which conflict with it and yet must be understood in its terms, for there are no others—so long as our culture persists in changing, it must face such cycles. That old and new will find eager partisans to give intellectual expression to the conflict, is inevitable; just as it is inevitable that peacemakers will finally effect a settlement in which will lie the germs of new wars. For the record reveals that it is the peacemakers, those who consciously strive to blend old and new in a novel pattern, who are the creators of that which, added as a permanent deposit, is the starting-point of further change. It is the peacemakers, the adjusters, Thomas, Spinoza, Leibniz, Kant, Hegel, Marx—whose ideas make further history.

This fact has an import both practical and intellectual. It makes clear what in a changing culture must be done, though it does not dictate what we shall do. We may, if we will, bound by sentimental ties to what is old and familiar, regard the new world, so terrifying and alien, with suspicion, distrust, and fear. It is well to be critical as we mark the more than dubious value of much that is taking the place of goods once so sure. We may set our faces like adamant against what is coming, we may seek refuge in another realm, we may give way to disillusionment and despair. Or we may be so intoxicated by the promise of the new that, forgetful of the achievements of the past, we shall throw ourselves wholly into the passionate struggle for its realization. It is well to prepare ourselves for the fight that is to come, and perhaps it is well to buttress our new faith with a sophisticated and dogmatic defense, and take up the powerful weapons of intolerant zeal and emotional conviction. We may try to throw overboard blindly what need not and cannot perish, and what we shall later have to bring back again, or we may contend that with our new instruments we are for the first time able to achieve all that the old world cared for.

All these things we may do, for all these things men have done again and again. But this is not what must be done. What must be done is to face resolutely both the old world and the new, and to attempt once more the age-old task of adjustment and reconstruction: to accept the materials offered by both past and present, and out of them build still another edifice. Those materials, taken together, dictate both limitations and opportunities. Much that we cherish will of necessity be excluded, and so will much that we hope for. But to incorporate the values of the past that criticism reveals as permanent with the novel values made possible by what we are creating, is the task that must be performed. And those who do not in some fashion work upon it will not be counted among the builders of the world that is to come.

The practical import need not be pursued at this point. Let us rather allow the history of ideas to tell us of the intellectual method by which such reconstruction can be effected. It points to the inescapable persistence of that slowly mounting body of intellectual techniques and values in terms of which novel ideas must be understood and judged. We must understand what is new in terms of the ideas we already have; we have no others. We can learn from experience only if we have already learned from experience. This may be a paradox, but it is also a fact. It indicates that the concepts by which we make experience intelligible, the ultimate intellectual values we seek, the standards by which we verify, are themselves the deposit left by a long experience with the world. It is to the test of this embodied experience that we bring the fresh experience we are seeking to understand. In the testing the tests are themselves tested, and a new deposit is left. What we have learned teaches us how to ask questions, and in the asking we learn how to ask better. Without tradition, without the past, there could be no experiment, no learning from experience; without experiment, without a never-ending asking questions of the world, there could be no past, nothing but a passing present.

This fruitful and necessary interaction of tradition and experiment, of reason and experience, we have built up rather consciously into an effective intellectual tool. We call it scientific method, and the history of natural science is a cardinal illustration of the technique of cultural change, of the use of the rational lessons of clarified experience to clarify and learn from new experience. Science is at once traditional, cumulative, and rational, and critical, original, and experimental; and its method is a continued criticism of experience by reason and reason by experience. But operating at a deeper level of this same interaction than our natural science is the philosophical tradition out of which it grew and in terms of which it is itself understood and criticised. That tradition has its own carefully built-up standards of testing and criticism, and its own appeal to human experience as the setting of all man's knowledge and values. When scientific tests have left too much unexplained, when they have failed to make intelligible too large an area of experience, it has recalled them to a confrontation of experience again, and from that encounter they have emerged deepened and enlarged. It has reminded them of that universal pattern of what is, those fundamental concepts and distinctions, which, whatever the language of a particular thinker or a particular tradition, seem forced on the mind by a common world and somehow expressed; and from that rational analysis they have emerged clarified and rendered intelligible. This basic criticism of science, like science itself, is a never-ending process, a process in which an intelligible pattern of ideas and fresh contact with the world are made jointly to illuminate our knowledge of that world and its possibilities.

The appeal to experience, like the appeal to reason, on whatever level it is made, is a moment in a process of criticism. This solid fact has implications. It implies that knowledge is extended and enlarged, and its concepts and methods clarified, not through experience alone nor yet through reason, but when experience and ideas are made to confront each other. It implies that the appeal to experience, so often taken to be either the beginning or the ending of inquiry, is in fact no start and no conclusion, but an intermediate stage in a ceaseless process. It implies that philosophies of experience which start with experience as a subject-matter are in fact starting with certain ideas of experience, and that those which end with experience as a conclusion are in fact ending with a certain experience of ideas. And a whole range of philosophies, including most of those called empirical, stand condemned as inadequate, unenlightened, and blind. We must start with tradition, and we must end with tradition criticised, clarified, and enlarged.

On the level of philosophic criticism, therefore, we are forced back on the classic tradition of European thought, on that basic pattern of ideas which has persisted throughout the long search for intelligibility. The classic tradition means Greek thought, and Greek thought means Aristotle—not an Aristotle to be opposed to Plato, but the Aristotle who expressed in words that confrontation of idea and fact which Plato makes us see dramatically. There, with a clarity from which the accidents of circumstance have dropped away, and with a singular freedom from problems of adjustment and partisan loyalty, we can find the structure of the world and man's experience of it rendered in intelligible language. It is the language to which, after many a long wandering in a far country, present philosophical thought seems to be returning. It is the language in which alone, whatever the dialect, the presence of man as an intelligent and valuing being in a world that is intelligible and valuable, of human life as a natural expression of a nature that sustains and responds to its interests, can be understood. Whatever their starting-point in particular intellectual struggles —and they have been many—whatever the presuppositions that circumstance has forced upon men, those who have been honest enough to follow out the structure of the world in the light of a comprehensive view of human experience have ended by speaking in terms that can be translated into that language. It is a language that can express every human experience, knowing and acting, art and religion—a language in which we can talk equally of man and the world and God.

This is not to say that the long odyssey of modern philosophy, from which we are today returning with many a wound and many a deep scar to the naturalism of Greek thought, has been in vain. Although without what Plato and Aristotle first said, all words would be meaningless, they did not say the final word. Emerging as they did from a single culture, they could not reflect on the conflict of cultures; creating a single science, they could not see one science leading to another. And neither the limitations nor the power of the classic tradition they created can be fully appreciated until it is seen from the perspective of all that we have since experienced and learned. Without the flesh and blood of that living experience, the classic tradition remains a rigid skeleton, sterile and dead. That struggle of two conflicting types of knowledge for man's allegiance, which became the basic intellectual issue in modern thought, in terms of which all other practical issues of adjustment have been expressed, has had many consequences. The conflict of a moral and religious tradition with new scientific concepts and techniques, of knowledge of the ends of action in morals, art, and religion, with knowledge of the structure of nature in natural science, has many sins to answer for. From the coming of Aristotelian science in the twelfth century to compete with the Augustinian tradition of Christianity, until the present-day acceptance of an enlarged and deepened scientific method as the one type of knowledge, it has dug a gulf between man and the world. It has led to philosophies which at their worst denied the reality of human life, and at their best left it irrelevant, supernatural, and unintelligible. But it did at least force men to confront the classic tradition with experience, to see it as functioning in an entire culture in rapid transition. And out of that renewed confrontation has come an Aristotelianism, extended and deepened, more Aristotelian than that of Aristotle himself. No, this critical enterprise of the last hundred years has borne its own fruits.

The classic tradition insisted that the world is by nature intelligible and valuable, and that thinking and valuing are in themselves natural events. Intoxicated, however, with the discovery of the intelligibility and value of the world, it read the universe not only in terms of its own particular schemes of understanding and living, which was natural enough, and easily corrected by further experience; it read it in those purely intellectual and structural terms which are the proper objects of knowledge, and failed to take seriously its own insistence that knowledge is but one among many human activities. So long as knowledge, as with Aristotle, was so framed as to make human life intelligible, this selective emphasis was perhaps no serious danger; but with the development of a much narrower if more potent intellectual method in the seventeenth century, the exclusion became important: what could not be so known was not real. Beginning with Kant and his successors, the critical appeal to a wider experience of the world in which man lives taught first that intelligibility must be sought, not merely in one but in all the activities of human life, and then that the very search for intelligibility itself has a natural setting. Not only are poetry, self-sacrifice, and religious adoration facts to be understood; nature lends herself to lyrical expression, to moral devotion, and to idealizing worship as well as to understanding, and all these activities of men have definite implications for the character of the nature that sustains them. Even more: ignorance, error, and the achievement of partial interpretations are as insistent facts as truth; and all these salient traits of human thinking are to be understood only when intelligence and beliefs are seen in their biological setting in the behavior of living beings adjusting themselves to their environment and manipulating its materials, and in their social setting functioning in specific ways in a cultural whole. Thus out of this confrontation of knowledge with experience has come not only the means of judging the success of particular schemes of knowing, in the light of the function they were developed to perform; there has come also an appreciation of the role of knowing itself in human culture.

The present return to an enlarged and deepened Aristotelianism—or empirical naturalism, in the jargon of the day—is thus the fruit of a process of criticism which, beginning in the attempt to put mechanical science in its setting in human experience, has ended by pointing to the setting of all science and all knowing, of the classic tradition itself, in the manifold activities of man's group life. And thus through the discovery of the broader biological and social context within which the search for intelligibility finds its place, that tradition has been rendered flexible enough to deal with those problems of changing cultures and shifting schemes of science which were originally outside its scope. In partial independence of this philosophic self-criticism, natural science, whose limitations a century ago made it impossible to bring under the operation of one intellectual method the physical analysis and the non-mechanical pursuits of men, has gradually extended its scope to embrace human life in biology and human activities in the social sciences, at the same time reconstructing its concepts and method to deal with all the higher activities of mankind. Today we possess at last a science that, insisting on the reality and importance of all man's experiences and enterprises, has the concepts through which it hopes to make them intelligible, and a philosophy that can embrace in one natural world, accessible to thought in all its parts and amenable to the operation of intelligence in all its processes, all the realities to which human experience points: symphonies as well as atoms, personality as well as reflex action, religious consecration as well as the laws of motion.

That thought and intelligence have as yet hardly made the most of their new opportunities, is a fact so obvious as to need no belaboring. That our modern naturalistic philosophies are as yet programs rather than achievements is equally patent. Yet it is also a fact with which we must begin, that they have set the general framework within which hard thinking and patient investigation may proceed. Not only has there passed the characteristic problem of nineteenth-century philosophizing, born of its cultural conflicts: how can man and man's interests and values be given a cosmic significance in the face of a science undermining the traditional theological guarantee of their central place in the universe? This problem's passing has carried with it the solutions as well, the philosophic idealisms which placed them outside a so-called "realm of science," the evolutionary philosophies which found a new substitute religious faith within that realm, and the negative answers of nineteenth-century mechanism and materialism. There has passed also that central "problem of knowledge" which persisted in modern thought so long as two different types of knowing were in conflict. Today it is no longer necessary to defend one type of knowledge against another, nor to justify any of the enterprises of the life of reason. Such enterprises have now achieved an assured and recognized status; they are once more an integral and natural part of the universe. And liberated from these traditional problems, thought can go on to explore the possibilities of human life and culture in the world it finds, to discover what must be done and how to do it, in religion, art, science, and social reconstruction. The difficulties are stupendous; but they are such as intelligence may hope to solve, not the dialectical products of contradictory assumptions, insoluble by definition.

If the world of thought we find offers once more a comprehensive nature with room for everything experience discloses, from electrons to God, and if it presents the instrument of scientific method as the tool for investigating their status, tracing their relations, and criticising their value, what then is to be done? Intellectually, the answer seems clear: we must develop a philosophy of nature adequate to human experience, and a philosophy of scientific method adequate to the task before it. Since we are today in the midst of the most fundamental revolution in physical science since the seventeenth century, there is much present concern with the philosophy of nature. It is presumably too early to attempt to formulate the structure of nature in terms of our radically novel and still shifting physical concepts, as it is certainly premature to try to press them into a new synthesis by a *tour de force*. It is not too early, however, to try to understand the fact that such concepts do shift, and that the structure of nature is successively reformulated, nor is it ever untimely to point to facts that any theory of nature must take into account. It is clear that a theory of nature arrived at by starting from mathematical physics will be highly selective of certain aspects of the nature within which we live. It is well to ask for clarification, therefore, as to what aspects the physicists do select, and why they select them, lest we be persuaded that the nature of which they talk makes unintelligible the nature in which we live. It is well to view the formulations of physicists in the light of the function of physics, lest we assume that physics made the world rather than that the world has given birth to physics and physicists. It is well to realize that the mathematical and logical structure of events which is found conditioning the processes of nature and is perfected in imagination far beyond the limits of any observable process, is still something discriminated and found perfectible in those processes. If we forget these obvious facts, we shall find ourselves in our latest scientific philosophies falling into the traditional errors of metaphysics, identifying nature with the latest formulations of its structural aspects, and facing the insoluble problem of explaining all the rest of the experienced world that is left over.

Until very recently there was a gulf between the philosophies of nature which started from mathematical physics and those which started from the biological and social sciences, between the various logical realisms and the more empirical naturalisms. Today, however, that gulf is being rapidly bridged, and we seem to be approaching a synthesis between the structural categories of mathematical physics and the functional and temporal categories of biology and anthropology. The physicists, face to face with their new world of fields of radiant energy, have been forced by that world to develop concepts strikingly similar, on the one hand, to those of Aristotle, and on the other, to those of modern philosophies of social experience. The concepts appropriate to the functional relations of physical events within a systematic and organic structure, are no longer radically disparate to the concepts appropriate to the more complex forms of human experience. We seem to be nearing the time when a common set of categories and a common intellectual method will make both intelligible in the same terms, when both atoms and human societies will be seen as illustrations of the common structure of nature. When that time comes, we shall no longer have two philosophies of nature, based on which group of sciences is taken as furnishing the more inclusive categories and methods. We shall have rather one nature, and one scheme of understanding, within which similarities can be illustrated and distinctive differences discriminated. We have already a common emphasis on the ongoing processes of nature, on the emergence of novel ways of behaving, on the genuine creativity of the life of the universe, and on a pluralistic yet organic type of structure adequate to describe the immense variety of natural processes.

Moreover, the very fact of the reformulation of the basic principles of physics today has made it abundantly clear that principles do shift, and that the structure of nature does receive new formulation. The history of our own natural science, to say nothing of that of other systems of thought, as well as any accurate analysis of scientific procedure itself, reveals that science and knowing is a human activity, an active process of interpreting the world we live in, something men do to work out and criticise beliefs. It is highly selective of the facts from which it starts, and of the particular structural aspects of the world it is concerned to seize and express. Any systematic body of beliefs—any science—is the expression and formulation of certain natural relations in a definite language with a grammar of its own. Men can not only change their language when their interest in knowing shifts, as they did in the seventeenth century; even when it persists the same, that language has to enlarge its vocabulary and extend its grammar to express new facts and new relations, as it has done ever since. In more Aristotelian terms, when it is no longer possible to say what things are in terms of one basic principle, that principle—as Einstein has shown—must be modified or pushed back to a still more fundamental principle to enable us to say what the new things are. The history of our own science is the history of the continual criticism and modification of the basic assumptions in terms of which the structure of nature has been pieced together and expressed. Science today, moreover, involves not only assumptions of expression, of grammar, but assumptions inherent in the human systems of spatial and temporal measuring from which it derives its data, and by which it verifies its conclusions—assumptions peculiarly subject to change. Knowledge, in a word, is not an immediate seeing, is neither the intellectual apprehension or vision of rationalism, nor the sensible vision and perception of empiricism, but is mediate and functional, an active process of criticism directed toward a selected end. Such a conclusion is supported both by psychology and by the technique of scientific procedure, and is illuminated when knowledge is seen in the light of its functioning within its appropriate cultural setting.

Such an analysis of the nature and procedure of scientific inquiry, moreover, does not leave the criticism of values to the poet or the mystic. If science is an activity, a technique for the criticism of beliefs expressing the structure of the experienced world, there is no reason why it cannot work upon beliefs expressing the relations of experienced values. If science employs basic principles as instruments for organizing beliefs into an intelligible system which experience can verify, it can also employ principles for organizing the goods discovered in the world into an equally verifiable system. That scientific, moral, and religious principles of organization are all alike cumulative and traditional, that a culture operates by bringing these achieved principles of verification to bear on fresh experience, is obvious. Experimental criticism of scientific as of all values can only determine whether they result in the kind of good recognized as ultimately good. But though such ultimate values, scientific, aesthetic, religious, or moral, are the premises of experiment rather than its fruit, they can be themselves modified when the organization they lend to experience leaves too much out of account. To view such principles, scientific or moral, as functional in specific ways is to provide a means of testing their validity, at the same time that they are themselves tests of the experience that comes within their scope. And thus all values are seen as amenable to the intellectual method that has proved so successful in disciplining beliefs about the physical structure of the world.

We must begin, therefore, with what we find—whether it be economic organization, moral standards, scientific beliefs and principles, or metaphysical concepts and distinctions. To this insistence our world is forever forcing us back. And since we find everywhere today both traditional beliefs, institutions, and values, and novel experience, facts, ideas, demands, and needs, we must begin with both. We can disregard either only at our peril—at the peril of an arbitrary, uncritical, and ultimately untenable choice. We cannot appeal to the immediate and uncriticised experience of the moment, in all its changing confusion; but neither can we neglect it. We can only face that experience with the full knowledge of the tests and principles and standards built up in every field through the long history of our culture, and use those tests and principles to organize the fresh experience we are creating. If we are honest, we shall find those tests deepening as they actually function in our world; if we are intelligent, we shall consciously strive to make them more adequate. But if we are wise, we shall employ our most potent instrument of criticism, the scientific technique, to discover the promise of the future and the treasure of the past, and what must be done to adjust them to each other. We must begin with what we find—so that we may find more than that with which we began.

What must be done with our several institutions should by this time be fairly clear. What has been illustrated with metaphysics and scientific method is equally applicable to all. What must be done will be done, whether or not we realize what we are doing. I would willingly illustrate it also from religion, a favorite theme. With religion too we must start with what we find. That is meagre enough, God knows—it is crude, sentimental, literal-minded, worldly, humanistic, practical, and inordinately concerned with means and instrumentalities. Yet perhaps even out of what we have we can develop a faith in a certain method and way. It is well to remember that it is all our institutions, our science and education, our art, our moral standards, our religion, our social groupings, from the family up, and not merely our political and economic organization, that must be transformed. Whether the transformation is forced upon us by our own unthinking acts, or whether intelligent criticism shall play a part, depends upon us, and our knowledge of our world.

That the economic revolution we are now involved in has been the major determining factor in revolutionizing our entire culture, and that the eventual reorganization of our culture will be largely dependent on the economic organization that is worked out, is so obvious as to need no emphasis. It would be easy to state in general terms what that economic organization must be—so easy that the statement may well be left to others. There are plenty of prophets today who can give us detailed pictures if we will, and the pictures are surely plausible enough. But economic revolutions, after all, are not produced by revolutionaries; they are produced by men working out the possibilities of the productive forces of society within the conditions set by those forces, and so far as the *form* of economic organization is concerned, it matters little whether those men think they are communists or fascists or democrats. It is quite possible that a political revolution will be one incident of our economic revolution; but neither are political revolutions caused by revolutionaries. They are caused by men too stupid or too stubborn to develop what is implicit in technology, and they replace those who will not with those who will. Whoever does it, and however they achieve power, what must be done with our economic machine will be the same; its organization will be dictated by its inherent structure, and will be achieved only by patient and critical inquiry into that structure. Most Americans would prefer that the inquirers should come to power in ways more consonant with our tradition than upheaval and dictatorship; it is surely at present premature to deny that they can. That preference is so large a part of what we find that it may well prove determining. It is clear likewise that both the form and the manner of the eventual economic organization of our society will have to grow out of the material that society offers, not out of the material of another society halfway round the world. Respect for human personality, and devotion to the conditions of its development, self-reliance, a widely distributed initiative, the essence of liberty—these things are too deeply ingrained in our life to be disregarded.[1] Their conditions have been revolutionized, and what they will become in our new world is still a matter for clarification. That any American form of collectivism and economic planning must contain many elements usually called syndicalistic, is fairly certain. One may consequently vote a Marxian ticket, but unless he be blind he must realize that the programs of present-day Marxian parties have little relevance to what must and will be done, though their presence may influence its doing.

And so the philosophy of cultural change supplies an attitude, a perspective, and an intellectual method, for determining what must be done in each of the many complexly interrelated institutions of our changing culture, from metaphysics to the family, from epistemology to religion. What must be done will be clarified when that attitude and method are brought to bear upon the materials, traditional and revolutionary, of that changing culture itself. There is surely plenty to do; but the tasks can be approached with a genuine satisfaction that intelligence can once more deal, not with the inherited dialectical difficulties of a tradition grown academic, but with the insistent problems set by our own world. And it may be given to us to rise, with the great adjusters of the past, above the strife of our own intellectual adjustment to a comprehensive vision of life, and to express in our own language the universal pattern of human existence. We may start with an ideology born of the class struggle, and yet in this very human flesh we may see God.

[1] For the information of future historians, as well as of agents of the FBI, this passage has been allowed to stand as it was set down in 1934. The author has at no time been tempted to adhere to Marxian principles, or to any social philosophy that would be called "socialism"—unless the welfare state administered by President Eisenhower be so dubbed. Like the vast majority of Americans, he has always been fundamentally syndicalistic in his social thinking, and he is convinced, and has been from his college days, that any form of social control of industry growing out of American conditions, and expressing the American temper and experience, must include a very great degree of economic decentralization or "economic federalism," that is, a widely distributed group initiative and group control.

Never having been a Marxian, the author has never felt that any European experiment in social reorganization claiming allegiance to "Marxian" principles has been a betrayal of his own social faith. In consequence, he has been able to preserve a somewhat greater degree of objectivity toward such experiments than have many American democratic socialists.

PART I

Toward the Theory of History

CHAPTER 1

The Theory of History

I REMEMBER once long ago asking a friend what he was particularly interested in doing in his life. This was in the morning of our days, and we both had our ambitions. "I want to study history," he replied. "The history of what?" I went on to inquire, quite naturally, it seemed to me. To my surprise, my friend was greatly perplexed at this simple question. "Why," he finally managed to come out with, "I'm not interested in the history of anything in particular. What I want to go on and study is just history."

Now, what this "just history" may be, that so many men seem anxious to study and write about, I have unfortunately never been able to understand. It is easy to observe that those who have in the past been devoted to it have rarely been agreed on just what it is: no two of the classic "historians" have understood what "history" is in precisely the same way. And it is today quite difficult to avoid rival schools of "historians" vociferously debating just what kinds of material their "history" should include. We have all been taught, I presume, that "history" cannot be merely or primarily past politics or past battles, but must include a great deal more than those very minor matters. Many tell us "history" must deal primarily with facts about the economic institutions under which men have lived. Others bid us study the great ideas that have meant so much to those capable of appreciating their significance, the ideas of science and philosophy. For some, it is the religion that has organized and expressed the life of entire cultures that seems of fundamental "historical" importance.

Section I of this chapter appeared in "History and the Social Sciences," in *Freedom and Reason,* ed. S. W. Baron and others (Glencoe, Ill., 1951). Reprinted by permission of the Free Press.

Art and literature, those consummate expressions of what the past has been and has felt, have their own devoted followers. Still others insist that the true "history" is of the beliefs and institutionalized habits of men, the beliefs which the masses have actually entertained, and which have determined the course of men's social relations.

Now it is not hard to understand sympathetically a genuine interest in all these various things. I can indeed understand and share in an interest in everything that men have done and thought and felt and made during their long sojourn on earth. I can even understand what used to be called "natural history"—though I find that today what Nature has done is not regarded as the province of "the historian," and enters there, if at all, only if it has done something to his "history"—usually in the first chapter. But I must confess I cannot understand even the meaning of the questions, which of these many different interests should "history" include, and which should it emphasize and make central? [1] Nor, if "history" is to include all of these interests, and is to be the complete record of everything that man has done on this planet, can I see how "history" differs from the entire sum of human knowledge. For every human activity can be viewed historically, in its temporal aspect: all that man has done and thought and discovered and come to know thus falls within the all-comprehensive "province" of the historian.

For these reasons, we are told, "history" must inevitably be selective. I am inclined to agree, at least in the sense that I myself, not being omniscient, have always found it necessary to make a selection. But I have never been able to understand why "history" has to exclude anything. I am wholly unable to understand why a detailed study of Hannibal's campaigns is not perfectly valid "history"; although I too know all the reasons why such study should not be inflicted upon the young. I was much amused to discover, in the late thirties, that the Columbia historians, though committed to the insignificance of military history, nevertheless imported from Cambridge an able historian of military strategy, so soon as it became apparent in 1938 that military

[1] I can make sense out of such questions only by analysing them as really meaning, What should *courses in history* in our schools and colleges include? This is a valid question; but it is a question about the aims of education, and clearly has nothing whatever to do with the nature of "history."

problems were about to become central. I am not unacquainted with the familiar observation, "That used to be what history was, of course; but now it is only the history of military strategy, not history itself." I am perfectly aware that "history" has itself enjoyed a history; and I flatter myself that I can with the best of them explain why different historians have been and still are interested in the histories of different things. But I must say that I can see no reason in the most complete understanding of why "history" has become what it is today, for answering in one way rather than another the question, "What *should* 'history' be and include?"

When pressed, the historian will tell us that "history" selects from the record of the past what gives us "understanding" of ourselves and our present shenanigans. I am perfectly willing to admit that that is just what the historian actually does. To be sure, I have never yet found an historian who did not dwell lovingly on an immense amount of past material, not because it had any discoverable connection with the "understanding" of anything else, but simply because he was fascinated by it. I have never found any historian so puritanical as to be really bound by such a narrowly pragmatic creed. Nor do I ever expect to. And it is of course terribly difficult to find any plausible theory as to why what has been selected from the past does enable us to understand.

One school of historians today is very insistent that "history" should aim to explain why we are acting the way we are, and how we got into the mess we are in. The history of that mess seems to me to be very important, and to illuminate what we should do about it. But I really cannot see why the history of our mess is to be identified with "just history" in general. If it is, then the history of ancient Egypt, for example, is hardly "history," for it seems to have made only a minor contribution to our trouble. This is a view I cannot accept, for I find Egyptian history fascinating. I cannot even regard it as the proper aim of "history" to account for how the Egyptians got into their messes; for their history seems to be about other things than messes, and is in fact largely irrelevant to them. And the same holds for the history of Greece. Despite the efforts of very able historians today, I am still not clear that the most important thing about the Greeks was their failures, though I hope I can point a moral as well as the next man. And though like their gods the Greeks were very human, I find that what interests me about them is not the way they resemble us, but the things they did that we cannot do. In any event, moreover, if "history" is really to explain why we are acting the way we do, I should think it would have to explain why we are painting the kind of pictures we do, and composing the kind of music we write, and why we are puzzling our heads over the general theory of relativity. But that, I shall at once be told, is not "history"; that is the history of art or of music or of physics.

Ah! says another school, history helps us to understand where we are because it explains why things have been as they have. It makes clear the "pattern of the historical process." This seems a promising answer, until we reflect that it means that what history explains to us is "history" itself. And this is very odd—*pace* Spengler, Toynbee, Sorokin, and other speculative positivists who in searching for a "pattern of history," for an "historical morphology," piously hope that they are being very "scientific"—which is an act of faith rather than of knowledge. For it is clearly not history that enables us to understand history, but science—anthropology, psychology, economics, and the rest of the social sciences. This wisdom as to the relation of the social sciences to history has been common knowledge for several generations. Moreover, even if "history" could miraculously explain history, we should still have no light on why we select the particular things we do to label "history."

There is of course a simple answer much in fashion today: "history" is really economic history. It is through the history of men's economic activities and relations that we can alone gain a genuine understanding of "history." But I observe that those who say this proceed to use economic history primarily to explain political history. What they are interested in understanding seems to be political struggles and fights; and they all point to further political battles in the future. I am inclined to agree that this is an excellent way to understand political activity; and it certainly sheds a good deal of light on many other things as well. But I am still in the dark as to why it should be politics alone that "history" is trying to understand. And with the best will in the world I cannot see that economic history throws much light on many other things I want to understand—why, for instance, British thinkers down to Bertrand Russell have persisted in making the same initial assumptions as William of Ockham, despite the absurd consequences it has been shown in every generation those assumptions entail; or why and how the theory of relativity and quantum mechanics have transformed Newtonian science. The histories of such things seem intelligible without much reference to how men have made a living—to what a fashionable jargon calls the "relations of production." But perhaps "history" in general is merely what economics *does* enable us to understand. If that were true, it would at least simplify matters.

As a result of perplexing questions like these, I have been driven to ask whether there is any such thing as "history" in general. At present, I am convinced there is no such thing. Nor do I know of any good reason why there should be men set apart as "Professors of History," or why there should be special "Departments of History" in our colleges and universities. Of course, I greatly enjoy and profit by what these men tell me, and I am convinced that they ought to be supported in some way.

In any rational organization of academic teaching, there would be no place for any separate and independent "Department of History." Rather, each department of knowledge concerned with a separate subject-matter would include members with a major interest in the history of that subject-matter, and of the intellectual efforts to grasp it. I do not intend to be invidious. I believe there is equally no rational reason for any separate and independent "Departments of Philosophy" in academic teaching. Every department should include members with philosophic imagination and horizons, and capable of philosophic analysis.

To be sure, I am not so addicted to the vice of pure reason as to have any immediate intention of starting such a purge, however justified it may be rationally. I am trying to emphasize certain fundamental facts about the nature of history. Everything in our world has *a* history, and the man who wants to understand any particular thing or field is well advised to inquire into *its* history. Everything, that is, is *historical* in character, and has an existence that can be measured in time. And this historical aspect which any particular thing has and possesses is an essential part of what it is. But "history" in general seems to have no meaning, unless it be taken as synonymous with knowledge as a whole. History is not a "thing" at all, it is not a noun, a "substance." It is rather a character, an adjective, a predicate. Or, put in somewhat more formal terms, "history" is not a distinctive subject-matter to be inquired into. It is rather at once a trait of all subject-matters, something to be discovered and understood about each of them; and a distinctive way of inquiring into any subject-matter—though by no means the only way.

And therefore I find no meaning in the questions, what should "history" include? What should the "historian" emphasize? There is no such thing as history, nor are there any "historians." Every history is the history *of* something, and every historian is trying to trace the past *of* something. In terms of that determinate "something," it is not hard to discover what *its* history must include. The various strands then fall into their proper place, once we have decided what it is, the historical aspect of which we are interested in. The history of our science will then be one thing, and the history of our present mess a somewhat different one; although in investigating either we shall often find ourselves concerned with the same factors that are in a different way involved in the other. There is no "process of history" in general; but every historian of anything will find himself discovering the "historical processes" by which that particular thing came about.

Actually, of course, there does seem to be need of "history" in the curriculum, and of "historians"—just as there is of philosophy. Each in its own way can contribute powerfully to the unification of intellectual perspectives. But this need is pedagogical rather than rational, and it is probably best satisfied when neither historians nor philosophers remain isolated in separate "departments" of their own, but cooperate with teachers whose interests are focused in other disciplines. But then—of what "department" can this not be said?

II

It has been shown why there is no such "thing" as "history": rather, any determinate existence has an historical aspect, and possesses a particular history of its own. These questions about the nature of history, and about what it means to be a history, and to have a history, belong to the general investigation which I call "the Theory of History," as do the other inquiries pursued in the various chapters in this Part.

By "the Theory of History" I mean an enterprise analogous to the one undertaken by Aristotle in developing the "theory of nature" in his *Physica*. The latter is an analysis of natural processes, and an examination of the fundamental characteristics such processes possess in order to be and to be understood. The "Theory of History" is conceived as the analysis of both human and natural histories, of their pervasive traits, and of the concepts in terms of which they may be found intelligible. The theory of history is consequently a branch of metaphysics, of ontology—or, as I should prefer to put it, an enterprise of metaphysical analysis.[2] That is, it is a critical examination of a certain kind of subject-matter, those traits or aspects of existent things that are said to be "historical," and of the intellectual instruments for dealing with that subject-matter.

Now "history" like "experience" is notoriously a double-barreled word: it means both what has happened, *Geschichte—was geschieht*—and the knowledge and statement of what has happened, *historia*.[3] Thus like "experience," "history" manages to raise in itself the whole "problem of knowledge": of the relation between what has occurred and the knowledge of that occurrence, between existence or Nature and discourse, with all its difficulties of statement and expression. With historical knowledge, the understanding of past events and their significance, any "realistic" position is peculiarly hard to maintain, for such knowledge is so obviously an *interpretation* of what has happened, and even an *addition* to what that happening was when it did take place. Since the "understanding" of the past is patently a matter of the historian's interests and categories, of *his* way of understanding things, rather than of the way in which things were understood when they took place, history and historical knowledge have for over a century been the great stronghold of the "idealistic" interpretation of knowledge. And when it is properly understood, as it has not been even by the left-wing Hegelians, the core of the Hegelian position on knowledge is, I judge, irrefutable. It is true that human thought and knowledge is the most important thing in the universe, and the most significant thing in history: for without human thought there could be no importance or significance whatsoever. And it is true that the past al-

[2] For a further statement of the nature of such "theories" or metaphysical analyses, see Chapter 5, pp. 134–37.

[3] "Historia" comes from the root adjective ἵστωρ, "knowing, learned": from which is derived the verb ἱστορέω, "to inquire into," and the noun ἱστορία, "inquiry, *Forschung*."

ways becomes unified in the perspectives of the present, and is inevitably understood as leading up to *our* problems and *our* ideas; for there is no other way of "understanding" the past. Hence all the many European "critical" philosophers of history [4] in the last generation, in their analysis of historical knowledge, have been philosophical idealists: Windelband, Rickert, Simmel, Dilthey, Cassirer, Croce, Collingwood.[5] Even those much influenced by Marxism, like Max Weber and Karl Mannheim, have expressed, by American standards at least, a ve idealistic "Marxism."

In significant contrast, the relatively few American thinkers who have been concerned with the critical analysis of history and historical knowledge—I am thinking of F. J. E. Woodbridge, Sidney Hook, E. W. Strong, and John Dewey; Morris R. Cohen, Maurice Mandelbaum, and A. O. Lovejoy; and, among historians themselves, Carl Becker, C. A. Beard, Allan Nevins, and Louis Gottschalk [6]—have been, not philosophical idealists, but proponents of a *realistic* conception of historical knowledge. These men have all emphasized the *pluralism* and the *contingency* of history, and the *relativity* of the historian's principles of selection and categories of interpretation to his own age and his own knowledge. But they have all maintained an "objective relativism" in historical knowledge; and hence they have all concluded that the historian can arrive at genuine knowledge, not merely at a world of his own imagining, like most of the Europeans. The soundest and most suggestive of these American critical philosophies of history are probably those of Woodbridge and Morris Cohen, who proceed from a fundamentally Aristotelian realism; and Dewey, who by his own devi-

[4] For the contrast between "critical" and "speculative" philosophy of history, see W. H. Walsh, *An Introduction to Philosophy of History* (London, 1951), Chapter 1, sections 2 and 3.

[5] For accounts, see the criticism from a realistic position in Maurice Mandelbaum, *The Problem of Historical Knowledge* (New York, 1938); and also R. G. Collingwood, *The Idea of History* (Oxford, 1938); Raymond Aron, *Essai sur la Théorie de l'Histoire dans l'Allemagne Contemporaine: La Philosophie Critique de l'Histoire* (Paris, 1938); and Pietro Rossi, *Lo Storicismo Tedesco Contemporaneo* (Turin, 1956).

[6] For a full bibliography of American contributions to the critical philosophy of history, see the one drawn up by Ronald Thompson in Bulletin 54 of the Social Science Research Council (1946), *Theory and Practice in Historical Study: A Report of the Committee on Historiography.*

ous paths arrives here, as elsewhere, at a position which makes supreme sense.

Hence, despite all the insidious temptations that history and historical knowledge offer to the seductive snares of an idealistic epistemology, I am offering in these papers an "American"—that is, a *realistic*—conception of historical knowledge. I am proposing to set forth, with an application to historical knowledge, the kind of "functional realism" as to knowledge I find in Aristotle. If certain historical continuities are observable between my ideas and those of other men who have lived after Aristotle, like Hegel, Marx, and Dewey—all Aristotelians at bottom—this is but an illustration of the fact that Aristotle's thought has itself enjoyed a history, and has become other and more than what it was when Athens first heard it.

Should I call the view set forth in these papers an "Aristotelian" conception of history, I should doubtless be misunderstood. I might even get involved in a fruitless controversy about what is "Aristotelian." I shall not therefore so call it; it *has not* been so designated. To be sure, the precarious state of my philosophical credit with certain moderns, which is greatly extended, predisposes me to seek the pure gold of the Stagirite. But it is enough to recognize my view as true. For Aristotle and I agree at least in this, that we both set Truth above all claims to intellectual proprietorship.

I propose, therefore, to take full advantage of the fact that "history" is a double-barreled word, and designates both the *significance* of events and the *knowledge* of that significance.[7] For men's actions and beliefs, and their institutionalized ways of acting and believing, are entangled in a labyrinth of causes and consequences, that is, in a complex network of natural meanings and significances. The historian selects and grasps those natural meanings or "involvements" that are relevant to an outcome historical events have themselves generated; and the history he

[7] What "history" does *not* designate is the mere *occurrence* of events. Our name for the record of such occurrences is a "chronicle." If the *New York Times* had been published from the first day of creation, we should have a most valuable "chronicle" of human history. But without further appraisal of what had been significant, we should have still no "history." Thus the illustration Russell always uses of a proposition about the past: "Caesar crossed the Rubicon," is indeed a proposition about the past. But it is not an *historical* proposition, for it states nothing about the *significance* of that event.

discovers and writes becomes itself a further natural event in the "history" that men's actions produce. Like all knowledge, historical knowledge is the power of using selected relations of events for realizing in detail the ends Nature imposes on men. It is functional, objective, and relative to determinate ends. It is relevant always to the particular values that are implicit in the respective natures of things.

The history that is a *knowledge* of significances is thus not a term to be defined. It is an inquiry into a subject-matter: into the "histories" that things—actions or ideas—have had. And the function of historical inquiry—what the inquiry that is "historical investigation" itself does—is to be determined, not by some arbitrary definition, but by the traits of that subject-matter, by the factors there present that must be grasped if those traits are to be understood. That subject-matter, the historical aspect of existence, is prior. The histories that are discovered and written down, that belong to "historiography," are the outcome of inquiry into it, into the historical traits of things.

Now the inquiry I am calling the "theory of history" is not to be confused with what is usually known as the "philosophy of history." "Philosophies of history"—that is, "speculative" philosophy of history—are very important productions of man the thinker and actor; and the nature of the world in general, and of human societies in particular, is obviously such as to generate them, especially during times of rapid social change, when men are peculiarly aware that they are living in an "age of transition," and are themselves "making history" in the face of live options and open choices. But "philosophies of history," when uncritically held, and not understood in the light of their function, are suspect today, and justly so. This is not for the reason the historian usually gives, that they are too "philosophical" and not "scientific" and "objective" enough. On the contrary, they are not philosophical enough. Not knowing themselves for what they really are, philosophies of history do not ask the right questions; or rather, they do not ask the right questions first, and hence they are confused and muddled on the questions they do ask.

Speculative philosophies of history are concerned primarily with two problems. First, does the history of our society exhibit any discernible pattern? What is the structure of the "process of history" revealed in the past of our society? Secondly, what is the nature of "historical causation"? What is the "dynamic factor" that has caused our history to have that pattern, and which, if it continues to operate the same way, will have similar consequences in the future? The first question is asked by those with a pretense to empirical method, who hope they are being very "scientific": by men like Comte, Spengler, Sorokin, and Toynbee. The second is asked by metaphysical theorists who are not afraid to label a cause: by men like St. Augustine, Hegel, or Karl Marx. These are important questions, and any critical reflection on history must consider them. But they are not the first questions to be asked: they are derivative, and demand much preliminary clarification.

Now I think there is what can be called a "science of social and cultural change," and that there is no reason to prejudge the question as to whether patterns can be discovered in such change—whether there are "laws" of social change. Though we may not have gotten very far with it as yet, such an inquiry is certainly possible. I judge it has been carried farthest by American social scientists, especially by the anthropologists of the Boas school, who alone have considered anything like an adequate range of empirical materials. But such a "science of social change" is clearly not the same thing as historical knowledge. It may well be fundamental in understanding particular histories, and history clearly furnishes it with much of its own materials. But to say that there are laws of social and cultural change, which may well be true, is definitely not the same as to say that there are laws of "history."

The problems of that rather adolescent science are important, and critical reflection on history must consider them. But these questions also are not the first ones to be asked about history. If they are to be fruitfully pursued, there must be an initial clarity on certain fundamental concepts and distinctions. Before proceeding to examine the processes of social change, the theories developed about it, and the way it is to be understood—the task of any science of social and cultural change; and before examining the pattern and structure of our society's past, and the dynamic factors that have been giving it that pattern—the task of a philosophy of history, which is directed toward the appraisal of the past and the present in the light of the future they suggest, there are certain prior questions that must be asked. And these are the questions that are the peculiar province of what we are calling the "Theory of History."

The problems of the Theory of History comprise, first, a group of general questions. What *is* "history"? What is it *to be* "a history"? What is it *to have* "a history"? What are the implications of the *fact* of history for those things that have histories? for the understanding and evaluation of those things? The second major problem of the theory of history is, How are the histories of things to be understood? And the third problem is, How do the histories of things enable us to understand and explain the things that possess those histories?

There is a fourth kind of inquiry in connection with historical knowledge, which deals with the techniques of the "critical scholarship" which establishes the record or chronicle of past facts and events, and is hence the indispensable prerequisite of all the other types. These problems of the critical interpretation of documents and monuments, together with the specialized ancillary disciplines this process draws upon, are usually grouped together as "historiography," and are dealt with in the working manuals, like those of Bernheim or Langlois and Seignibos. Such critical scholarship is here taken for granted as indispensable, and the technical questions it raises, so long as philosophical problems are not involved, I am content to leave to the experts on *Geschichtslehre*.

But I am definitely not content to relinquish to the technicians the question, What are "historical facts"? or to accept without question the notion of "critical" or "scientific" historians, like Henri Berr, for instance, that the historian must first establish and collect all the "facts"—presumably on white index cards—and only after this has been done proceed hopefully to search for some "historical synthesis" or "interpretation" of these facts.[8] If this wholly Baconian notion of intellectual method, that enough "facts" will somehow precipitate a structure of themselves, actually works with success in history, then history enjoys the dubious distinction of being the only field of knowledge in which this is the case. Events are in truth infinite: they may serve as raw material for various kinds of inquiry. But events become "facts" only in the light of their relation to some *hypothesis*—as Claude Bernard could have told Berr. In all inquiry, the "facts" are not the brute "data," but *significant* events, significant only as *evidence for* some idea or

[8] See Henri Berr, article "History" in *Encyclopedia of the Social Sciences,* for a revealing expression of this naive theory of procedure.

theory, and they are normally discovered only through the use of that idea. It is the general experience of the historian that he asks questions for which the relevant "facts" are *not* to be found in the existent record; he has to dig them out painfully himself. The facts of the record of any particular history are thus selected *by* that history together with some hypothesis it has generated. The most illustrious victim of this Baconian will-o'-the-wisp of Berr's was Lord Acton, who had a whole library full of index cards, but never found the "synthesis."

When we examine what is involved in anything's having a history, or in understanding the history of anything, we encounter a very complex situation, with many factors to be discriminated, and many different types of possible historical inquiry, each type with its own distinctive function. That is, the historical character of existence makes it possible to seek a number of different kinds of understanding and explanation. It is not here proposed in any sense to limit the scope of historical inquiries, or to exclude any of these different types. Rather, it is hoped to provide a *framework* within which each of the various types of historical inquiry can find its appropriate place. We have already suggested four major types of historical inquiry: 1) the theory of history; 2) historiography; 3) the science of social and cultural change; and 4) the philosophy of history. All four presuppose a fifth type, the establishment of the record or chronicle.

In the preliminary questions with which we set out, it has been suggested that "histories" are plural, adjectival, and determinate. They are always histories *of* something, involving a selection, from the infinite objective relatednesses of past events, of those events and relations that have been important and significant for making that thing what it is. The histories that things possess as aspects or traits of what they are, are, as the histories of particular determinate things, themselves plural, selective, and determinate. As to the nature of these "histories," it remains to show that they are also progressive and cumulative, and develop and grow with the occurrence of fresh events and further consequences. As a history thus grows with the further passage of time, and produces new eventuations, the selection from past events which it includes will alter: events and factors that earlier were not important will come to be selected by their historical outcomes as highly significant. The past events do not themselves change; but as a history grows, its *selection* from them changes. The past, as sheer events, does not alter; but what is *significant* and *relevant* in the past of anything changes cumulatively as that thing itself changes and develops.

A "history" thus always involves the relation between an outcome in a present, and the past of that present. It will have both a determinate "focus" in a "present," and a past from which that focus selects what has a bearing on that particular history. Any thing, at any date in the past, as well as any thing in our present, will be found to possess such a "history" which can be objectively investigated from the vantage-point of *its* present.

These questions about the nature and delimitation of particular histories will be examined in Chapter 2. In addition, the chapters in this first Part will deal with the two major problems of the theory of history: first, How is the history of anything to be understood from its focus in a present? secondly, How does the history of anything, so understood, illuminate and contribute to the understanding of what that thing has become and now is? More briefly, these two problems are: How does a present explain its past? and, How does that past explain its present?

The first question is the problem of understanding histories. It is here considered in Chapter 2, "On the Understanding of Histories," together with the prior questions about the nature of histories. The second is the problem of the historical or genetic method, and of the various uses of historical knowledge to understand what has had a history. This second problem proves to be the most difficult and perplexing of all those questions involved in the existence of the fact of history. Some of the many issues it raises are considered in the two Chapters 3 and 4, which examine "History as an Instrument of Understanding."

CHAPTER 2

On the Understanding of Histories

Historical investigation [says Santayana] has for its aim to fix the order and character of events throughout past time in all places. The task is frankly superhuman, because no block of real existence, with its infinitesimal detail, can be recorded, nor if somehow recorded could it be dominated by the mind; and to carry on a survey of this social continuum *ad infinitum* would multiply the difficulty. The task might also be called infrahuman, because the sort of omniscience which such complete historical science would achieve would merely furnish materials for intelligence: it would be inferior to intelligence itself. . . . An attempt to rehearse the inner life of everybody that has ever lived would be no rational endeavor. Instead of lifting the historian above the world and making him the most consummate of creatures, it would flatten his mind out into a passive after-image of diffuse existence, with all its horrible blindness, strain, and monotony. Reason is not come to repeat the universe, but to fulfil it. Besides, a complete survey of events would perforce register all changes that have taken place in matter since time began, the fields of geology, astronomy, paleontology, and archeology being all, in a sense, included in history. Such learning would dissolve thought in a vertigo, if it had not already perished of boredom. . . . The profit of studying history lies in something else than in a dead knowledge of what happens to have happened.[1]

A considerable part of Section I has appeared in Part I of "Controlling Assumptions in the Practice of American Historians," in *Theory and Practice in Historical Study,* Bulletin 54 of the Social Science Research Council (New York, 1946). Much of the material in the rest of this chapter was used in a talk in a symposium on "Historiography of Philosophy" held at the meeting of the Eastern Division of the American Philosophical Association at Wesleyan University, Middletown, Connecticut, on December 29, 1938, and printed in the *Journal of Philosophy,* XXXVI (1939), 460–74.

[1] George Santayana, "History," in *Reason in Science* (New York, 1905), pp. 51–53.

IN VIEW of the situation Santayana thus graphically depicts, it is clear that every written history must be a selection of so-called facts made with some particular emphasis. This means that the historian must employ some principle of selection: he must choose what he will include as "significant" for his history. In writing the "history" of the United States, he must decide what is "basic" for that history.[2] Even though he permit himself four lengthy volumes to set forth "The Rise of American Civilization," and can hence afford a broader base,[3] he cannot escape the need for a principle of selection. There is no such thing as a "complete" history, not even the interminable productions of the Chinese scholars.

Moreover, if seventeen years elapse between the two written histories, the principle of selection employed in the later one will probably differ appreciably from the principle that served for the earlier. This will be not only because in the interval the historian has found out more "facts," and now has a greater store from which to choose those that are really "basic" for a much shorter work. It will be due fully as much to the circumstance that he has grown in the stature of his wisdom. He has come to understand the world and its ways and the pattern of human experience with more of maturity and insight, we hope; at least he now understands it differently. And he understands it differently in large part because there is now something different to understand. The history-that-has-happened during those seventeen years—the history as "actuality"—has not stood still. That history, like all the histories-that-happen, has been progressive and cumulative. In 1944 the United States was not what it was in 1927. And the American nation possessed in consequence in 1944, quite apart from all "interpretation," a different history from the America of 1927. Hence the historian, facing the problem of selecting those facts in the American past that seem basic for 1944, will not be able to make just the same selection that he made in 1927.

It is thus not only the historian who must be selective in understanding and writing his histories, in his historiography. The histories that things possess—what has occurred, history as "actuality"—are themselves *plural* and *selective,* in two major senses. In the first place, every

[2] Cf. Charles A. Beard, *Basic History of the United States* (New York, 1944).
[3] Charles A. Beard, *The Rise of American Civilization* (New York, 1927).

history is the history *of* something, and these "somethings" are plural: each has a history that is the particular history of the particular past of that particular something, different from the history of any other something. There can be no "history of everything," no "history of the world as a whole." For the world is not a whole—for human experience and knowledge at least. Histories are thus plural and many, to the degree in which our world is plural and many. This pluralism of histories is thus grounded in a general ontological pluralism. Or rather, the best evidence for an ultimate metaphysical pluralism is the encountered plurality of histories.[4] This encountered plurality of many things with many different histories can be called the plurality of histories in the present. In the second place, histories are temporally plural: they are progressive and cumulative, as we have seen in the case of Beard's two Americas.

Thus the history the historian will write, and the principle of selection he will employ, will be undergoing continual change, because the histories things possess are continually changing, always being cumulatively added to. With the occurrence of fresh events, the meaning and significance of the past is constantly changing. Of course, what *did* happen, taken as a sheer brute event, does not change, no matter what further events take place. Caesar still crossed the Rubicon the exact day he did, William invaded England in 1066, Lincoln was still shot in April, 1865, the American heroes still dropped their bomb on Hiroshima in August, 1945, no matter what consequences subsequently flowed from those momentous happenings. The events as accurately *chronicled* never change; no one, not even the idealistic interpreters of historical knowledge, has ever maintained such a patent absurdity. But as we have seen the historian is not and cannot be concerned with all that *did* happen. He is and must be concerned with those events that *did* happen which turn out *later* to be "basic" for his history. He can not be concerned with the entire past, with all its infinitesimal detail; he is concerned only with the "basic" or *significant* past, with that selection from all that did happen which *has* happened—with the history of what *has* happened as significant and meaningful events. And it is precisely this "basic" past, this *meaning* and *significance* of the past, that is continually changing, that is cumulative and progressive. Writ-

[4] See Chapter 7, "Empirical Pluralism and Unifications of Nature."

ing the history of the United States, the historian uses what is basic and significant in that history-that-happened for 1927, or for 1944, as the principle that will control his selection of material. What is significant in American history he will understand in one way in 1927, and in a somewhat different way in 1944. For the historian's understanding of the significant past, like that past itself, is progressive and cumulative.

There is really nothing mysterious about this obvious fact that men's understanding of what is significant in their past changes with the lapse of time. For all understanding is in terms of causes and consequences. Now, our understanding of causes naturally changes and deepens, as we find out more about the operation of causes—with our changing and developing schemes of explanation of the causes of what has happened. And equally naturally, our understanding of consequences changes with the working out of further consequences in the history-that-happens itself.

In the first place, our understanding of the causes of what-has-happened changes as we manage to extend and build up our sciences of man's social behavior. Thus the rise of the Greeks was explained by Herodotus in terms of one scheme of understanding, or "science"; by Thucydides, in terms of another; by George Grote, in terms of a third; by Marx, in terms of a fourth; and by contemporaries like Zimmern, Rostovtzeff, and Westermann, in terms of a fifth and still more adequate science. Each of these schemes of understanding and interpretation selects somewhat different facts: hence each comes out with a different "history."

Again, when we are content to explain what groups of men do by attributing their actions to the "guiding hand of Providence," we will, like the early New England historians, write histories of the operation of God's will and providence, and we will select facts that illustrate it. Or, like Bancroft, we will record "the movement of the divine power which gives unity to the universe, and order and connection to events." When we have come to understand the mysterious ways in which God works, his wonders to perform, as the working out of the God-given genius for politics of the Teutonic "race," we will, like H. B. Adams, trace the "origin" of the New England town-meeting to the primitive German mark. When we have read John Stuart Mill's *Logic,* and absorbed his Baconian conception of the nature of science, we will eschew all guiding hypotheses and indefatigably collect "facts," hopefully trusting that somehow good, in the guise of some "synthesis" that will make it all clear, will be the final goal of all this ill. We will then be strictly "scientific" and "critical" historians, like those great pioneers who won respect for "history" as an academic discipline in the historical seminars set up during the 1880's at Johns Hopkins, Columbia, and elsewhere. When we have seen a great light, and been converted to the gospel of St. Marx, we will write histories like those of Simons, Gustavus Myers, Lewis Corey, or Curtis Nettles. When we have learned from James Harvey Robinson that the historian must master all the social sciences, and have read—or at least abstracted—all the books in that wide field, we will understand the past in terms of all the different hypotheses of all the social sciences, and will, like Harry Elmer Barnes, adopt a "multiple causation" theory as our principle of selection. Our understanding of the *causes* of what has happened will change in these ways with our changing—and we hope, increasingly adequate—schemes of scientific explanation.

Secondly, our understanding of the consequences, and hence of the "significance" of past events, changes with the further history-that-has-happened—with what comes to pass in the world of events, as a result of the possibilities inherent in what has already happened. Thus, World War I was understood in one way as leading to the adoption of the Covenant of the League of Nations. It was understood in another way as the Russian revolution worked itself out, and began to appear as a much more significant consequence of that war than the abortive effort at establishing an international organization. That war took on a further significance with the rise of the Fascist and Nazi regimes, and with the resumption of German economic expansion in Central and Eastern Europe. Still later it began to appear as the first stage of the Russian domination of the European continent. And now—fresh understanding awaits each new date and further eventuation.

Or take the significance of American participation in that struggle. Twenty years ago, the entry of America into World War I was understood as the result of British propaganda and the machinations of the munition-makers. Events after 1939 changed all that. After Pearl Harbor, America's part in World War I was seen as its first and unsuccessful attempt to curb German aggression and establish a military guarantee of the status quo. With the resumption of post-war power politics, it became the initial emergence of the United States as a superpower, whose irresponsibility might well prove a major menace to peace, and should we drop a few H-bombs, make us the most ruthless combatant in history. With the Pentagon curbed by the White House, 1917 began to appear as America's first assumption of responsibilities commensurate with its resources, as a tryout for its developing role as the well-meaning if rather clumsy defender of the free world and the architect of peace. And next year—!

New consequences flowing from past events change the "significance" of the past, of what has happened. Events which had been overlooked before because they did not seem "basic" for anything that followed, now come to be selected as highly significant. Other events that used to seem "basic" recede into the limbo of mere details. In this sense, a history-that-has-happened is not, and in the nature of the case cannot be, fully understood by the actors in it. They cannot realize the "significance" or consequences of what they are doing, since they cannot foresee the future. We understand that history only when it has become a part of our own past; and if it continues to have consequences, our children will understand it still differently. In this sense, the historian, as Hegel proclaimed, is like the owl of Minerva, which takes its flight only when the shades of night are gathering, and the returns are all in. The ultimate significance of any history-that-happens will not be completely grasped until all its consequences have worked themselves out and can be discerned. The "meaning" of any historical fact is what it does, how it continues to behave and operate, what consequences follow from it.

For example, at an historic moment during World War II Winston Churchill said: "With the fall of Singapore we are beginning to realize the meaning of Pearl Harbor." Note the word "beginning." For the "meaning," that is, the cumulative consequences of that specific event, were obviously not completed when Churchill was speaking. They have not been completed yet. For they depend on how things will still turn out, on the future.

In this sense, we understand any history-that-has-happened, any strand of our past leading up to the present, in terms of necessary reference to the future: our principle for selecting what is "basic" in that history involves a reference to its predicted outcome. Our emphasis will be determined by what we find going on in the present. But what we find there is not as yet fully worked out or realized. Rather, the present suggests what will eventuate in times to come, some realization in the envisaged future. Thus, we understand what is "basic" in the history of present things in terms of what we call some "dynamic element" in the present, some "present tendency," as we say, directed toward a future end. The present is full of such "tendencies": it suggests many different possible futures, according to which of the different conflicting tendencies displayed in the present proves controlling. The historian of present things selects one of these possible futures as "just around the corner," as we say, and uses that future as a principle by which to select what is "basic" among the multitude of past facts at his disposal. In this sense, an understanding of our past depends on and involves the future—a projected and predicted future based on an analysis of the present. We discover a "future" in our present, and we then understand our past—the past of our present—as aiming at that predicted future.

For example, our papers are full of attempts to understand what has been happening in our recent history—at the moment, what has been happening in the Middle East. Most of this discussion inevitably turns out to be a prediction of what is going to happen: we cannot understand what has already happened without reference to a projected future. Thus we cannot understand the Administration's foreign policy, toward England and France, toward Egypt, toward the Arab world, toward Israel, toward the United Nations, toward Russia—we cannot understand what is "basic" in the history of what that foreign policy has been, without trying to predict how it is going to turn out. We are all confident what the future is going to bring—though our predicted futures differ radically. As we say, we are now beginning to see the significance of what that foreign policy has been, as we find out what it has already led to.

The historian of present things must thus choose among the various possibilities in the present that tendency, that predicted future, which he judges to be dynamic or controlling. He chooses as his principle of selection the "real pattern of events," what is "being realized," what is "working itself out," as we all say. Now, since the future is not foreseeable in detail—though many elements in it can be predicted, and all human action is based on such predictions of what will happen if other things occur [5]—the historian's choice of a principle of selection necessarily involves a certain choice of "allegiance," an act of "faith" in one kind of future rather than another. This future need not at all be one we would approve: our own sympathies may well be on "the other side." Thus Greek thought about history, with its cycle of degradation from an initial Golden Age, was in fact controlled by the fascination of inevitable doom: Thucydides ended with a tragedy. Henry Adams, who could not reconcile Grant's administration with belief in progress, had a perfectly good "future" in the degradation of energy. Spengler reads the past in terms of the predicted decay and death of an entire civilization, conceived in terms of a biological metaphor. And many a contemporary political historian finds all events crystal-clear in the light of a foreseen and imminent disaster. Thus the Alsops are excellent historians, though one can be quite sure their predictions of doom will never be realized: something worse will come to pass in the meantime.

Thus, to take the growth of science as the "dynamic factor" in the intellectual history of modern times, means that we judge it of most significance today. "The future is with it," we say, meaning we are for it. No Catholic would choose just such a principle of selection; for him the future would be different, and consequently his understanding of the developments since Copernicus and Galileo. In the same way, to take the growth of the group control of technology as the principle for selecting what is basic in our economic past, is to

[5] I take it for granted that the future cannot be "foreseen," by men at least, however it may stand with God. Many elements in it can be "predicted": that is, all invariant relations of the "if-then" type. But what the antecedents will be cannot be "foreseen." Particular events are not subject to scientific determination.

Because men cannot "foresee" the future, their predictions are never "correct": other events have consequences which interfere. No decision is thus ever "right," no practical problem is ever "solved," except in the sense that men are forced on to focus their attention on the new problems their supposed "solution" has generated, often far worse and more insistent than the one dealt with. Hence that goal or end we judge to be "dynamic" or controlling in the present is never fully reached. The future always turns out to be significantly different from what was predicted: we have overlooked something in our analysis of the present, and hence in our forecast of the future.

express a similar "allegiance." It is to make the problem of establishing such control central in the present. In terms of that principle of selection, the dominance of *laisser faire* during the nineteenth century will be understood as a "stage" in the reconstruction of the earlier medieval group controls. No "rugged individualist" would choose that focus; in his history he would select a different past.

But to say that a principle of selection is "chosen" does not mean that such choices are arbitrary. Men do not arbitrarily "choose" their allegiances and faiths, even when they are converts; their faiths rather grasp them. Grace, we are told, is prevenient, and it is God who sends faith. The history-that-happens itself generates the faiths and allegiances that furnish the principles for selecting what is important in understanding it. Men do not "choose" arbitrarily to be Catholics—or rugged individualists—any more than they "choose" not to be. Some men indeed have their faiths and allegiances forced upon them by "facts," by knowledge; though presumably for no man is this wholly the case. For these, facts discovered do impose the selection of the controlling tendencies and implicit ends in the present, in terms of which they can understand the past. For such men, knowledge does declare what has to be done: the furtherance of scientific discovery, the achievement of a group control of industry, the working out of a viable international organization.

This is especially true when men are in responsible positions, and have to act to get something done. Thus Herbert Hoover, though a "rugged individualist," was compelled by facts to go further than any of his predecessors in setting up group controls. This practical and functional knowledge of what has to be done, like the technical knowledge of how to do it, the "know-how," is relatively free from the "arbitrariness" and the irresponsible "relativism"—the "subjective relativism"—of so-called "theoretical knowledge," which is usually not "knowledge" at all, but a mere "having of ideas," mere "ideology." In terms of these ends, that have to be achieved, these goals forced on us by facts, men understand the past and the present, using these ends as principles for selecting what is "basic" in the histories they write.

Yet such principles remain for action a choice, and for knowledge and understanding an assumption and hypothesis: they call us to act on predictions imposed by knowledge when we know we cannot actually foresee what the future will become. For the intelligent, such ends are given and determined by events understood. Within limits, there is a choice of means as to how these ends may be realized. Perhaps this is but another way of saying, that where choice is possible, we are there dealing with a plurality of means. The choice of those means is itself forced by facts, and dictated by knowledge. Yet it remains a choice, a "faith"—at best, an intelligent and critical faith in certain means: in the rejection of war as an instrument of policy, for example, or in the determination to employ democratic methods.

II

It is well to be clear from the outset, that "a history"—*the* history some determinate thing possesses—is an aspect or trait of what that thing *now is*. A history is hence not itself a subject-matter, but is rather an aspect, an "essential property," *of* some subject-matter. Nor is a history an efficient cause. The history of a thing is not the cause of its being what it is, but is rather the resultant or precipitate of those complex processes that have generated that thing: a history is an *outcome*, not a cause. A history is not a process: it is not a verb. A history does nothing. Processes do things, and the result is a history or histories. The history of a thing can be said to be part of its formal cause, to belong to its essence, to what it is. But *what* a thing is has never *made* it what it is: a history does not cause or make itself, nor does it cause or make anything else. The things that have histories do; and they act in the way they do because of their histories.

A history is hence not a "process." A process is a subject-matter to be inquired into, it is an encountered substance: and it is an efficient cause, a verb. Processes are the subject-matter of science, which distinguishes them and analyses their structure as they operate in the present. Histories are full of processes at work; but "history" in the singular is not itself a "process," any more than the world as a whole is a single process. Nor is the history of any particular thing a process; though it will exhibit a complex of processes interacting with each other. "Process," that is, has meaning only if it manifests an invariant structure, only if that same structure is repeated in various instances. A "process" is always an instance of a kind, of a way of operating: its structure is a "way" or "law," a universal, or adverb. In contrast, a history is always a particular: it is always unique and unrepeatable, and never an instance of any universal structure. Whenever we can truly say, "History is repeating itself," we mean we have found a process at work, whose structure has been exemplified before. Hence the historical record of events and changes does not explain anything: it is itself something to be explained and understood, and that not by "history," but by science—by the structure of processes at work to generate histories.

Events happen; and because they *have* happened, other events *are.* A history is what *has* happened, not what *did* happen: a history is not the brute events chronicled in the record, but the events selected from the record as significant and intelligible for that history. It is what *has come* to happen because something else *did* happen. The totality of what *did* happen we can never know, in Santayana's superhuman and infrahuman sense, but only what *has* happened. It is a statement of the historical character of existence to say that what *does* happen will *have become* different when it *has* happened. What it *is* depends upon what it *will be* when it *has become* a past. This is what it means to find "novelty," "creativity," "originality" in the world. But it is not the past, it is not history, that is "creative." It is the present, and the future operating in the present, that creates the past, and makes history. It recreates the past, which is the material for the present to work upon.

The past is thus not a cause of the present, but a resultant, a precipitate, a cumulative achievement. The past is always "our past," the past of our present. It is the material *with which* we work, and *upon which* our "tendencies" operate. "The past" is *our* past, and as essentially related to our present, is never "over." This past of our present we may call "the Envisaged Past."

But the future likewise is not what *will be,* what *will* eventuate. What *will be,* will be different from our future, when it has become a present. *Our* future is rather the determinate possibilities of the present, what is predictable on the basis of our analysis of it. But the present contains also a host of indeterminate possibilities, unpredictable factors and tendencies. *Our* future is what we can predict; but what will be in its actuality cannot be foreseen—at least by men. Just as the past when it was a present was not what it has become in our present, so the future is not what it will become, when it has become a present. What will be, will be: but this is not equivalent to saying, "What will be already is," or, "The future is now what it will become." To say that the future will be determinate when it has become a present is not to say that it is determinate now. This future that can be predicted from our present may be called "the Envisaged Future."

In contrast to the envisaged past and the envisaged future, our present is the subject-matter that can be directly experienced and dealt with, examined, analysed, and used to test and verify hypotheses: it is the entire context within which inquiry can be significantly carried on, as contrasted with speculation. As such, the present includes the record of the past: astronomical tables, geological strata, fossil remains, archeological deposits, written documents, and monuments.

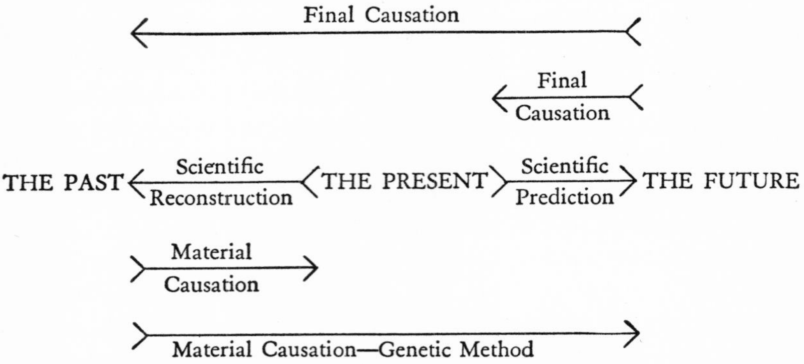

Both the "envisaged past" and the "envisaged future" are thus perspectives from our present, arrived at by analysis of that present, and then used in turn to illuminate it. This double movement in both cases is characteristic of historical inquiry. The reconstruction of the past and the prediction of the future—the outward movement from the present—is effected by bringing our scientific knowledge to bear upon the specific materials disclosed in our present. The understanding of the present in terms of the past and of the future—the inward movement toward the present—is a bringing to bear of this envisaged past and envisaged future upon a further analysis of the present. The understanding of present and past in terms of the future is teleological, a matter of predicted outcomes of present tendencies; the understanding of the present in terms of the past is a matter of material causation, of the genetic method.

It is well at this point to guard against a misconception. It has been said that the "history" of anything is what has happened in the envisaged past of that thing. The understanding of that "history" consists in looking backwards from a present, tracing the continuities or persistences of materials to be found in that history, uncovering the operation of the various factors and processes that have modified and reconstructed those materials, and understanding those processes of modification in terms of our best available scientific knowledge of such processes. The history of materials, social or intellectual, lies in what men have successively done with them and to them: it involves both originality and reconstruction, and persistent continuities. Human history is made by men thinking and acting in characteristic ways, upon the problems those ways of thinking and acting have generated. To grasp the significance of a history we must understand both the continuities and the changes in the histories things have had, and then use the joint presence of those continuities and changes to illuminate what those things themselves have become and now are.

But it has *not* been said that only things or ideas in *our* "present" have histories, or that the only possible vantage-point from which to trace and understand the history of anything has its locus in *our* "present." The past is full of past eventuations or outcomes, each one of which can be taken as a past "present"[6] from which to envisage and understand *its* history. Anything at any date or time will be found to possess a history that can be investigated from the vantage-point of *its* "present," or *focus*. And even if the historian begins, not with such a past eventuation, but rather with the history, say, of *our* science or *our* philosophy, he is indeed led at once to those past "presents" or foci in which our materials and ideas were formulated, and finds he must investigate the history of those formulations from the focus of their loci in the past.

Yet even if the historian chooses arbitrarily to inquire into the history of some past idea, philosophy, or institution, he finds that in the end

[6] The awkwardness of this locution makes it desirable to generalize the notion of the "present" from which a "history" is selected and understood, into the notion of the "focus" of a history, a notion central to any reflection upon histories.

he cannot wholly escape the vantage-point of a focus in his own "present," with its own scheme of understanding, and its own consequences and outcomes. He may set out to trace the history by which Newtonian science came into being, or the history that eventuated in the Thomistic synthesis in the thirteenth century. He cannot remain blind to the revolution that has overtaken Newtonian science in the twentieth century, to our present-day way of understanding that classical mechanics, and to its significance in the world of Einstein. He cannot disregard, in dealing with what Thomas took from Aristotle, the revolution in the interpretation of the Aristotelian documents introduced by Werner Jaeger. For instance, Gibbons's *Decline and Fall* is inescapably an "eighteenth-century history of Rome," in its pattern of understanding, which unmistakably belongs to the Enlightenment; and in its way of taking Christianity, in terms of what Christianity *had become* in the eighteenth century.

Thus any focus may be selected by the historian from which to trace and understand a history. The history of Egypt as contributing to the Periclean age will find its "focus" in the Periclean age; the history of Egypt as contributing to the empire of the Ptolemies will find its "focus" in that empire. If one be content with such an arbitrary choice of focus in some past or *proximate* "present"—that is, "proximate" for that history—then reference to *our* present will not be called for, though it will be implicit in the scheme of understanding we shall employ. For example, Rostovtzeff can write a history of the Hellenistic empires as leading up to the Roman conquest—which is *his* focus—without bringing in the significance of that history for 1943—very much! But he does emphasize economic history, because that is our twentieth-century way of understanding the past. In other words, Rostovtzeff was writing a "modern," "up-to-date" history of the Hellenistic empires. No eighteenth-century scholar could possibly have written his book.

But if the question be raised as to the justification for taking that particular past eventuation as the focus for historical investigation, then there must and will be a reference to a still more "ultimate" focus, in our present. The "focus" of a history must always be relative to something. The "proximate focus" will be relative to the historian's particular enterprise of understanding. The "ultimate focus" will always be found in the historian's own "present." So long as historians live in time, such "presentism" is inevitable.[7]

III

In an interesting section of the last chapter of his *History of Historical Writing,*[8] "A Prospectus of the New History," Harry Elmer Barnes, analysing the methods of contemporary American historians, finds them facing two different and perhaps incompatible tasks. The first is "to trace the genesis of contemporary culture and institutions"—as F. J. Teggart put it, to discover "how man everywhere has come to be as he is." [9] In this enterprise, "the criterion of the significance of the various aspects of culture must be their cogency and relevance with regard to the present age." The other task is "to reconstruct as a totality the civilizations of the leading eras in the past." Here "in attempting to reconstruct the civilization of the age of Pericles the criterion of the importance of events and interests should be the estimates placed upon them by the Periclean age, not by those of the period of the historian." [10] Like many other historians Barnes sharply sunders these two inquiries, and questions whether both can be undertaken in a single work.

Let us examine this taking of a vantage-point in some past "present," this search for the "estimates of the Periclean age" and the significance

[7] Chester M. Destler, in a rather confused article in the *American Historical Review,* LV (1950), 503–29, "Some Observations on Contemporary Historical Theory," identifies what he calls "presentism" with "subjectivism" and "relativism," and attributes all three to "an epistemological revolt from modern science." Many diverse views are lumped together in this article. Mr. Destler seems not to realize that all the philosophers he mentions are concerned to defend a realistic view of historical knowledge against the European idealists; at least he recognizes that like Dewey I am neither a "subjectivist" nor a "subjective relativist." The passage quoted from Dewey's *Logic:* "The conceptual material employed in writing history is that of the period in which a history is written" (p. 233), means that the historian uses the best science available in his day to understand the facts of the record, which are certainly "independent" and "objective." I gather that Mr. Destler agrees with this "presentism" of Dewey's. What the "exclusive presentism" criticised may be, I cannot imagine. I should think that any historian, though he must live in his present, would be by definition concerned with his past.

[8] Norman, Oklahoma, 1937.

[9] F. J. Teggart, *Theory and Processes of History* (Berkeley, 1941), p. 226.

[10] Barnes, *History of Historical Writing,* p. 380.

events, ideas, and institutions possessed "then." In our histories we all try to do something of the sort; and in so doing we certainly manage to understand something. But what is it we are doing when we try to understand "from the inside" the "Periclean age," or the "Middle Ages," or the "Reformation," or the "Enlightenment," when we try to get the "feel" of such unities in terms of foci immanent to them? As many Germans in particular have pointed out, following Nietzsche's search for "unities of aesthetic style in the manifestations of the life of a people," there are certainly such genuine objective structures there to be discovered. It is indeed possible to divide the past neatly into such "periods of synthesis," with intervening "ages of transition"; [11] though it may be significant that whenever we do this, we always find ourselves in an "age of transition," never in a "period of synthesis." It may also be significant that the attempt, with a Pater, a Henry Adams, or a Henry Osborn Taylor, to get the feel of an age from inside, seems always to approach a work of art, the historical novel, or even that triumph of Hollywood, a Cecil de Mille spectacle.

Such structures are certainly there, such relations exist to be singled out: that is why we find so many "insights," so many perceptions of connection and relatedness in works so perverse as Spengler or Toynbee. And vantage-points or foci are there—many of them! What seems arbitrary and "subjective" is why we should emphasize one structure rather than another, this focus rather than that; for there is specified no basis of selection in terms of which the structure chosen could be criticised or verified. Should we, for example, understand the "Periclean age" in terms of what we call the "Greek view of life," or in terms of the progress of Greek geometry, or of Greek economic organization, with its triumphs in banking, or of Athenian imperialism, or of the rise of the Greek middle class? All the structures and foci these terms suggest are objectively there. Which is the unity, the focus, we are to choose? What will dictate our choice?

And such a view, furthermore, suggests a pattern of successive syntheses, a pattern of which Hegel and Marx have made much. But unfortunately the syntheses display very ragged edges. Does the thir-

[11] I was guilty of a book like that myself once; unfortunately, in 1926 I had not found out about the "age of the Baroque," and considered it a "period of transition." That is what the poor historian is up against.

teenth century in Western Europe, for example, belong to the "medieval synthesis," or to the "expansion of Europe" in the Crusades? Is the fourteenth century to be taken as "the breakdown of the medieval synthesis," or as the "rise of modern values and ideas"? Are we to understand the fifteenth in terms of the "Renaissance," or of the "commercial revolution"? Which of these is the incident in which? Is it the mathematical science of Oxford, or the Aristotelianism of Paris, that will furnish the clue to the thirteenth century? When on earth did the "Romantic period" begin? When did the "Enlightenment" end? Many a man clearly went on being "enlightened," quite oblivious of the fact that he was now living under "Romanticism." Some of us are perhaps still not aware that the "age of liberalism" is dead. Is there then no clear pattern, but only amorphous "facts"? Or are there many patterns? They seem all to be "there," but to be "relative." To what? Some tell us that history displays a "dialectical interpenetration of opposites." There is certainly plenty of "interpenetration."

And what, after all, are these "leading eras" into which we neatly parcel out the past? What is "Newtonian science"? What is "liberalism"? "Nationalism"? "Capitalism"? What is "the Renaissance"? Where is it to be found? In Italy, Germany, France, the Low Countries, or England? In the ninth, the twelfth, the thirteenth, the fourteenth, the fifteenth centuries? What is "Greek culture," and how is it to be discriminated? Is it Athenian literature and philosophy, or Alexandrian science, or Dionysian religion? Are we in fact, as Barnes would have it, dealing with *the* past—or with *our* past? Are we not really choosing the leading eras in *our* past, in *our* inherited materials? All these patterns and foci—what are the important eras, what is their succession, what are their foci or "styles"—are always *relative to* something. And what they are *relative to* is clearly *our* present.

But they are not "arbitrary": what shall be the perspective we shall choose is itself dictated by history. Thus Greek culture has always been a "leading era" in the past of all later cultures in the West: but it has always been something different—to John of Salisbury, to Thomas, to Ficino, to Galileo, to Winckelmann, to Hölderlin, to Nietzsche. And again, if we ask, how did Greek culture look to the Greeks? we must add, to what Greeks? To the Spartans? To Thucydides? To Alcibiades? To the followers of Dionysos? Our choice could only mean, how it looked to that element that looks important *to us*. To take some focus other than our own, which we must do, is thus ultimately to take our own at one remove. Greek culture is not part of *the* past, except as a body of records and documents, to which archeology is daily making startling additions, but of *our* past. There can be no other significant past. And *our* past is not buried in *the* past: it is living in the present, in *our* present.

IV

It has been illustrated where we get if we start out by taking "history," or "the task of the historian," as all-inclusive, instead of recognizing that histories are plural, adjectival, and determinate—that they are always histories *of* something, of the *relevant past* of that thing; that they involve a selection, from the infinite relatednesses of past events, of those events and relatednesses that have been important and significant *for* making that thing what it has come to be. If we frankly start by selecting something definite and determinate to investigate the history *of*—something with a locus at any point in time, anywhere in our past—then that history will not be "arbitrary." It will be capable of perfectly "objective" investigation, just because it will be *relative to* that definite thing.

This is merely an illustration of the general principle, that nothing can be "objective" in the way we all want our knowledge to be "objective," historical knowledge as well as all the rest, unless it is "relative"—"relative *to*" something else. Things are "objective" only in terms of their relations. If anything is taken "by itself," out of all relation to anything else, ἁπλῶς, "absolutely"—then the taking will inevitably be an arbitrary choice. If there be no relations to other points of reference, there can be no "reason" for that choice: it will be a "subjective," not an "objective," choice. In other words, "relativism," being *relative to* something determinate, is a necessary condition of any "objectivity." Every "absolute"—everything that is unrelated—is an arbitrary, groundless, "subjective" choice. To fail to take things as related is to destroy all possibility of objectivity.

This "objective relativism" of historical knowledge, as so far developed, has not yet managed to answer all the questions. The selection of the relevant history of anything demands a further "focus" in that thing—either in our present, or in its past "present," as the basis of selection. The relevant past of anything, its history, is selected by some focus in the eventuation of that history. Thus, it is not enough to investigate the history of "our science," or the history of "our economic system." We must first determine what *focus* in our science, what *focus* in our economic system, will select those relevant pasts. This notion of the "focus" of a history is hence fundamental, and the determination of that focus remains a basic problem. To that problem we shall now address ourselves.

At the end of Section I of this chapter, we found that the focus of any history of present things is the eventuation in the envisaged future suggested by present tendencies. That future focus we then stated purposely in very general terms—as the establishment of group control of industry, the working out of international organization, the fostering of further scientific discovery. This was not only because, since the future is not foreseeable, such generality is safer. More particularly, it was to emphasize the fact that what is predicted from an analysis of the present and imposed as an end is not a fixed career. What men envisage is an end, together with a problem of means. The future focus is thus more precisely the problem of how something that must be done is to be brought about. "What has to be done" is something given. The envisaged future poses insistent problems and issues. The past has left us a deposit of materials and resources, setting the limits and conditions within which a choice of means is possible. That means, once chosen, further determines what the future will be when it has become a present. God—or the future—proposes, but man disposes: he forces God to propose something else. And what God—or the future—proposes, is always problems and issues. Man responds and answers. To be sure, man never "solves" the problems with which the future confronts him. He may come near a solution, especially in matters intellectual: but he then finds that what he has done has generated fresh problems, and he is forced to turn to them. They may well be so insistent that he forgets the old problems. Thus, we had to get rid of Hitler and the Japanese militarists. But in doing that necessary job, in the way we chose to do it, we got the Russians and the atom bomb on our necks. Thus do men progress in history. But what men have accomplished in trying to deal with the problems forced on them remains, as the past that is left to work with, as the materials with which to meet new issues. The "past" that is thus left in the moving present is a kind of storehouse of incomplete solutions. And the course of history becomes a game of questions and answers between the future and the present, a conversation between the envisaged future and men—in the current jargon, a "dialectic."

History as confronted and lived through by men is thus fundamentally *problematic* or *functional:* it is a finding of the ways or methods to bring about the ends which history itself imposes upon men. The envisaged future is always presenting men with issues that must be met. Men are always doing something: they are so acting or so inventing new ideas as to create difficulties and tensions for themselves, oppositions that have somehow to be resolved. And their attempts at resolution generate further problems in turn. The past furnishes us with the long record of how past problems were worked upon. Facing our own issues, we turn to our resources, our materials—the means and methods at our disposal. And we understand those materials and resources in the light of their respective histories, of the past problems and action upon them that forced men to create those materials and leave them to us. Our problems—the foci forced upon us by our envisaged future—lead us to select certain materials from our past, and to understand those materials, that selected past, in terms of the problems that generated them, and to which they were a working solution.

It is such *problems* that form the ultimate foci for selecting the facts and events that are relevant to and significant for any history. We have just been speaking of present problems as forming the focus for the history of the present, or of anything in our present. The "present" —or the "present state" of anything: of an institution like marriage, or a body of ideas like physics, or a human activity like painting—is the "locus," the vantage-point, from which we must look backward in trying to understand the history of that institution, science, or activity. But though the vantage-point has its locus in the present, that present state is not yet a sufficiently precise or definite *focus* from which to trace its history. We must find a more specific focus than the mere "present," a definite focus *in* that present locus, for selecting and organizing the relevant facts, events, and conditions that will enter into that history. And that specific *focus* in the present situation of whatever it is we are examining the history of, is precisely the problems presented in that thing. Thus the history of the institution of marriage will find its focus in the problems forced upon men in connection with that institution, the conditions that have generated those problems, the changes they have forced, etc. The history of physics will find its focus in the problems forced on physicists by the present state of physical knowledge and theory, what discoveries and theoretical achievements generated those problems, and how. The history of painting will likewise set out from the focus of what painters are today trying to do and why, what their problems are, and how they came to face those particular problems.

But this holds true not merely of the history of the present, or of present things alone. It is not merely when the locus of which we are trying to trace the history is in our present, that the specific focus is formed by the problems analysis will reveal in that locus. It is true also when we are considering the history of some past eventuation, some past "present," in which the proximate focus is to be sought in that locus in the past. The focus for selecting the materials of that history leading up to a past outcome will be equally the problems confronted. It is in terms of the problems forced on thinkers by the coming of Aristotelian thought, that we select, organize, and understand the history of thirteenth-century thought. It is in terms of the problems forced on a mind brought up to take the Aristotelian world of individual processes very seriously, by the mechanics and the mathematics of the second half of the seventeenth century, that we understand the thought of Leibniz—in terms of what Cassirer would call Leibniz's *Aufgabe,* his task. It is equally in terms of the focus of its generating problems that we understand, say, the English agricultural revolution of the eighteenth century. Woodbridge tells of his teacher Ebbinghaus, who would really explain the thought of a philosopher when he abandoned his notes and asked, "Was will der Mensch?" "What's the fellow really trying to do?"—What is his *problem?*

Any past, any history of anything, is to be understood in the light of the *succession of problems* faced by the men who created that history: what they were trying to do, how they were trying to do it, what resources they had at their disposal, what limits those materials imposed, what possibilities they left open, how they were chosen and closed.

Consider, for example, the history of architecture. If that be taken as something more than the customary chronicle, if it be a genuine "history," it will be understood in terms, e.g., of what the medieval cathedral-builders had to build: what the function of a cathedral was; of the problems of vaulting, arching, buttressing, etc.; of the problems of glazing; of the problems of raising money: enlisting the guilds, or rich donors, or city fathers, as patrons; of the problems of symbolism, of setting forth a bible in stone; of the problems of civic pride that had to be expressed and gratified; of the resources available: the accessible stone or brick; the skills, techniques, and artistic traditions to be worked with, the styles, designs, forms inherited; the expectations of the people, their taste and demands. Like any materials and resources, all these things are to be understood in the light of their respective histories. All set the conditions to which doing the building well, perfecting the implicit possibilities, had to conform—all determined the "artistic" problems. For a New England Georgian meetinghouse, for a Hopi pueblo, for a California Franciscan mission, for a modern skyscraper, all these factors would be different: in each case a wholly new set of problems would be imposed, and a new achievement attained. But the history of any type of architecture would involve a host of analogous factors, all unified in the particular problems confronting the builders and challenging them to do their best. And though the history of architecture is not in itself an "evaluation," it is obviously not only relevant but essential to any evaluation of the success of the architects in accomplishing what they were trying to do.

In contrast, consider our collections of so-called "timeless art," or art "without epoch." Here the basis of selection is purely an aesthetic criterion—that of a sensitive artist today. But the point is, such a collection is definitely not history. Likewise, for the great majority of us, however much we may be attracted by its achievement, African art has "no history"—we simply are ignorant of the problems involved.

And I suspect that any "science of social and cultural change"—which we have defined as the inquiry into the "laws" and "patterns" of the processes at work in histories—would be concerned primarily with the processes involved in problem-meeting. It would deal with how historical problems are generated, through "diffusion," the getting of new materials, techniques, and ideas from outside that culture, or through "invention," the working out in the culture of new solutions to old problems, with the tensions and maladjustments resulting, both in intellectual and material techniques. And it would deal with how problems are dealt with: with the patterns of adjustment, assimilation, compromise, and reconstruction; of reeducation, of modifying old habits, rebuilding institutions, and changing beliefs. It would examine the part played by conscious thought: by reflective criticism, by philosophic reconstruction, by "scientific methods." It would set forth the part played by social choices, by legislation, and their basis in group conflicts; and the part played by dramatic upheavals, by "revolutions" in control. It would show how all these methods work through modifications in the institutionalized habits of belief and behavior—through "psychological" processes. The "science of social and cultural change" would thus deal with the patterns of processes involving means and ends in problem-facing, with functional patterns. And it would treat the efficient cause of such change—the "dynamic," the "driving force" —as frankly a concern of the technique of the "art of social change," which tries to understand the past in terms of the present means to social action: how the means and methods one hopes to employ today have operated in the past.

However one approach it, any analysis of the factors involved in a history takes one ultimately to a functional structure, a structure of means and ends. Indeed, there are so many facts and so many patterns of relation, so many structures and types of structure discernible in the history of anything, and it is so manifestly impossible to include them all in a history, that any selection will remain "arbitrary" and "subjective" unless it is dictated by some problem or necessary choice generated in that history itself. Only in such a problematic, functional context—only by realizing clearly, in any field whose history we are exploring, "These are the fundamental problems and choices today," or "These *were* the problems, this was the *Aufgabe,* in some past or proximate 'present' "—can we hope to understand or write the history of anything "objectively." Only thus can we escape the difficulties of Barnes and the "stylists," and their hopeless search for the "estimates of the Periclean age itself." Inquiry cannot hope to discover those "estimates," which vary "arbitrarily"; but it can discover the *problems* of the Periclean age. Cassirer's *Aufgabe,* the "task imposed," is a rather better term than "problems." It means something imposed, that must be faced, *faciendum.* "Problems" is too weak: it suggests that men "thought them up," and could escape them if they wanted to.

Only thus can we understand objectively, for example, the history of the Romantic era. It is notoriously difficult to find any common traits, common pattern, or "style" in that movement. But we can hope to find the *common problems* in terms of which we can understand its history. As Jacques Barzun writes, "Clearly, the one thing that unifies men in a given age is not their individual philosophies, but the *dominant problem* that these philosophies are designed to solve. In the romantic period this problem was to create a new world on the ruins of the old" [12]—i.e., to criticise the inadequate synthesis of the eighteenth century, and to reconstruct a more adequate one.

The historian *must* make a selection. From the infinite variety of relatednesses that past events disclose, he must select what is important or "basic" for his particular history. If that selection is not to be merely what *seems* important *for him,* if it is not to be "subjective" and "arbitrary," the selection must have an "objective" focus in something to be done, something he sees forced and imposed on men, some *Aufgabe* or *faciendum,* some job to be accomplished. The history of what is important *for* and relevant *to that problem*—of the causes and conditions that generated it, the materials and resources men had to draw upon, how they dealt with it—will then be perfectly "objective," in a sense in which no mere recording of arbitrarily selected "facts" could ever be.

This is the "objective relativism" that is characteristic of historical knowledge, as it is of all types of knowledge. Knowledge is "objective" only *for* some determinate context: it is always a knowledge of *the* structure and relations essential *for* that context. In historical knowledge, the context is always a teleological and functional one, pointing to a structure of means and ends, of "means *for*" or "relative *to*" ends

[12] Jacques Barzun, *Romanticism and the Modern Ego* (Boston, 1943), pp. 21–22.

and eventuations. In that context, the relation between the means and the outcome will be "objective."

In historical knowledge, the focus in any history—the focus in a problem in the envisaged future—will be *relative to* that time and situation —it will be "the" problem, "the" issue, "the" *Aufgabe for* that history, what has to be done "in those times." It will be what Paul Tillich calls the "Kairos." This problematic focus of a history will be "historically relative," and "historically conditioned"—and for that precise reason, it will be "objective." The fact that this focus, this *Aufgabe,* this Kairos, is continually changing with further history-as-actuality, is the reason why history-as-written has to be continually rewritten, why it is never enough merely to add further new chapters to a history selected by a now antiquated focus. "Objectivity" means always being *objective for* something, just as "necessity" means always being *necessary for* something. There can be no "objectivity" without relations to an objective; there can be no warranted idea without an ideal.

In summary, then, on the first of the two major problems of the Theory of History, the question of how histories are to be understood, this "objective relativism" means concretely: The history of anything is what has happened and become relevant in the envisaged past of that thing. The understanding of that history consists in looking backward from a "focus," tracing the continuities or persistences of materials to be found in that history, uncovering the operations of the various factors and processes that have in the past modified and reconstructed those materials, and understanding those modifications and reconstructions in terms of the best scientific knowledge available today—of what Dewey calls "the conceptual materials available in the historian's present." The focus in the present of any history first selects *its* past, and designates the particular historical changes that brought about its present state. These changes are then themselves explained by drawing upon the best science of changes in that "present" in which the history is being understood—a science of cultural change in which certain patterns or constant operations of human behavior have been arrived at through the experimental analysis of observed behavior. The record of the past of course furnishes material to such a science of cultural change, in the form of instances of the kind or pattern of behavior that can be observed in the present. But it is in terms of our present science of human behavior, of our psychology, anthropology, and social sciences in general, such as they are, that we must ultimately understand past human behavior, if we are to understand it at all.

But this science of the processes at work in human histories will not of course of itself explain the presence of the particular materials that enter into actual processes. To understand the processes by which ideas and institutions are changed and developed, will not of course explain what particular ideas and institutions are there to be changed. In contrast with a "process," which is always one instance of a universal, a "history" is always a particular, a concrete individual, with a unique material of its own. In that particular history, universal "processes" are at work, and the changes that take place in that history are to be understood in terms of the appropriate science of those universal "processes." The particular materials that are changed by these universal "processes," however, are explained not by the universal processes of change, but by tracing their *histories* to those points where they were formed or transformed—by universal "processes" again to be themselves explained by the science of formation and transformation. Thus a "history"—as a concrete individual, a τόδε τι—is to be understood both in terms of the origin of its materials, and of the operations of human thought and action upon them. The "origins" are always themselves unique histories; the "operations" are illustrations of a science of human operations. To grasp the significance of "a history," we must understand both the continuities and the changes in the histories that things have had.

CHAPTER 3

History as an Instrument of Understanding: The Genetic Method and Historical Determinism

HISTORIES are not only things to be understood and explained. When so understood, histories themselves become instruments for understanding those things of which they are the histories. The joint presence of the continuities and changes in the past of a thing, when once envisaged, can be used to illuminate what that thing has become and now is. Nothing is so clear or obvious as the fact that this is the case; yet nothing about history is so puzzling as the precise nature and function of this illumination that historical knowledge brings. A knowledge of the history of things *is* essential to an understanding of them, and ultimately, of ourselves and our world; yet when we ask *why* and *how,* we are at once plunged into a thicket of thorny questions.

There are a host of impossible explanations of the undoubted fact that a knowledge of the past does illuminate the present. We are told, for instance, that history helps us to understand where we are today, because it explains "what we have been through," and "why things have been as they have": it explains "the pattern of the historical process." This sounds promising, until we reflect that what it means is that what history explains to us is history itself. And this is puzzling: for it is clearly not history that enables us to understand history, but science.

And we are still suffering from the effects of the idea of evolution, whether in the form given it in Hegel and the various Hegelianisms and Marxisms, or in the Darwinians, or in Spencer and the sociologists.

All alike suffered from the delusion that the mere record of the past somehow explains the present, that there is a fixed line of development which "causes" and explains the changes that illustrate it, a necessary dialectic or evolutionary progress of history; and that human institutions and ideas evolve, unfold, and move through time, in a kind of vacuum, by a sort of inner force. Now obviously the record of what has happened is not itself the explanation of anything, but rather presents a series of problems that demand to be explained. Even if we do manage to force the facts into some intelligible pattern, that pattern will be, not the cause of the facts, but itself a result to be explained. Nor does one "stage" of history cause another: causes are to be found, not in the past, but in the experimental analysis of the present. The past is not the cause of the present, but rather itself a resultant of other causes.

Thus Herodotus understands the rise of the Greeks as due to the favor of the gods; Marx, as due to the tensions generated between the forces of production and the relations of production, and the resulting class-conflict that is precipitated; and contemporary historians, as due to the factors involved in our own more complicated social sciences. The record is the same for all: so far as written documents go, it has been largely available and known since the seventeenth century. It is the schemes of science that have changed. Herodotus actually traveled through Greece, Asia Minor, and Egypt, and has left us marvelous stories and penetrating observations. But today, thanks to archeology, we know far more about the *history* of those civilizations than he did. He only *observed* them: we *understand* them. In fact, it can be said, the farther off we get from them in time, the more completely we understand their history.

It is thus clear that the attempt to understand Greece *wie es eigentlich gewesen* is not only impossible, but is not even a valid ideal of knowledge. Yet we must have some understanding of what Greece was; for Greece is one of the most vital intellectual forces today. And if we are to understand the ideas with which we must work in our world, we find ourselves inevitably seeking to understand what they meant to the Greeks who first invented and used them. The past is the storehouse of our materials, which we try to comprehend by the history we write, not by the history our fathers made. And so we select from the scanty record what we can find comprehensible, and interpret it by means of our science and thought; and the result, incomprehensibly enough, helps us to understand that science and thought better!

How, then, does a knowledge of its history "illuminate" the present? How does it contribute to an understanding and an evaluation of the materials in any present? How does a knowledge of the history of anything function as an instrument for comprehending that thing? Just what about that thing does it enable us to explain?

It is easy to say that a knowledge of the past explains everything, that the history of a thing tells us all about it. It was so said by the advocates of the historical or genetic method in the full flush of its triumphs in nineteenth-century natural and social science, and in the hey-day of the revelation of evolution. The excesses to which these claims were pushed by the uncritical has naturally provoked a reaction. For it is just as easy to say that the record of history itself explains nothing, but rather offers a problem to be explained: that history has nothing to do with evaluation, and that to think that it has is to commit the genetic fallacy. It was so said by Morris Cohen, by Sidney Hook, and by the whole crop of logicians during the past generation: and such a critical view furnishes the main drive in Woodbridge's treatment of evolutionary thinking.

Now it is clear that history does not explain some things: it does not explain itself, as the simple-minded have in effect said, and it does not explain the "origin" of anything. But it is equally obvious that history does make clear other things: it certainly furnishes a great deal of what we can call provisionally and non-committally "illumination." Just what it does and just how it functions needs careful clarification. I propose therefore to undertake a defense of the historical or genetic method; or rather, to attempt a reconstruction of that method into a defensible form. And I want to indicate its proper place in the functional or "problematic" view of history I am setting forth.

In his classic critique of the genetic method, Sidney Hook has well characterized the historical method in its familiar form:

> It starts out from the idea that all objects of historical analysis have had a development and that this development can be rendered significant, or understood, by tracing the spatio-temporal continuity of its structure—whether it be of an institution, or folk-legend, or tool—as far back as possible. . . . No notion is more widespread than that knowledge of the past is the key

to the present. "How did it get that way?" is a question considered by many to be the preliminary indispensable to understanding the state a thing actually is in.[1]

And Hook has also given the most forceful critique of such "historicism":

Reflection will show that the reverse is true, that knowledge of the present is the key to the understanding of the past. Or to select a more specific illustration, no amount of knowledge of the mind of primitive man will add one jot to our knowledge of the mind of man today; on the other hand, the more we discover about mental processes going on today—in the illiterate adult, the infantile, the superstitious—the more insight we can win into the intellectual life of the primitive. . . . Granting that every institution or historical situation has had a development, the most exhaustive knowledge of its development cannot of itself lead to an understanding of 1) why this institution ever originated; 2) why it persisted; and 3) why it developed in the direction it did. . . . At best historical continuity is a *condition* of survival and not a cause.[2]

The genetic method, then, maintains that tracing the "historical continuity" of anything is an adequate explanation of that thing. Thus any discussion of it soon bumps into the notion of "the continuity of history." Now this notion stands in great need of clarification. In terms of the present analysis, "the continuity of history" is a wholly vague and meaningless phrase. "History" in general is not "continuous." Rather, there are determinate "continuities" that may be discovered in "histories." Every *process* at work in histories is continuous; and the histories themselves have an aspect of continuity, or they would not be unified histories. But they must also have an aspect of discontinuity, of novelty, of new factors coming into operation, or else they would not be histories at all. Thus a falling stone has no "history," though its motion is continuous and its velocity cumulative. For its acceleration remains constant. On the other hand, a disease can be properly said to have a "case-history," though it be "typical," and "run its course"; for its "acceleration" is not constant, but new factors are coming into play.

[1] Sidney Hook, "A Pragmatic Critique of the Historico-Genetic Method," in *Essays in Honor of John Dewey on the Occasion of His Seventieth Birthday* (New York, 1929), pp. 157, 156. Quotations used by permission of Henry Holt and Company, Inc.

[2] *Ibid.*, pp. 156–57, 158.

Hence "evolution" is not a "history," if it be taken as of the unilinear, Spencerian type defined by Spencer's famous formula; though there might be specific histories in a Spencerian world, the result of the impingement of different evolutions with different rates upon each other. Hegel's formula does describe a history, because it introduces novelty as well as continuity; though if it be taken as genuinely "dialectical," that is, as deductive a priori, it ceases to be a history.

In fact, "continuity" is said to obtain in histories in three main senses, which are often confused. 1) In opposition to change or novelty, "continuity" is taken to mean the continuance or *persistence* of materials—physical objects, customs, habits, or ideas. 2) Change is taken as itself continuous, and "continuity" hence means the *gradualness* of change, as opposed to leaps or mutations—as in Darwinian evolution, as opposed to "revolution." Change is held to proceed by small steps, with no necessary continuance or persistence of anything. This is the general nineteenth-century conception of change, as "freedom broadening down from precedent to precedent." 3) "Continuity" is taken as synonymous with the fact of history itself, of the historical character of existence, as the persistence of something that "has" a history, and unifies that history, but undergoes whatever changes happen to it, so that they can be viewed in a serial order of antecedents and consequents as changes of that thing. Continuity in this sense means *uninterruptedness* of function in an institution or idea, not the persistence of materials or forms with a changed function, and is quite compatible with drastic changes in the way of performing that function: e.g., as with marriage, or technology, or the idea of God.

"Continuity," that is, may mean either *persistence,* or *gradualness,* or *uninterruptedness* of function. All three senses point to certain aspects of histories; though it is obvious that the first two, continuity as persistence and as gradualness, do not hold of all factors in every history. A history would be no history at all if everything in it persisted; and it is plain that many histories exhibit drastic changes, revolutions, or mutations.

The well-known passage from E. B. Tylor's *Primitive Culture* illustrates each of these three kinds of historical continuity:

Looking round the rooms we live in, we may try here how far he who knows only his own time can be capable of rightly comprehending even that. Here is the honeysuckle of Assyria, there the fleur-de-lis of Anjou, a cornice with a Greek border runs around the ceiling, the style of Louis XIV and its parent the Renaissance share the looking-glass between them.

These are illustrations of sheer persistence of forms.

The ridiculous little tails of the German postilion's coat show of themselves how they came to dwindle to such absurd rudiments; but the English clergyman's bands no longer so convey their history to the eye, and look unaccountable enough till one has seen the intermediate stages, through which they came down from the more serviceable wide collars . . . which gave their name to the "band-box" they used to be kept in. The books of costume show how one garment grew or shrank by gradual stages and passed into another.

These are instances of gradualness, and of persistence of form coupled with loss of function.

In books, again, we see each writer not for and by himself, but occupying his proper place in history; we look through each philosopher, mathematician, chemist, poet, into the background of his education,—through Leibniz into Descartes, through Dalton into Priestley, through Milton into Homer.[3]

Here is the persistence of material with a new function, continuity of means coupled with new problems and new ends.

Now just what does tracing a continuity of the first or the third type in a history tell us? It points to the relevant *antecedents* of the materials in a particular and determinate history. It "reveals" the *source* of those materials, and it "discloses" the particular operations or processes that generated them. These processes must be of a *type* that is experimentally verifiable today; but the concrete processes, and the particular materials they operated upon, are found in the record, by tracing a history. The formation of any belief or institution in the past will thus be an *illustration* of human nature as it is observed today, but a *revelation* of how human nature operated in the past.

Thus tracing a history will disclose the specific function of a way of acting or believing in the past, and how well that way did its job.

[3] Edward B. Tylor, *Primitive Culture* (New York, 1889), I, 17 ff. For comment and criticism, see F. J. E. Woodbridge, *The Purpose of History* (New York, 1916), Chapter III, "The Continuity of History."

It will not of itself reveal the present function of that way, or its adequacy today. But it will illuminate the differences between the conditions then and now, the consequent decline in adequacy, or the changes in the very function performed. It is thus that history is relevant to evaluation in the present, though it does not in itself furnish such an evaluation. For example, to understand how the doctrine of national sovereignty was formulated during the era of the Protestant Revolt does not indicate whether or not it is adequate for our era of jet-plane technology, though it does suggest that the inquiry is worth making. Rather, when we find in our closely-knit world that national sovereignty fits in with international waterways like the Suez Canal like grit in a bearing, and are forced to face the problems with which that confronts the United Nations, the history of national sovereignty explains why we have the problem, focuses attention on the modified functions it must now serve, and reveals how well it once performed a function we can no longer afford to let it perform. Or, an understanding of why it was that the fact of knowledge became a central philosophical problem in the eighteenth century, through revealing the assumptions that then generated it, frees us from the necessity through the mere persistence of those assumptions of finding it a problem today. This is the liberating and emancipating function of historical knowledge, so often and so justly extolled.[4]

One thing that tracing historical continuities does *not* do, is to explain "origins." Historical knowledge may "reveal," point to, give the locus of "origins," but it does not "explain" them. Now the term "origin" is used in the discussion of histories in at least three different senses. It designates 1) the *coming into being* or genesis of something at a time before which it did not exist. Tracing of the history of the thing will lead us to the occasion when that occurred; but it will not explain the occurrence. Such a genesis is explained by the operation of processes verifiable today, by an Aristotelian *ὑπὸ τίνος*, a "By What." Histories are of course full of such geneses or beginnings. "Origin" means 2) the *source* from which something is derived, the Aristotelian *ἐξ οὗ* or "From What," the material cause. Now knowledge of the source of materials may be interesting, but it sheds little light on what has been or can

4 See James Harvey Robinson, *The Human Comedy* (New York, 1937), esp. first and last chapters.

be done with them. The enormous labor that has been spent on tracing the "sources" of various writers in literary history might well have been directed toward what the writer did with his materials, wherever he got them. A generation ago the standard course on Shakespeare spent so much time on the sources of his plays that it had little left for a study of how he used those sources. The former was judged to be literary "scholarship," the latter was not.

It must be recognized that any "source," like any "coming into being," is always specific and determinate, and must be relevant to the particular context or inquiry. Thus we derived the Constitution from the convention of 1787, no matter where the Founding Fathers got their ideas, and from the specific interpretative decisions of the Supreme Court. We got the honeysuckle design from the Assyrians, no matter whence they derived it. We obtained geometry from the Greeks, no matter how they managed to develop it. Inquiry into such sources is relevant to the understanding and evaluation of our materials just in the measure that it is specific and determinate, and reveals the specific function of those materials, whether they be the honeysuckle design or geometry. In contrast, the "origin" of religion, or of marriage, or of poetry, or of myth, is vague and irrelevant unless it be merely a disguised and mythical way of indicating a selection from the manifold functions those institutions are now observed to be serving. The same holds true of *"the* origin of *the* state," or *"the* origin of 'capitalism.' "

"Origin" is taken to mean 3) *antecedents.* In this sense, "origin" designates the mere fact of historical continuity of the third type. In such an inquiry no real "ultimate origins" or real "beginnings" are discoverable—none, that is, that are specific and determinate. The search for mere "antecedents" suggests in itself no principle of selection, no functional context or problem to furnish a selective focus for a history. It is sheer description, like Mill's account of causation. In the context of a history, that is, we can profitably distinguish the "By What" and the "From What," but not the "After What."

"Origin" is thus used in the sense of "coming into being," of "source whence derived," and of mere "antecedent." Only the first two contribute to an understanding of the present; and neither, without reference to other active factors or processes, is adequate to "explain" how anything "comes about." We can therefore agree with Sidney Hook's statement of the results of a criticism of the genetic method, without taking it as the end of our inquiry:

It has gradually become clear that a detailed account of a thing's development cannot serve as a substitute for an analysis of its *nature.* Not that knowledge of a thing's development does not contribute to our understanding of its nature, but rather that such knowledge of the past serves at best as a suggestive aid to the experimental determination in the present of what the thing really is.[5]

II

That this is not a conclusion, but a point of departure for further inquiry, I wish to illustrate with a passage from Woodbridge that I have found extremely illuminating:

When we say that the evolution of anything discloses its *history,* but not its *nature,* we should not prejudge the possibility that there may be things the nature of which is only historically definable, the nature of which is, we may say, just their concrete history. A grain of wheat in its chemical and physical composition is a thing quite different from what we call a seed, the grain of wheat which implies what only its history can make apparent at the time of harvest.[6]

This notion of an "historically definable nature" is most instructive. Woodbridge takes as his illustration the seed, a living thing, an instance of a natural process of growth. This instance of a living organism indeed raises various questions when his further analysis is applied to human histories. But the relation found between the temporal structure or pattern of the seed's growth and the mechanism involved does seem to clarify and illuminate the relation between the temporal structure of human histories and the mechanism they are dependent upon.

It is conceivably possible that we might know the chemical and physical composition of all seeds without any nook or corner left unexplored; that we might then be able to detect differences in their composition which would allow us to classify them with accuracy, so that one kind of seed could be distinguished without error from any other kind; and yet that we might find nothing which would indicate what the nature of those

[5] Hook, "A Pragmatic Critique of the Historico-Genetic Method," in *Essays in Honor of John Dewey,* p. 156.

[6] F. J. E. Woodbridge, "Evolution," in *Nature and Mind* (New York, 1937), p. 143.

seeds is as displayed in their growth. It is considerations like these that give to vitalistic theories their recurring interest. Yet we should emphasize two things: first, that under the supposition we have made, vitalism is scientifically unnecessary; and secondly, that vitalism would be scientifically necessary only if after fully ascertaining the composition of all seeds we were unable to distinguish between them or to classify them as of different kinds. It may well be that every living thing in its germ has a mechanical constitution as specifically and individually distinct as the specific form and individuality which its maturity reveals. The evidence points that way, and as long as it so points, vitalistic theories are naturally viewed with suspicion. No; the supposition I have ventured to make, has not been made in order that we may entertain once more a theory which retreats defeated again and again after every fresh appearance, but to emphasize the fact that the nature of a thing may be progressive. Time may enter into its substance.[7]

This analysis of the career of the seed as an "historically definable nature" I choose to push a little further, because I wish to use it in analysing human careers and human histories. The characteristic and specific temporal pattern of the seed's career is found to be correlated with a characteristic and specific "mechanical constitution," so that every such constitution or structure indicates such a temporal pattern, and such a pattern implies that such a "constitution" is present as a mechanism. If there is to be that pattern, then there must be that mechanism: it is "essential" to the occurrence. But the "nature" of that mechanism—what it can do, its powers—are revealed only in their operation, in the specific career and temporal pattern correlated with it, in "the nature of those seeds as displayed in their growth." A complete chemical analysis of the seed would not lead us to "expect" such a growth; but confronted by that growth, we find such a seed to be a necessary factor or condition of its occurrence. That is, a certain chemical constitution, of the genes, etc., is essential to that historical nature or pattern, without in any sense *being* that nature. The nature is not definable chemically, but only historically. We know that if those genes are changed, by X-rays, e.g., there will be a different pattern of growth; though even could we analyse the chemical change completely, we could not tell *how* the pattern would be changed. We should have to observe the new pattern, and then correlate it with the new chemical constitution.

[7] *Ibid.*, p. 144.

This chemical constitution I shall call the "material" of that career. It is a set of "passive" powers; but what those powers *can do* is discoverable only when they operate in the career. The "constitution" is chemically analysable in isolation: it operates as a set of limits, boundaries beyond which the operations of the seed's processes of growth cannot go. The Mendelian laws, for example, are the statement of such a set of limits. A "mutation" is a significant change in that constitution, and hence in both its powers and the limits it sets; and consequently it will make possible a new determinate set of operations, a new "historical nature." A mutation is thus an "origin" as a coming into being or genesis. But how the limits have been changed must be observed before they can be correlated with the changed chemical structure.

The specific chemical structure is essential to the historical nature, but it is not the only factor essential. Other factors are needed to set those factors in operation, to serve as stimuli or "active" powers. The soil, moisture, and sunlight interact with the seed as efficient causes or dynamic factors. They are selective of the powers of that constitution, determining which of them shall be realized within the limits set. They may destroy the seed; they may alter its limits or change its chemical constitution, and thus cause a mutation and originate a novel character in the pattern of the career. To do so they must be of the "same order" as the mechanism of the seed: that is, they must be capable of interacting with it. A gardener can plant the seed, but he cannot make a garden by wishing or thinking alone; he must use instruments capable of interacting with the seed, physico-chemical means.

But though the chemical constitution of the seed, and the interacting factors, are both essential to that historical nature, they do not *define* it: they *are* not that nature. That nature *is* its concrete history, the history of that interaction. The growth of the seed is progressive: "time enters into its substance." This does not mean that there enters in or is present any additional "vitalistic" factor or controlling "entelechy"; it means that the process is itself "vital," a life-history, a career in time, to be described as a history of interactions, to be recorded as the rings of the redwoods have recorded each its own unique "vital nature."

Limits are set by the chemical constitution and the interacting factors: they cannot normally operate beyond certain rates, and it will take a certain time for the seed to come to maturity, flower, bear seeds, and decay. We can state the "normal life-history" of such a seed, that is, under "normal" conditions of interaction. Such a normal life-history will be a statistical generalization. It will be no revelation of the powers of that seed under *other* conditions, as agrobiologists like Wilcox have shown; and as anyone who has ever planted a garden knows, those powers and limits are not dependent on the seed's constitution alone, but on the interacting factors as well. Irrespective of the rate, there is found a certain fixed sequence which can as yet only be described; though when described, it might well be correlated with more elementary chemical processes, like rates of chemical deposit, etc., at certain temperatures.

III

Now when we turn to human histories and careers, we find the same relation obtaining between the "historical nature"—the particular history—and the factors and mechanisms found to be essential to it—between the temporal pattern of the history, and the "constitution" or material of the history. Here too that temporal pattern or history must be first given, before we can analyse how its different factors, the different historical processes at work in that history, have interacted in particular. And the powers of those processes—what they can do—are likewise revealed only in their concrete operations. When we have found those temporal natures, we can then correlate them with the organization of their materials and of the dynamic or interacting factors.

For example, in the histories of societies and cultures, or of their parts or aspects, like institutions or ideas, there are many discoverable patterns of organization, comparable to the chemical constitution of the seed. There is the *economic organization,* a set of institutionalized habits for controlling technology and its fruits; the *technological organization,* a set of habits for turning natural materials to human use; the *intellectual organization,* a set of systematized and operative beliefs and attitudes; the *political organization,* a set of institutionalized methods of adjusting conflicts; the *religious organization,* the most inclusive of all, a set of habitual ways of acting, feeling, and even believing, holding that society together and expressing its common experience; and other organizations as well. Each of these organizations of social habits is a group of "limits" or "boundaries" beyond which human action in that society cannot go, a set of "passive powers," giving a determinate form and direction to what men can do in that society.

The "history" or "temporal pattern" of that society is consequently "determined"—that is, confined within certain prescribed channels or limits—by each of these organized structures of habits. Thus "social determinism," or "historical determination," in those historical natures that are societies or cultures, means quite literally "confinement" of its activities within "termini" or bounds set by its institutionalized habits. Now, these determining or limiting organizations of habits are not themselves "active powers," or "dynamic factors": they are very definitely *not* social or historical "forces." They *do* nothing whatsoever, but are *ways* in which things are *done;* they are adverbs, not verbs or processes—they are *limits,* not activities. This is fundamental for any understanding of social or historical "determinism."

Thus "economic determinism" does not mysteriously invoke nonexistent economic "forces"; it refers to the limits set to the possible economic interactions in a society by the "relations of production" that are habitual in that society. Thus under our economic system—or any other—the only governmental program of dealing with unemployment that will receive the support of the business community is national defense and war—as both Hitler and the New Deal found out, and as has been learned by subsequent American administrations, both Democratic and Republican. "Political determinism" points to the limits set to possible activities by the prevailing habits of political action. Thus, in the absence of representative government, all political differences become "conspiracies," as in Russia. With representative habits and methods, it is necessary to take account of public opinion, and to employ all the resources of Madison Avenue to persuade or bulldoze people to follow your policy. "Intellectual determinism" points to the limits set on action in a society by its store of available knowledge, methods, and attitudes.

Now, in general, the more inclusive the organization, the more "determined" it is itself by the activities it serves to organize, the more it is limited by those materials, the more "derivative" from them it is. For example, a political organization, as the habits of adjusting differences and conflicts within a society, or within an institution or group, is obviously dependent on or limited by the conflicts of interest or habit it smooths over, by their intensity, and by the need for unified action. That is, the political problems of securing cooperative action through adjusting conflicts of interest, habit, and desire, are themselves largely "determined" by factors in the particular "organization of habits" within which the conflicts take their rise. Today, these factors giving rise to conflicts are largely economic. But they are also religious, as in Ireland, India, and Boston; or they involve moral patterns of living, like birth control and prohibition. Or they are "nationalistic"—perhaps these are only a contemporary type of religious factor, and are so intense because we have as yet been able to devise no adequate political method of dealing with such religious emotions. The "political organization" is itself determined by the intensity of the conflicts it must deal with, and by the need for unified social action. Whether the political methods of the French Republic can solve the problems of conflict in Algeria, whether those of the British "commonwealth" can solve those on Cyprus, whether those of the United States can solve the problems of desegregation—these are themselves problems still to be determined.

But the political methods available themselves "determine" the conflicts they exist to harmonize; that is, the intensity of the conflicts is a function of the lack of means of adjustment and compromise. If you can hope to win in the next election and get something of what you want, your temper will remain below the boiling-point. If there is some institution, like the old French Senate, or the Supreme Court before Roosevelt got it on the run, then you will get up steam to "capture the state." The situations in Cyprus or South Africa are cases in point. And every form of political organization generates its own institutionalized complex of behaviors and habits, with clustering vested interests, including a bureaucracy that impedes and limits adjustment. The political power to enforce cooperative action notoriously has a relatively independent career of its own, as we have seen in men as different as Stalin and Roosevelt.

The religious organization, as the most inclusive organization in a society, is the most determined by that culture, the one most clearly a "reflection" of it, like the priestly religion of Bergson's closed society, or the emerging American religion, or the social religions of Europe.

On the other hand, the intellectual organization or "science" of a given culture, in the measure that its beliefs about nature are controlled by the structure of nature itself, is least subject to "social determination"; while its "social science," the attempt to organize intellectually its beliefs about society, is notoriously much more narrowly determined by its materials, and much more limited by the habits and attitudes of the group whose problems it formulates and tries to deal with. This is the basic difference between the various "organized systems of beliefs" of different cultures, and the functional knowledge of how to do something—between the countless schemes of "intelligibility" or "understanding," all socially determined or limited, and the type of "science" generated in our own society, which has been increasingly determined by the functional structure of its subject-matter—that is, by the relation between means and ends, which can be verified as a means to manipulating that subject-matter.

Now the world and its several subject-matters exhibit an infinite diversity of structures or relatednesses through which they may be intellectually grasped. On various selections of these structures, many different "organized systems of beliefs" or "schemes of intelligibility" —many ways of understanding—may be based. Each scheme or way will be socially determined to serve some specific social function, in addition to serving the general psychological function of making men "understand" or feel at home in their world by providing relations they can count upon.

Our own science is likewise thus socially determined: its function and aim is kept "within the bounds" of the "power to do something," the power to manipulate natural materials, by the organization and pattern of habits in our society. Our science is socially limited or determined to inquire into and understand in terms of those selected relations that are the natural structure of modes of operation, the relations of means and ends, the functional structure of processes. That is, our science is socially determined to be an art, a technique, a technology; and we "understand" something when we know how it is brought about, when we can manipulate it, and thus produce what we want, and thereby "verify experimentally" a functional relation of means to ends.

The history of the working out of this type of science in our society explains why it is socially determined to be functional or technological knowledge: indeed, this is a clear illustration of the use of historical knowledge as an instrument of understanding. The growth of the arts and crafts, and the accumulation of capital, led to the demand for a "useful knowledge" of ways of operating, or functional structure, long before the means and methods of gaining such knowledge were perfected. Thus the problem was socially set or generated, how to build up a type of technological science like ours. How that problem was set, is "revealed" by tracing its history, and "explained" by recourse to our science of social change. This problem was faced, when it confronted men in the sixteenth century, with resources consisting of two other kinds of science: 1) the classifying and linguistic scheme of the Aristotelian schoolmen, especially as turned from a religious to a practical function in Northern Italy; and 2) the techniques of the essentially aesthetic science of Greek mathematics, likewise bent to a "practical geometry" in Italy—though the idea of a mathematical science of nature for practical ends had been already generated in religious interests. The nature of these materials is all "revealed" by their complex histories, and "explained" in terms of an elaborate set of social determinations.

But that history of materials out of which our science was built makes it clear why it took so long for an essentially technological science to develop frankly the form of a technique, a means of manipulating things—to make central the structure of means and ends, of modes of operation, and to work out the appropriate techniques in mathematical procedure. The historically conditioned nature of those materials imposed limits upon them, and made them refractory to the new uses to which men were bending them. Their history explains why they were refractory, why the materials presented the problems they did. Our present scientific knowledge explains the measure of their success: why their use enabled men to do what they did. They succeeded in the measure that they did grasp the instrumental structure of things, and thus served their socially determined function of being "useful knowledge," of how to manipulate, just to the extent that they were determined by the structure of natural modes of operation—by the way things really act.

Thus social organization determines the aim and function of the science generated in a society. Then that science, if it be the knowing how to do things, determines the other organizations in turn—it imposes new limits upon them. This is the situation typical of the complex relation between the different types of social or historical determination.

Our science is still subject to many other kinds of determination, which help to set its problems and limit its attitudes. "Science" is itself an institutionalized complex of behaviors and habits, each with an inertia and a persistence of its own. Russell has pointed out that whereas American rats placed in mazes rush around madly until they chance upon the way out, German rats sit down and calmly figure out the answer. This is a place where the history of materials and the tracing of their "sources" is important, for it leads us to the different intellectual "traditions," with their characteristic assumptions and ways of thinking, that are so important for understanding. This determination by an intellectual tradition is most obvious in the case of "theories," the schemes of interpreting and organizing experimental results, as contrasted with techniques and procedures—that is, in just the measure that "understanding" in terms of a familiar pattern takes precedence over functional knowledge.

But in the measure that our science has become a functional knowledge of how to do things, and concentrates on means, the natural ways of operating of materials, it has gained relative independence of these other social determinations. And the most significant "mutations," or novel factors introduced into our culture, have since the seventeenth century come from science, which has been the chief "dynamic factor."

We have been examining the complex "constitution" or "structure" of a society, its various organizations of habitual activities, which, taken together, correspond to the "chemical constitution" of the seed. These organizations, we have seen, form a set of specific powers imposing "limits" or "bounds," and thus determining the activities of men in that society. But just as in the case of the seed, what these determinations or limits set to the powers of a society by its various "organizations"—its "constitution"—actually are, is revealed only in its history—in its "historical nature" as exhibited in the temporal pattern of its growth. A society *is* an "historical nature"; that is, it is *not* its limiting organizations alone, taken at any given moment—they constitute merely its formal structure—but it is rather its concrete history: "time enters into its substance."

And significant changes in the limits and the powers of these organizations—what the biologist calls "mutations"—have been generated in all of them. Science has its discoveries, technology its inventions, politics its "statesmen," religion its "prophets." Each organization has its own history, in which the others appear as "interacting factors." And that history must be given before it can be understood and used to analyse our materials. Thus the history of science is not merely a history of scientific problems, but also of the way in which those problems have been determined or limited by technology, the economic organization, religious habits, etc. And the history of the economic organization is not merely the history of economic problems, but also of the way in which those problems have been determined or limited by technology, by scientific knowledge, by religious habits and beliefs, by political methods, by habits of behavior like national allegiance, etc. It is thus a matter of the particular focus taken—or imposed—which set of problems the historian makes central.

IV

We have so far taken Woodbridge's notion of an "historically definable nature," his example of the seed, and his statement of the relation between the temporal pattern of its career and the chemical constitution of the seed—between the formal cause of that career and its material cause, the material or mechanism involved in that career. We found that the chemical constitution could be analysed in isolation from the seed's temporal career; but that as a mechanism *in* that career, it functions as a set of determinate "passive" powers limiting possible interactions with the environment. That environment provides a set of stimuli or "active" powers, as well as a further set of passive powers of its own. The distinction between "active" and "passive" powers is always relative to the particular context; what is really active or dynamic is the process of interaction itself. The career of the seed—its life-history or vital pattern—is the record and conservation of those interactions, their cumulative consequences.

These processes of interaction are of a certain type or "order" determined by the constitution of the seed itself: they are *physico-chemical.* But the pattern of the career or life-history is of another order, biological or *vital,* that is, temporal and cumulative. This "vital" and temporal pattern of the seed's career is not an "active power"—it is not an efficient cause, though it may be said to be a formal cause—but is rather a resultant of physico-chemical interactions. Nor is it, like the chemical structure of the seed, a "passive power," or limit. It is the record of the actual interactions of seed and environment, of the cooperation of their joint powers. What those joint powers can do—what the powers of the chemical structure of the seed, and of the environment, and of the chemical processes of interaction between them, actually *are*—is revealed only when they cooperate in a concrete career: it is not revealed even in the normal or typical life-history or career of the seed. This biological, temporal, "vital" pattern neither causes, controls, nor limits the chemical interactions that produce it: it *is* rather the career which those interactions, within the limits imposed, actually cause.

Now when we go on to examine how far human histories and careers are like the career of the seed, as a prelude to examining in such histories the relation between material causes and mechanisms to the formal cause or pattern of the career, that is, the relation between the recurrent processes in histories to the pattern of that history itself, we find ourselves considering the nature of "historical causation" and "historical determinism." We have found that the "constitution" or structure of any society, culture, or institution can, like the constitution of the seed, be analysed in isolation from the history of that society. We have distinguished a number of organized behavior-patterns or structures: economic, technological, intellectual, political, religious, etc. But in the history of that society these organizations function as a set of passive powers, determinate powers limiting possible interactions, determining or limiting the ways in which men can act, what they will do. Men act in all the ways described by these different culture-patterns, or organized institutionalized forms of behavior. They provide both a set of limits or passive powers, and a set of appropriate stimuli or active powers. Each way of acting interacts with the others, and is both stimulated by and limited by the rest. What is really active or dynamic, that is, what changes the patterns of acting, the organizations of group habits, is the process of interaction between activities taking place in accordance with these different institutionalized ways of acting. The career of the society—the historical and temporal pattern of its changes

—is the record and the conservation of those interactions, their cumulative consequences.

We have examined the way in which these various "organizations" in a culture set limits to or determine possible actions—and therefore the "history" of that culture. We have been led to a formal analysis of causation and determinism in histories. Such "historical determinism" we have viewed as the *limits* set by the organized patterns of behavior that make up the structure of a culture. It is pluralistic, involving a multiplicity of different sets of limits or determinations, with varying degrees of independence and "derivation," but mutually interacting on each other. Each set has a career of its own, but each is "determined" by all the others. These institutionalized behavior-patterns are not themselves "active powers" or "dynamic factors." The active powers in histories are not "habitual ways of behaving," but what men actually do; and such concrete human action is determined not only by social habits, but also by conscious and reflective attempts to deal with the problems forced upon men, and with those generated by the unforeseen consequences of their dealing with the problems they have tried to solve. Such reflective human action is another kind of process that histories reveal. It is what makes it impossible to understand human histories merely in terms of their material and formal causes alone; they must be seen in the broader functional context of efficient and final causes, of means and ends.

The processes of interaction in histories are of a certain type or order, which is determined by the "constitution" or structure of the culture itself: they are *psychological,* that is, human ways of behaving. But the temporal pattern of the society's career—its actual history—is of another order: it is *historical,* that is, temporal and cumulative. Now this "historical pattern," like the "vital pattern" of the seed's career, is not a) an active power or cause, but is the resultant of human actions; nor is it b) a passive power or limit. It is the record of the actual operation of the powers of human nature as organized in its social institutions. What these "powers" of human action *are,* as socially organized—what men *can* do in their group behavior—how they will act under various conditions, is revealed only in their concrete histories. It is not revealed even in the "typical" or "recurrent" patterns exhibited in many histories, and repeated in some, those patterns that form the subject-matter of the science of social change. These recurrent patterns neither cause, control, nor limit human actions and their interaction—though such action is limited by the concrete "organizations" of habit.

Again, just as in the case of the seed, the "dynamic factors" in human histories must be of the "same order" as the organizations of human behavior which make a culture what it is; that is, they must be capable of acting on human behavior. That is why the notion of "human behavior"—of habit and of institutionalized forms of acting—is fundamental in the analysis of human histories, just as "physico-chemical processes" are fundamental in the seed's career. Just as the material cause of the seed's career is its chemical powers and constitution, so the material cause of any human history is the institutionalized, socially organized behavior of men, and in just the sense in which that career can be understood in chemical terms, as the chemical interaction of various factors in the environment with the chemical constitution of the seed, so human histories can be understood in *psychological* terms, as the interaction of the various factors in the human environment with the behavior-patterns of human groups.

The career of the seed is not its "chemistry," and the history of a group is not its "psychology." But just as the gardener, whatever his purpose, must use physico-chemical means in planting his garden, and bringing about the distinctive careers of his seeds, so action of any kind in human histories, whether of geographical environment or of conscious and reflective human purpose, must be capable of influencing the behavior, attitudes, and beliefs of men.

In the seed, we have distinguished two types of *recurrent pattern,* chemical and vital; and in human histories likewise two types, psychological and historical. These types of recurrent pattern are in addition to the concrete and particular pattern or structure that *is* the unique career of that seed, or *is* that individual history.

	Recurrent:		*Unique:*
Seed:	Patterns of organized Chemical Processes	Vital Patterns	A Career
Society:	Patterns of organized Psychological Processes	Historical Patterns	A History
	Mechanisms	*Resultants*	

The unique career of the seed is chemical in its mechanism: it is the resultant of chemical processes. But it is vital in its form: it is temporal and cumulative. The individual history is psychological in its mechanism: it is the resultant of human actions. But it is historical in its form: it is temporal and cumulative. This holds true also for the recurrent or typical patterns in the second column, which can be illustrated in unique careers and individual histories. They too are in form vital and historical, respectively; but they are not unique, they are repeatable. They can be taken as the patterns of specific organizations of chemical processes or of psychological processes, in contrast to the more general ways of behaving of the simpler chemical processes, or of the more elementary psychological processes, listed in the first column.

Thus, just as the seed, in its "normal environment," has a characteristic "life-history" or career, so the actions of the group, in its "normal setting," may exhibit characteristic and recurrent historical patterns: for example, the business cycle, the pattern of cultural assimilation, the pattern of political revolution. Such recurrent historical patterns are often called "patterns of 'historical processes.'" But this is confusing and misleading: it is like speaking of "patterns of 'vital processes'" in connection with the seed, as though the processes at work in the living career of the seed were other than chemical interactions. It suggests that the processes at work in histories are other than human actions. Such a way of speaking is apt to obscure the basic fact, that such recurrent processes are *not* operative "forces," as are chemical interactions, or human actions, but are rather cumulative resultants or registrations. They neither cause, control, nor limit human actions: they in no sense "determine" the course of history.

These recurrent historical patterns are a) psychological in their mechanism, just as the vital patterns of the seed are chemical: they are typical patterns of human behavior under typical conditions, subject to all the determinations already listed. But they are b) historical in form: they are not deducible from the "laws" of human behavior analysed in isolation from the complex social and historical setting in which it is illustrated, as under laboratory conditions, for example, or as generalized from a wide variety of contexts. They are temporal and cumulative: like the normal life-history of the seed, they display a fixed sequence and order of stages. In human histories, the recurrent temporal patterns are, like the normal life-history of the seed, statistical generalizations. But they are neither so "typical" as the vital patterns of the seed, nor are the elementary psychological processes, the specific interacting factors that are the mechanisms or causes of these historical patterns, so difficult to analyse. The "environment" of a human history is never normal, save in the most general terms: "cultural assimilation," e.g., itself has a history. And the environment of a human history, unlike that of the seed's career, consists largely of other careers: it is social and historical. Hence in a history there is no clear distinction between that history and the "dynamic factors" in its environment. Depending on the focus we take, any factor may be treated as "dynamic," while the rest will then appear as "limiting" or "determining."

Strictly speaking, the recurrent patterns of the first type—those in the first column, the chemical pattern and the psychological pattern—are likewise statistical generalizations of ways of interacting with the environment. These ways, formulated as chemical or psychological laws, do not set any limits or determine the interactions. What does set limits is the constitution together with its environment: if either or both are altered, new ways are displayed. The patterns are "recurrent" only in so far as these materials and conditions remain the same. Hence the recurrent psychological patterns neither cause, control, nor limit human actions and their interactions: the limits are set, not by these elementary psychological processes, but by the concrete organizations of human habits.

The concrete career of the seed, or the concrete human history, is always unique: it is the cumulative record of many specific interactions. The recurrent patterns, both those in the first column, the chemical and psychological, as well as those in the second, the vital and historical, are the product of different degrees of abstraction or isolation from these concrete and unique careers and histories. The two first are more generalized, from a wider variety of varied contexts. The patterns of the chemical processes are the most generalized of all, and hence the most constant through the widest range of contexts, because they are most abstracted from any particular career. They have been established under laboratory conditions. Yet even here biochemistry shows that by altering the environment, marked changes in the pattern will be produced, especially in the rates of chemical accumulation.

With the psychological patterns, the typical patterns of human behavior under typical conditions, such "abstraction" is much more difficult. Laboratory conditions here seem able to deal only with the most isolated kind of behavior, like reaction times, the learning curve, and such segments of behavior. We all know how short a way "experimental psychology" has been able to go with organized human behavior. As Graham Wallas used to remark, it has run into great difficulties when it tries to go much further up the scale than the decorticated white rat.

Moreover, the structure of human behavior, both individual and group, the organization of responses that corresponds to the chemical constitution of the seed, and may be called the "constitution of human nature," has itself had a history, and no laboratory conditions can isolate it from that history. "Human nature" not only like the seed exhibits different powers in different environments: in those different environments it actually *has* a different "constitution." For "human nature" is not significantly the wealth of possible responses with which the newborn infant is endowed, any more than the "constitution" or "nature" of the seed is the possible actions of its constituent chemical elements. It is the *organization* of those elements, or those responses—the particular set of organized habits generated by the social institutions of the society into which the infant is born, that make up its environment. Human nature is thus not "constant" and "original," but fundamentally historical in character: human nature is an *historical nature,* like the seed's career.

Hence the psychological patterns in histories are themselves *historical,* like the particular behavior patterns of the various "organizations" of social habits, economic, technological, intellectual, political, etc. And they are *plural,* varying in different cultures, classes, and groups. We can hence "predict" how men will act in the envisaged future; but we cannot predict the changes in their action that will be effected by changes in the determining organizations or institutions. We may be sure of the persistence of present ways where change is not forced: it is clear we can expect no drastic change in general in the near future, no matter what revolutionary institutional changes are brought about. But we cannot predict those forcings, nor the long-term changes. Hence there is ground for no facile optimism. There is no method of drastically changing human nature overnight, or next year; and there is no certainty what changes in human nature any institutional change will produce, even in the long run. There is certainly no available art of how to change human nature. But likewise, there is no justification for an ultimate pessimism, no ground for believing that "you can't change human nature," that men will always act as they are acting today.

If this historical and plural character is true even of "psychological patterns," it is all the more true of the recurrent historical patterns. They are likewise historical and plural: they are the cumulative record of psychological processes or ways of behaving; they are "recurrent" only when the same psychological processes and the same conditioning organizations of habit are present, and both these have histories.

v

We have been analysing the relation of material to formal causes in histories, the relation between the structure of the materials of histories, social organizations or institutions, and the temporal pattern of those histories. That is, we have been analysing "historical determinism," or how the structures of a society limit its possible histories. We have found that the materials of a history are always psychological, habitual ways of behaving, "human nature" in the concrete sense of particular socially conditioned organizations of activities that function in that history and themselves have a career. Human ways of acting are the "substratum" or *τό ὑποκείμενον* of any history: they are what persists, is acted upon, and modified in that history. And since it is these materials that set the limits to and determine the powers of what men can do, all historical determinism is thus *psychological*. This is largely true even of the determination or limits set by natural conditions: by geographical environment, climate, available raw materials, etc. The limits such conditions set are not only limits set *to* human action: their limitings are a function of the available knowledge and technical skill. Consider how differently South Africa has limited the Kaffirs and the English, or Peru the Incas and the Guggenheims. In any event, these "natural limits" have today been pushed back so far that their restrictions are now basically a matter of human social organization. Thus, in the thirties it was said that Germany "needed" raw materials. But she "needed" them only in the sense that she was unable to pay for them, except in aspirin and cameras—a matter clearly of social organization. Today Europe is being greatly "limited"—and perhaps determined to various rash actions—because oil from the Middle East has been cut off. But the oil is there in abundance, and the technical skill to get it to Europe is part of our know-how. The limiting is by the inflamed "nationalistic" emotions directed against "colonialism"—something only too patently "psychological."

It is well to insist on this psychological character of historical determinism, for it enables us to escape what we may call "historicism," a fallacy analogous to the fallacy of "vitalism" in analysing the career of the seed.[8] Because the biological pattern of the seed's career is "vital," or "living," we are tempted to convert that temporal pattern of living into an active and controlling force, "life." Likewise, because the temporal and cumulative pattern of a human history is "historical," we are tempted to convert that historical pattern into an active and controlling force, "history." In the face of this temptation, which has not always been resisted, it is well to point out:

There are no "vital forces" in the seed's career—except in the sense in which there can be said to be "dormitive powers" in opium. These mere "nominal essences" are, to be sure, convenient classifications, and they serve to point to the real problem, what chemical processes are involved? Likewise, there are no such things as "historical forces," except "human action"; i.e., men doing certain things in certain ways that have had histories. Yet our histories and our thinking have been full of such "forces" as "nationalism," "democracy," "individualism," "collectivism," "liberalism," "imperialism," "communism," "fascism," etc., all conceived as "powers" that can be "born," "grow," "spread," "promise," or "threaten." In 1848, we have been told, "nationalism" triumphed over "liberalism"; and thereafter "imperialism" captured "nationalism" and ruined "individualism."[9] This is a typically "vitalistic" view. I am not suggesting that such terms are wholly meaningless. But

[8] I am aware that the term "historicism" has been used to designate other positions, all of which are uniformly considered by those who use the term to be fallacious. But what these positions are, what they all agree in maintaining, and why they are all considered to be "fallacious," are questions to which I can find no clear answer in the voluminous literature that raises them. Hence I propose to use "historicism" with a precise meaning.

[9] I am afraid that Carlton J. H. Hayes, on whose admirable textbook I cut my eyeteeth, is sadly guilty in this matter. His later mortal fight against "nationalism" could not fail to make that "nationalism" appear to him as a force to be combated with every weapon in his power.

they do not designate "forces," nor even any concrete way of acting or organization of behavior. They denote rather certain aspects of many different ways of acting, selected by their reference to some particular problem. Thus "liberalism" has a determinate meaning only in some specific functional context—in terms of some definite issue—and I am still trying to find out what problem Americans had in mind when they were engaged in hating "fascism"; since they seemed quite willing to act very much like the people they disliked.

The same criticism applies to all the components of human histories, to the different organizations making up the structure of a society. Thus there are no *intellectual* "forces," except in the sense that men with certain beliefs and knowledge act differently from those without. The ideas men entertain and act on certainly make a difference—when men act on them. But ideas are not forces unless entertained by men, not even when entertained by God—for in human histories God can act only through men. We have gotten over the "idealistic" notion of the independent action of ideas, if any idealist ever entertained it: Hegel clearly did not.

Again, there are no *economic* "forces," except that men doing things in certain ways produce certain characteristic consequences. It is always possible for them to do different things in the face of their problems, if their environment, the organization of their activities, has changed. These adjectives or classifications, "intellectual," "economic," etc., are convenient in designating the ways in which men act "intellectually," or "economically": they distinguish ways of acting. But unless they are translatable into such ways of acting, they remain merely nominal essences, like the seed's "vital forces."

Nor are there any "laws," "tendencies," or "directions" in history in general, save in the most positivisitic sense, as pure descriptions or registrations of the course of events; and even then, if the context be taken broadly enough, as in Sorokin, they all reduce to "fluctuations." Such tendencies or patterns are discoverable only in the context of selected histories, and even there they are not the expression of the operation of any "underlying forces" that could be correlated with them, but rather the expression of the results of the complex interactions of men acting in many different ways. We cannot take these tendencies as the basis for prediction, or count on their continuance, unless we have found the ways of human behavior of whose interaction they are the register, and have discovered the "human mechanism" involved, the particular psychological processes.

There are thus no "historical forces" or "historical laws or patterns" that operate as controlling forces dictating what men can and will do. What men can do is "determined," not by their history, but by what they *are,* by their "nature." This nature is itself "historical." But this means, not that their history dictates what they *will* become, not even that it is their "history" which "determines" or "limits" what they *can* become; but that the same kinds of activity, carried on within a multiplicity of limits, that have given them a history in the past, will continue to give them a similar history in the future; and in a "dynamic" or changing society will change their "nature," those organized habits that set the limits.

A society or an institution is what it is—or better, is becoming what it is becoming—because of what men have done in the past. And what it is, is to be understood as the fruits of what men have done before. But what it will become is "decided" not by what men have done, but by what they are doing and will do with those fruits. What they *can* do with those fruits—the powers of their materials—is "determined" or limited by what those fruits have been made into, by what men have done with and to them in the past. But though these inherited materials, and through them the past history they embody, set limits to or "determine" what men can do with them, what those limits actually are cannot be discovered until men try to do something with them. That cannot be discovered in a merely formal context, by analysing the structure of those materials in isolation from working with them, but only in a functional or teleological context, by using them as means toward envisaged ends.

And though men's materials, the fruits of the past, *determine* or limit what men *can* do, they do not *decide* what men *will* do with them, nor do they decide what new or altered limits will be imposed by what men will do. That unique and particular "decision"—the human action itself—depends, in addition, on the problems men see, on how clearly they see them, and on their ability and skill in bringing their materials and resources to bear on meeting the new problems. It depends, that is, on factors to be found not in a merely formal context, but only in a genuinely functional or problematic context—when, in the need of action, men use their materials as means to doing something about those problems. For one of the kinds of activity that has given men a history in the past and changed the organization or limits of human nature, and will continue to do so, is the activity of intelligent problem-meeting.[10]

So far, we have been pressing the analogy between human histories and the seed's career. This is possible in a purely formal analysis, when we are considering as we have been the relation between the two structures alone, the structure of the materials and the structure of the temporal pattern. But wherever we started we have always reached the point where questions were raised that are not answerable in terms of such a formal analysis alone, and point to the need of a further functional analysis. For human histories do differ significantly from the career of the seed; and this difference between a "history" and a "career" becomes of major importance when we try to use our knowledge of histories as itself an instrument for the further understanding of what has had that history.

The constitution of the seed is much more unified than the structure of any society, culture, or institution. No society or institution has a single structure or constitution: it possesses rather a plurality of interacting structures or behavior-patterns. In consequence, while the seed, like any organism, has a *career* as a whole, a society has no such career, for it is not a whole, nor does it possess the unity of an organism. A society, in consequence, possesses not a career but a *history*.

A *career* is a temporal continuity in which there is a *persisting subject,* a *ὑποκείμενον*, that acts and is acted upon, "develops" and "evolves." The best illustration of a career is the "life" of a living organism, a seed or a man. Careers belong to wholes that persist through time, and preserve an identity amidst change. They enjoy a career as a whole just because they are wholes. Of the fortunes of such wholes, we can tell the stories or narrate the careers, beginning at the beginning, and following through the events in which they figure.

The histories of societies, institutions, and ideas are *not* careers. There

[10] Footnote on "Sin": "Decision" depends on "will" as well as on knowledge, and will is limited by "sin." But sin itself has a history, and the limits it imposes are continually being altered. Sin, that is, is not "original"; it is itself an "historical nature."

is a *history* of these things: when we look backwards, we can trace the "sources" and the "genesis" of the factors found in the present, the antecedents that led up to what has eventuated, and is relevant to the problems now confronting us. But there is no "career," in the sense that we can find any "beginning," and then follow the "development" of what has persisted as a whole, as in the case of the life of the seed or of a man. For there is no whole that had a "beginning," or persisted. What has eventuated is not a whole, it is rather a plurality of ways of acting, interacting, and generating problems, which form the foci for selecting histories. We can trace backwards the antecedents of present problems: we are thus led into a plurality of "histories." But we cannot follow the career of any society or institution, and trace its consequences: we are led out if we try into a multiplicity of other careers, with indefinite ramifications. Looking backward, we find continuities of materials stretching into the past, with a focus in present problems. These continuities reveal further foci in the past, the problems that generated those materials, which in turn lead us back to the further past continuities of their materials. But looking forward into the future, we see, not such continuities, but problems, choices, new solutions. We see breaks in continuity, changes, contrasts with the past, happenings, events, actions; we see not "habitual ways of behaving," but "what men actually do," their "decisions"; not "why" they do it, what "limits" their action, "why" it limits it, "how" the limits got there. That is, we see the history that is to be understood, not the history that gives understanding.

The historian, bringing to the unification of a present focus our organizations, institutions, and ideas, is indeed tempted to view them as unities or "wholes," rather than as unifications in a functional context, and to attribute to them in consequence an antecedent career. These habits unified in such a problematic context, whose histories we can trace, can indeed be regarded as having had a career "potentially," before the problems were forced on our attention, and we can now be said to be "selecting" that career, and bringing it to light. This is what Hegel meant by "an Idea coming to self-consciousness": we now understand what was *really* going on, *we* bring it to the light of reason. An idea, for instance, may be said to have been enjoying a career, in the sense that its implications have been gradually developed and worked out. But such an idea *is* essentially the fully developed idea, not the one that started its supposed career with such development only potential. And it seems less dangerous and misleading to say that the developed idea or institution has had a history, than to say that a potential idea is enjoying a career. The latter view, in the hands of Hegelians and evolutionists, has led to mythical treatments: histories have been transformed into mythical stories of careers.

Thus once again our analysis of "historical natures" has taken us to a functional or teleological structure of means and ends in which those natures are unified in the focus of problems. Our examination of the use of historical knowledge as an instrument of understanding has thus brought us to the same *functional* and *objective relativism* to which we were led in the former analysis, in the preceding chapter, of the understanding of history.

CHAPTER 4

History as an Instrument of Understanding: Historical Decision

THE FORMAL analysis of histories carried through in the preceding chapter has pushed us to a functional analysis of their teleological structure. Histories have their focus in an outcome or eventuation. Within the limits or determinations set by the structure of their human materials, the social organizations of human behavior in a society, human action effects a "decision" that leads to that outcome. In turning to this "decision," we turn from the consideration of material and formal causes—the limits and determinations set by the social structure upon the temporal pattern of a history—to efficient and final causes, to the "dynamic factors," or "active powers," that can serve as means to ends and eventuations.

"Historical causation" involves both sets of factors: the *formal* pair, material and formal causes and their relation; and the *functional* pair, efficient and final causes and their relation. The second set is usually neglected: "historical causation" is then treated as though it were identical with "historical determinism," and exhausted by it; whereas in fact "determinism" is only half the story. When "decision" is overlooked, the "limits" set to human action in histories are taken as what brings those histories to pass—as though what men for psychological reasons *cannot* do were what makes things take place! All the various so-called "historical determinisms": geographical, climatic, racial, psychological, economic, and the rest, treat a "limit" as though it were an efficient cause or "dynamic." That is, they are all non-functional, and as such metaphysically unsound.

Historical causation includes *historical decision* operating within the limits of *historical determinism*. It is the "decision" that actually brings about the eventuation, and thus the history itself. Problems are forced on men by "history," that is, by what men have already done in the past in meeting earlier problems. In any history there is presented not only a possibility of thought and action, but a possibility of thought and action in very definite and limited channels, with a compelling demand to be realized. The "implicit ends" in a history may not be realized. But if they are, it is only because men have studied those ends and have discovered the means by which to bring them about. Men live always in a limited world, not in a world of boundless choice. And their choice of the means to use in facing their problems, the problems that are set before them and must be "solved" whether they will or no, is freest in the measure that men recognize and know these limitations. What must be done, what men are, what they can do, how they can do it—these are all things "there" to be discovered. What is not there already is whether men will do it. That depends on the discovery, on whether men know, and how far they know.

What is forced on men is the end—the tendencies working themselves out, the dynamic activities that are changing other ways of acting, and pointing to further changes in the future. This imposed end generates problems of means in detail: just how these changes are to be dealt with. "What has to be done" is determined by what has been done—it is "given," or forced on men. Men do not set themselves problems: what they have done and are doing sets the problems, which appear to them in the envisaged future, the projection of what they are doing—how their institutions are operating, the tensions, maladjustments, and conflicts they are generating. The past leaves a deposit of materials and resources, which set limits, "determine" what men can do in dealing with those imposed problems. Within the limits of "historically determined problems" and "historically determined resources," men act: they "decide" what way the problems will be met, they do what they will do. Their historical decision generates new problems in turn.

The problems thus forced on men by "history" are plural but interrelated; they become unified with further knowledge, and with the further advance of the history-that-is-lived itself. Thus in one restricted field of the impingements of technological invention on social control, we have forced on us the traffic problem, the parking problem, the accident problem. The better they are seen and understood, the more knowledge of facts is gained, the more the problems become unified. And the more they are seen to be unified, the more choices and decisions will be made with reference to that unification. The process is clear in wartime, or in the cold war; but such occasions merely make explicit what is always there but not realized. Thus ultimately we come to focus on the "basic problems for these times": our knowledge of the facts forcing such a unification upon us leads us to formulate the "real issues."

These problems are further unified as more history is lived: for the plural problems are never fully unified in any present. The "real problem" remains a faith—a rational faith to the extent that it is forced by knowledge. Thus, was winning the war the real problem in 1945? Do we not now know that Churchill saw further than Roosevelt? And is the containment of Russia the real problem today? Such problems never become fully conscious; men see specific problems, and the "larger pattern of history" is revealed only later—it is known fully only to God. That is, it is a function of our knowledge of the historical processes of social change, coupled with our historical insight into the particular factors involved. Can men ever know what Hegel called "the world-historical problem" they are facing? Could the Joan of Arc of the fifteenth century know what the St. Joan of Shaw knows? Or could the Socrates that walked the streets of Athens know what the Socrates of Plato's *Apology* knows?

A "philosophy of history" is just such an attempt to appraise the present in terms of the problems seen to be "world-historical." It is the attempt to be self-conscious about what we are doing. At its best, it is an instrument of analysis, an hypothesis as to what is "dynamic" today. It considers the present in terms of possible action, of the ends implicit in it, and of the means to their attainment. It is an instrument of politics, of social action. It involves a choice among the determinate possibilities of the present, of that tendency or predicted future which we judge to be controlling. But even when the envisaged future is most carefully based on an analysis of present tendencies, rather than on hopes, it remains a faith—hopefully, an intelligent faith—that the future will display a certain character.

How the problems are seen, how the materials and resources are understood, what skill and abilities are present—these are ultimately intellectual problems. This is the sense in which the ultimate determinism in histories is an *intellectual determinism,* and depends on what men know how to do, the extent of the "social intelligence" available in that society. This is maintained even in Marxism, which makes knowledge controlling now that it has been gained: the Marxian understands, he knows the "correct" decision to make. Thus, on the Marxian analysis, all the "objective conditions" for a revolution were present in the United States in 1933; only the "subjective conditions" were lacking: men did not know it.

The ultimate limit set to action is the state of science available. This will itself be limited by all the other social determinisms. Some may know how to meet the problems, yet their knowledge may not be generally recognized or applied, because of such social conditioning—because of the limits set by the economic setup, the inability to forego a tax reduction, for instance. The economists may know how, the Marxians may know better, and you and I clearly know best of all. But none of us knows how to get others to recognize our wisdom. It is easy to view this unhappy situation as due to the "stupidity" of others, or their "selfishness," or their "class bias," or the "propaganda of the interests," or the "power structure" of our society, or the "capitalistic system," or just "the system." But in the last analysis it is clearly due to our own ignorance—of how to put the Truth across! Here we come to the ultimate limit indeed.

These limits to the operation of human intelligence may indeed be looked upon as "sin." This is excellent for the religious purposes of contrition and penitence: "sin" is one of those unifying connectives or symbols that play so large a part in the techniques of religion, even when the limits are not further personified, as well as unified, as the Devil. But to view these limits collectively as "sin," is, for the sake of understanding them and doing something about them, to commit a fallacy analogous to that of "vitalism" in the case of the seed: to take the determinate outcome of a complex cooperation of factors as an unanalysable "force." This remains in the realm of mere labeling: it is content to give a name to how human nature operates in a specific social situation, without trying to discover the mechanism by which it is led to do it, in the human constitution, and in the way that constitution cooperates with the social structures in our culture. Sin is not unanalysable: it is a unification of the limits set by a complex cooperation of processes, all of which can be broken down. Sin is not a force, but a set of limits. And it has a history: at any given time it is a set of specific and determinate limits, setting definite bounds to what can be done in particular problems. There will always be some limits to what human nature can become—there will always be sin, enough sin to satisfy the prophet or the theologian, enough for him to use for his important religious purposes. But there is no specific limit that is immutable and cannot be pushed back. We can hence look forward to bigger and better sins—or rather, more refined and better sins.

The same holds true of another fashionable unification of these limits to the operation of knowledge, the taking them as the "impulse to power and domination," as Bertrand Russell has done; [1] though this has the advantage over sin that it is not taken as so unanalysable, and can be attributed to the aggressions resulting from a faulty education —probably far too facile an account.

Or these limits may be taken as "ignorance" in general, a symbol in another contemporary gospel, which ignores the social conditioning of that ignorance. "Ignorance" is, to be sure, an ultimate limit, just as "invention" or "discovery" is an ultimate dynamic or cause of social and historical decision, in producing the social changes that generate the problems that force action. But since both ignorance and invention in general lie outside human control, they are useless for any historical understanding, or for any program of action, and hence for any philosophy of history. Like sin, "ignorance" has a history, and is at any given time specific and determinate. Both have meaning in histories, in the present or the past, only as definite limits in particular problems.

The prophet can use "sin," the social scientist and the educator can use "ignorance," each employing his own label for the unification of the limits he encounters, corresponding to his own techniques. In fact, the limits are plural, complex, and constantly shifting. Their unification through such connectives or symbols serves as an instrument

[1] See Bertrand Russell, *Power: A New Social Analysis* (London, 1938), esp. Chapters 1 and 18.

for the functional analysis of problems. By grouping the limits around the major obstacles encountered, they throw into relief the most promising means for dealing with those problems. In terms of the problems, the limits and the resources for dealing with them are separated out and opposed. Thus Dewey insists that we must

> discriminate between the two forces, one active, the other resistant and deflecting, that have produced the social scene in which we live. The active force is . . . scientific method and technological application. The opposite force is that of older institutions and the habits that have grown up around them.[2]

Thus it is not ignorance in general, but a very specific kind of ignorance, that sets limits: technically, ignorance of how to do the particular things that must be done; and politically, ignorance of how to get men to apply the knowledge that experts already possess—itself a problem of political techniques.

Knowledge of methods and techniques is thus the dynamic in all historical decision. No matter what form of action is indicated as the most effective present means of meeting the imposed problems, its use depends upon knowledge—knowledge of the problem, of our resources, and of how to make our knowledge operative with men. And a philosophy of history, using the problem as a focus, will view the past in terms of the operation of that means, or "active force," and of that obstacle, or "deflecting force." Thus historical knowledge, as an instrument of functional analysis today, makes possible an understanding of the present in terms of the factors in a problem: it is essential to "seeing" and "analysing" the problem. Historical knowledge "reveals" the genesis or origin of the problem, points to the active force that is generating a tension, to the points of tension themselves, thus locating the obstacles or "deflecting forces," and also to the instrument for dealing with the obstacles.

II

Let us now turn to the process of *historical decision* itself. This falls into two main parts, the analysis of the way in which problems are generated, and the analysis of the way in which they are confronted

[2] John Dewey, *Liberalism and Social Action* (New York, 1935), p. 77.

and measurably composed. In the first analysis, how problems are generated, we are greatly aided by what has already been accomplished in achieving a scientific treatment of the processes of social change, mainly by the anthropologists. The two processes distinguished as involved in the generation of historical problems are diffusion and invention. *Diffusion* is the getting of new materials, techniques, and ideas from outside a culture. Thus the long assimilation by Western Europe of the successive layers of the thought of the ancient world was a complex process of "diffusion." Or, the spread of Western technology and science to the whole world is a large-scale process of "diffusion." We are at the moment seeing the diffusion of elements of Russian culture throughout the non-European world. This diffusion is always a complex process, varying from sheer imposition to eager adoption. Thus we have the very different incidence in which the Plains Indians took from the Europeans Christianity, the horse, firearms, and firewater. In the Oriental cultures, on the other hand, certain Western ideas, like nationalism, have had much greater appeal than even Western techniques of production.

Invention is the discovery, from resources within a culture, of new ways of meeting old problems. Often, in fact, inventions are produced which only then suggest their quite unintended uses—consider the discovery of new metals or chemical substances, whose possibilities then remain to be explored. The classic instance of an invention whose uses had to wait a generation to be found out is the sulfa drugs.

Both diffusion and invention are "active forces," creating tensions when they bump into obstacles or "deflecting forces." Invention is the ultimate "dynamic"—the discovery of how to do something new. In this sense, it is the ultimate "efficient cause" of social change, which is hence intellectual, located in the "intellectual organization" of a culture. Invention is the "ultimate cause" of generating problems. It is not the ultimate cause of resolving them. What is ultimate for such resolving, that is, for "historical decision," is the pushing back or removing of the "deflecting forces." This is a "political" problem, of getting men to act together in new ways.

In the Marxian analysis of social change, new inventions in the field of the "forces of production," in technology, compel men to change the "deflecting force"—in Marxian jargon, the "relations of production"—by political action, by a "revolution" that will "capture the state." Hence for the Marxians the "ultimate" or "basic" cause of "historical decision" is the *political action* that transforms the economic organization of society.

In the analysis of John Dewey, the "ultimate cause" of "historical decision" is the pushing back of the "deflecting force" by an *education* that is essentially *political* in character, and is directed toward getting men to act together in new ways, involving a political change of their institutions.

Both the "revolution" of the Marxians, and the "education" of Dewey, are essentially "political" techniques, on which both rely, together with the more ordinary political processes. Thus in the last analysis, the process of "historical decision," of problem-solving, like that of the generation of problems, depends on knowledge and invention. It is an intellectual problem—specifically, a problem of the political methods and techniques for pushing back the "deflecting" force. This is a crucial intellectual and technical problem today, demanding careful inquiry.

But the science of social change, though it can illuminate the process by which tensions and problems are generated, will not "reveal" which "forces" or organizations of human activities are "dynamic"—apart from the concrete problems of particular histories. Such knowledge demands in addition the historical knowledge of the factors operating in particular cultures. In our own society, these "dynamic" factors are largely "technological," concerned with the Marxian "forces of production." Has this been always true of other societies? Have not new religious ideas proved fully as disruptive in them? Islamic societies exhibit plenty of tensions, but hardly much change in their method of production. Or is Chinese history to be understood primarily in terms of technological change and the resulting economic problems generated?

Even for our own modern society, the Marxian analysis seems far too narrow. Even the invention of material techniques introduces "active forces," dynamic factors, relatively independent of any "forces of production." Consider the printing press; or the invention of contraceptive devices, and the consequent emancipation of women.

Invention takes place in all the social organizations. Thus Luther and Calvin invented a new technique of salvation outside the medieval Church. This invention was quite as "dynamic" as the various technological changes with which it was bound up. I am not quite sure whether Freud has invented another technique of salvation destined to prove quite as disruptive as Luther's to our inherited techniques.

In the political organization, the invention of representative government during the Middle Ages provoked major repercussions. And the invention of the idea of "nationalism"—that connective for organizing the most powerful emotions of men into a driving force—seems to have been far more dynamic in our world than the idea of industrial technology—even in Russia. There are also the educational techniques of mass literacy and of mass communication, with all they include. This is to say nothing of our achievements in the techniques of destruction, the military techniques that are forcing on us so many new political techniques.

It remains to analyse the process of "historical decision" itself. This really belongs to the "science of social and cultural change," and it has already been suggested that we can learn most about these processes from anthropology, from which we have hitherto drawn our illustrations. Now we shall approach the process of historical change directly, and try to delineate the "historical pattern" of such problem meeting. We shall attempt to get beneath the observable pattern itself to the psychological processes which are its mechanism. Since we are now considering not the mere limiting or determination, but the decision itself, we shall try to find the intellectual, educational, and political patterns involved—the ways of discovering new means, and the ways of getting men to believe together and act together on those means.

A history is always relative to a determinate tendency or direction of movement in the present, pointing to what will eventuate in an envisaged future if that tendency continues to operate—if men continue to act collectively in that way, and if no unforeseen contingencies intervene, the consequence of other ways of acting, or of the actions of other groups—like war, which upsets all predictions, or new discoveries and inventions, the most unpredictable of all factors.

This "most important" or primary tendency is seen as "limited" by a "deflecting force," "held back," prevented from displaying its "real powers." New ways of acting, which we foresee will be much more effective in the envisaged future than at present, are now restrained and limited by other ways. Their operation is "inefficient," and conceals "unreleased potentialities." Or a new idea is not seen in all its significant implications; men are held back by traditional habits and ways of thinking. Thus "evolution" meant at first primarily a new substitute for Providence; and only later were its more revolutionary intellectual bearings realized. Or the idea of "relativity" in physical theory was initially taken merely as proving the particular philosophy of science already worked out by the taker.

This is fundamental in intellectual history. Ideas have a logical structure of their own, which definitely limits the ways in which they can be pushed. And ideas also have an active power of enticing men onward—that is, men have an active curiosity that leads them to explore ideas when they are not held back by practical considerations. Under rather rare circumstances, men are freed from practice to explore ideas, to undertake what we call a "disinterested" analysis. Thus Spinoza was able to carry to the limit the denial of all potentiality, Leibniz was able to explore the implications of the idea of the great chain of being, Hume was able to push his analysis of the assumptions of the empiricist tradition, Bradley was able to push the presuppositions of the idealist logic.

The "active force" is not only limited by the "deflecting force," it also interacts with it, modifies and changes it. At times—perhaps normally—this process goes on unconsciously, without men being particularly aware of the modifications induced. In this way, humanitarian values crept into religion in the last century, the Presbyterian Church lost the true faith of Calvin, the Catholic Church went American—set the Knights of Columbus side by side with St. Francis, for example. In this way, the status and function of art were "corrupted" by capitalism, in this way the very substance of education was almost wholly lost by the rapid growth of that basic American religion, the faith in education.

Tensions are thus generated, not only *between* the active and the deflecting force, so that the older ways seem increasingly incompatible with the newer ways. The novel ways are themselves "impeded": an inner tension develops between what men might do and what they can do, which grows intolerable, and becomes a conscious problem for those committed to the new ways. At the same time an inner tension develops in the older ways. Not only are they at odds with the newer ways, not only do they render men unable to deal with and direct the new. The older ways are themselves sufficiently modified to lose their former power to perform their old function. They begin to "decay," they are "corrupted," they have "lost their power to function." And this becomes a conscious problem for those still committed to the older ways.

Since most men concerned are committed to both old and new, the tension between the two, which is generating these other internal tensions in each, becomes a central problem. Practically, men find themselves insecure, in an impasse, in a blind alley, in a state of paralysis, in a breakdown—their ways have disintegrated. Intellectually, they have lost their faith in the old, lost their assurance, their sense of direction given by the old ideas or standards and values—they are disillusioned. But they are unable to accept the new ways or ideas if they do not perform the same function as the old ones did before their disintegration. So men demand practically a new technique or organization of behavior that will do for the new "active force" what the older institutions used to do. Intellectually they demand a new "faith," a new "direction," a new "synthesis," that will fit the "essential values" of the old—that is, the values they are not willing to give up —together with the newer beliefs.

This is the well-publicized "predicament of modern man." Since it has been his predicament for at least seven hundred years, he ought to be fairly used to it by this time, and need scarcely take it as hard as his many self-appointed protectors hope he will.

In every cultural change—in every problem that becomes a focus for a history—four main parties are normally formed. The first are the *drifters,* the indifferent, who are led to "accept" the new without realizing what it really means or demands. They are unwilling to abandon the old and habitual, but they persist in its "forms" rather than in its "substance." Consider the mass of Presbyterian church members; or consider American "educators"—as contrasted with teachers. From the standpoint of any of the other three groups, these drifters are the most muddled and unintelligent of all. Yet without them there would be no "problem," and no possibility of a "solution"—until such partial assimilation of the new and partial disintegration of the old has taken place. The drifters are the raw material of change; they have to be won over eventually, if the change is to be incorporated in a new cultural pattern.

The second party are the partisans of the new way, or the new idea—the *radicals* or extremists. They see the possibilities in the new "active force," and are impatient at the limits the deflecting force imposes. They are especially impatient with the confusions of the drifters. They may well respect the old ways, and the old ideas, for what they could do when they were new. Psychologically they are apt to resemble the partisans of the old. Thus logical positivists are if anything more dogmatic than metaphysicians—not to mention the many resemblances between Communists and Catholics.

The radicals resemble the reactionaries in taking the problem seriously, with no intention to compromise. They have a "fighting psychology," and techniques: the new is the "one thing needful," the end for which any means is justified. They disregard and sacrifice other values and ends, which neither the drifters nor the mediators are prepared to do; the latter have a broader if less intense sensitivity. But the radicals also feel deeply the same need felt by the reactionaries. They have found something to perform better the same function the old way or idea performed, which they take with equal seriousness. They possess a rival faith offering the same kind of salvation. Hence they are "literal-minded," like the reactionaries; whereas the drifters and the mediators are, as we say, more "imaginative." They are apt themselves to split up through discovering still better techniques—consider the Protestants, or economic radicals: the Marxians, the Trotskyites, and their splinter groups. And they take the new idea, or the new organization of habits, as an answer to the old problem; they do not see that the eventual implication of the new is to make the old problem irrelevant.

The third group are the partisans of the old, the *reactionaries,* attempting to stem the tide, like the Fundamentalists in American religion, or like Mr. Hutchins among American educators—though it is unusual today to find either theologians or college presidents outside the first group, the drifters. The reactionaries may be shortsighted and blind, but they are usually not muddled. I am not too sure of Mr. Hutchins, however.

The fourth group are the conciliators, the *mediators,* the "statesmen" who work out the new organization of behavior, the "philosophers" who in terms of some new concept or new method, manage to effect a synthesis or adjustment in which the essential values of the old are seen as compatible with the new insight. This group ultimately prevails; it wins over the first group, the drifters, and what they have worked out, or invented, the novel organization of activities or beliefs, proceeds in turn to generate new tensions and to lead to new problems.

Social change normally goes on without much conscious attention. The "active forces" modify the traditional ways of action and belief, and the major changes, in any quantitative sense, are certainly so accomplished, like the thief in the night. They are already largely effected when they become conscious problems. The reactionaries always organize their forces too late; they "succeed" only when they adopt the substance of the demands and methods of the radicals. This happened notoriously with the Catholic Reformation of the sixteenth century, and with the "counter-revolution" in the bourgeois revolution—Napoleon and Metternich equally accorded the basic laisser-faire that the French revolutionaries had demanded. And it is being followed in the reaction of "liberal capitalism," in England and America, against the collectivistic revolution: Mr. Eisenhower and Mr. Macmillan alike accept the "welfare state." When the changes have become conscious problems, then the generation of tensions and problems is seen in terms of past "continuities," of gradual changes, explicable in terms of the past, of history.

The dramatic or "qualitative" changes in history—the dramatic reorganizations of ways of acting, or of ideas—the "mutations," the "renaissances" or "revolutions"—are effected in various ways in the different social organizations. In science we have developed a technique, so that it is normal and accustomed that the fourth group should prevail. When a tension develops between accepted scientific theory, and a specific hypothesis worked out to account for newly discovered facts, there is little taking of sides—though there *is* such a thing as scientific controversy between the radicals and the reactionaries: the classic instance is to be found in the life of Pasteur.[3] Rather, the invention of a new theory is expected and waited for, which shall include both—as in the classic instance of the development of wave-mechanics to deal with all the discrepancies about light and quanta emission.

In philosophy, which confronts new conceptions of "science" or intelligibility itself, the parties enumerated are normally found, and the philosophical revolutions are thus worked out. The classic examples have been the acceptance of Aristotelian science in the thirteenth century, of the mathematical order of nature in the seventeenth century, of Romantic social science in the early nineteenth century, and of evolutionary science in the late nineteenth century.

In practice—in politics, or in the social control of the processes of technology—the fourth group is often lacking: there is no invention of a new organization of behavior. The particular problems of conflict between the new ways and the old, and of the group interests bound up with them, are normally adjusted in detail. The adjustments register the balance of the different tensions. They are the work of "politicians," who differ from "statesmen" in their inventiveness, and in the breadth of their compromises and reorganizations. Most men, that is, most groups, see the particular problems and tensions to be relieved, not as unified, not as parts of a "broader conflict," or of an "historical movement." They have no "philosophy of history"; they are drifters, "mere opportunists." To both the second and third groups, they appear as mere "appeasers."

If the tension can be thus relieved in detail through the political process, the "active forces" go on operating through a series of compromises. We call this "collective bargaining," or "the democratic method." It achieves a balance of the self-interest of the different groups concerned, in terms of the strength of their desire to do what they want to do, of their compulsion to do it, and of their "effective power." The success of this process depends upon the enlightenment of its participants: on how far they see the limits set by the forces involved, both "active" and "deflecting," upon how far they know how to get the most

[3] See René Vallery-Radot, *Life of Pasteur*.

under such conditions, without provoking new tensions, broader and more acute—thus increasing the forces mobilized against them—that is, it depends upon their political skill.

This process of political adjustment is possible, to the extent that all tensions and conflicts are made subject to collective bargaining or political compromise. Whenever that is not the case, the tensions increase and tend to become unified. The second and third groups then gain at the expense of the first. There then develops a general conflict between the active forces and the reactionaries. Such a unified conflict is of course the complete failure of political techniques. It has occurred only once in American experience, in 1861. But the lack of such technical skill—the failure of democratic methods—is most conspicuous in international bargaining today. The ignorance of Western diplomacy, under the moralistic conduct of Mr. Dulles, its complete lack of knowledge of how to effect democratic "collective bargaining," the readjustment of effective national interests, or even of how to establish the conditions of such a process, are only too apparent today. But the failure of political methods is obvious wherever a unified conflict develops—a genuine "class conflict," for example.

In such a situation, "political success" occurs when one side "wins out," and what had previously been excluded from discussion or compromise is now open to it. The process of dealing with specific tensions can be carried on once more. There are new "alignments," new organizations, new legislation, fresh "invention," the "releasing" of the powers of the "active force," a modifying of the limits and an adapting them to the active force, a setting of new limits, a general "catching up."

The most drastic social revolutions occur when the complete decay and breakdown of the older ways gives the radicals, the third group, a relatively unimpeded scope. But it is not the revolutionaries who become the reorganizing statesmen: it is not the Jacobins, nor the Old Bolsheviks, but the mediators, the fourth group. The Revolution is organized by the "son-in-law" of the Old Régime; the Revolution is "corrupted"—i.e., it has to take account of limits.

For a revolution—or an international revolution, a war—leaves all the problems of readjustment and reorganization still unsolved, and still to be worked out. At most, it decreases the power of the "deflecting forces"—by introducing new ones.

Or a new religion is proclaimed, a new prophet delivers his message, expressing the "active religious force" of his times. Then the priests and theologians proceed slowly but surely to incorporate once more all the old wisdom. Is this a "corrupting" of the new religion, or is it an enriching?

In the new synthesis effected by the mediator or statesman, what is the relative force of the new and the old? In its appeal to men, what is tough, and has to be given its due? It is clear that technology is very tough, and has an irresistible appeal: this is our modern insight. Technology will in the end force an adaptation to its demands. In any modern technological culture, it forces on men a very similar pattern of adaptation, no matter what their social "theories" or "principles." Science is likewise very tough, and demands that men's other beliefs be harmonized with it. This is especially true of the science that is the folklore of a technological culture, and is itself largely a technique and a know-how. Science that merely gives understanding, that is "theoretical," is much weaker: and social theory that is not indispensable for policy-making is weakest of all. One has only to compare what happened to the theoretical structures of German social scientists under the Nazi dispensation, with the way their practical techniques of financing and influencing opinion were seized on and fostered.

This analysis has been generalized from intellectual and cultural histories. There is hence the temptation to assume that human history is a "logical" process, as Hegel concluded. It is therefore well to insist that in ways of acting, in political behavior, there are no logical incompatibilities, and no logical reconciliation is needed when a new way is incorporated. There is no present organization or way of behavior that cannot, if need be, be adapted to any other—even though the ideas in which the two are now thought of may seem to be incompatible. Even with beliefs, there are no two that are ultimately logically contradictory and cannot be entertained by the same mind and held together in a socially accepted synthesis, if the urge to do so be strong enough. There are plenty of psychological incompatibilities between older beliefs and new ones. But in the long run there are no two that cannot be "reconciled," either by making the necessary distinctions, or by finding some further postulate that will bring them together. Such is the power of the human mind, as one contemplates its past and present achievements in reconciliation.

III

The actual focus of any history is a problem that has been generated by a tension developed between newer and older human ways of acting and believing. It will thus normally be a problem of reorganizing human behavior or beliefs—of effecting some adjustment between ways of acting or believing that have come into conflict.[4] It will be a problem of human relations and attitudes, of getting men to apply and act on the knowledge and techniques that are available, and not one of inventing new ideas or techniques within the specific fields where tension is creating problems. In so far as invention of this latter kind succeeds in relieving the tension, that tension does not become a conscious and unified problem, and that invention will then enter into the historical continuity of other problems. Thus if new scientific knowledge comes into conflict with traditional moral values, as over the invention of contraceptive techniques, or of psychotherapy, that conflict will be solved, not by more scientific knowledge, but by intellectual adjustment on another level—by philosophic criticism and reconstruction, and by political adjustment, by shifts in the political power of different groups, as reflected in legislation.

The problems that serve as the foci of histories are thus human rather than technological. Medicine, for example, is an art; and hence technical factors, medical problems and discoveries, are central in its history. This is indeed all that the usual "histories of medicine" deal with; they are interesting enough as chronicles or annals. But the real history of medicine as an art is the history of medical practice: of the way in which the knowledge available to the medical profession has been made available to different groups in society. There is one history of the achievement of an increasing group intelligence within the medical profession, of the solutions achieved to technical problems by which

[4] The Marxian insight can be so generalized and stated in psychological terms, as Karl Mannheim managed to do after his coming to England. Cf. his *Man and Society in an Age of Reconstruction* (New York, 1940).

any physician today, however mediocre personally, knows how to do vastly more than any doctor of a century ago, however able as an individual, and is thus markedly more "intelligent," medically speaking. But medicine has a more fundamental history, the "medical history of our society," of the relative failure to make that professional or group intelligence a genuinely "social intelligence," with a focus in our problem of the wider "socialization" of medical practice.[5]

Or religion, another art, has likewise a complex technical history—of the techniques of worship, liturgy, iconography, etc.; of the technique of social organization, church polity, etc.; of the techniques of organizing beliefs, theology and philosophy; of the techniques of salvation, the insights of its prophets. All these technical histories, like any such, are histories of its present resources and materials, and instruments for analysing them. But the basic history of religion is of its getting men to accept its techniques and know-how: the history of its rise and spread and fortunes, of its appeal and missionary success, of how it organized human actions, feelings, and beliefs, and what happened to it in consequence.

Thus intellectual history in general is usually taken as the history of the genesis of our ideas, of the thinkers who worked them out, and how they confronted their intellectual problems—that is, as a technical history. But more fundamentally, intellectual history would be concerned with how those ideas came to be adopted, how they influenced men's other beliefs and actions, what tensions they created, what problems they generated, and to what further new ideas they led. It would become the intellectual history of a culture, the history of the social function of intellectual change. It would consider the social problems that led men to work out new ideas, the social determinations that channeled their efforts in certain directions, rather than others, the tensions they generated, and the consequences that developed when men were freed from social determinations to elaborate the implications of the ideas.

The selective problem thus becomes ultimately one of enlisting cooperative group action—of getting men to *act together* in new ways. It is thus a *political* problem. The focus of an intellectual history becomes specifically the problem of getting men to *believe together* in

[5] In the American scene this presumably does not mean "state medicine."

new ways. It is thus an *educational* problem. The conscious problems that serve as foci for histories because they are goals of action, are thus political or educational. Since they normally involve reorganizations of both actions and beliefs, they are usually both. By "educational problems," getting men to believe something new together, I do not of course mean mere schooling, though I am far from pessimistic about what schools can do. American schools are far from being the most conservative of all social institutions, as European schools are on the whole—indeed, the preservation of *something* of the past is precisely their most difficult problem. But the fundamental reorganization of beliefs is a matter of "political education," getting men to share new ideas as a basis for action. And such political education is probably best generated by common action and common concern with common problems. That is why professional or vocational organization is so important for such political education, since a man's profession involves his deepest and most sustained common action, and generates his most persistent habits. The greatest advance in such political education would be effected if every one were expected to join a union.[6]

The central place of such political education makes it clear why on the one hand appeals for "good will" and preaching seem so futile. What is needed is not good will alone, but new ideas and new behavior. And it makes clear on the other hand why calls for "more social science" or for a "more adequate social science" seem likewise to miss the point. What is needed is not so much more knowledge, as to get men to apply the knowledge and techniques already "available," but locked up in a small group of "experts," while the mass of men cannot apply, or even accept and understand, that knowledge, because the many social determinations prevent them from doing so.

Of course, such "political education" may well be considered as itself presenting a technical problem: it is dependent on the knowledge how best to get men to apply the knowledge that is available. Such techniques can obviously be made the object of intensive inquiry and investigation. It is clearly nonsense to say, our social science, or our "social intelligence," is of no avail, because of men's "sin," or their

[6] I should be a syndicalist on purely educational grounds, even were there not so many compelling economic reasons for that form of organization in America.

"drive for power," or their "irrationality," or their "group economic interests," or their "class bias," or any of the other excuses we make to ourselves. These facts of human behavior are just the "deflecting forces" any social science or social intelligence worth its salt would learn how to deal with! Such techniques for reorganizing beliefs and behavior will doubtless be very different from the techniques for dealing with natural materials; but such a genuine "social technology" is obviously of fundamental importance. How can men's actions and beliefs be best consciously reorganized? What obstacles are too hard to attack directly, which it would be better for the present to accept? Which are most easily modified? What is the best leverage? A genuine social science would have a central concern with these fundamental problems of political education, and with the methods for solving them.

Since the methods of "political education" are thus basic for the problems of history, the history of the *methods* of adjusting and reorganizing habits does seem to possess a kind of ultimacy. In social history it is the problems of political method and techniques that furnish the central organizing foci. And in truth British historians are apt to make the techniques of liberty and of parliamentary government central; Marxian historians, the method of the class struggle; German historians, their own distinctive political devices; and American historians, the "democratic method." For the same reason, in intellectual history philosophy has always seemed to present the basic organizing foci. For philosophy *is* the method of criticising and reorganizing beliefs, and the philosophic problems of adjusting different ideas to each other are obviously analogous to the political problems of adjusting different ways of acting.

At his proudest the philosopher is the statesman of ideas, organizing some new synthesis of intellectual materials, within whose novel constitutional framework men can henceforth carry on their intellectual pursuits. At his humblest he is the politician of ideas, effecting through his analyses compromises and working-agreements to live and let live. It is because the starting-point of the philosophic enterprise is the adjustment of intellectual tensions and conflicts, that the *history* of philosophy finds its focus for understanding to lie in problems of method, rather than in their culmination and fruit in imaginative vision. The *history* of philosophy is thus the history of the working out, the development, the application, and the refinement of intellectual methods. And this is likewise why the method of philosophic criticism and reconstruction, though it is always very intimately bound up with the prevailing "scientific method," is never wholly exhausted in it, but always retains something of the art of the politician of the mind.

IV

The present which we use our historical knowledge to understand we have found to be "problematic": it is full of "tendencies" big with the future, forces "dynamic" in the sense that they hold powers not now in operation, potentialities that promise more drastic modifications in the future. The present is thus full of tensions that are increasing. In the envisaged future, we predict, they will have grown intolerable, and will have to be faced. The present tension points to a future crisis: it is thus that problems are forced on us. An excellent illustration is the title of a recent book on religion: *Five Minutes to Twelve.* As Dr. Faustus found out, history is always understood at 11:55 P.M.; or else at five minutes before sunrise. Hegel was all wrong about the twilight: the only historians abroad then are—just owls.

Sub specie aeternitatis, or in the eyes of the Man in the Moon, it is more likely that we are at "two A.M. on a moderately blowy night," as James Harvey Robinson used to say. He saw mankind as just beginning to emerge from the great apes, and hence could view its history as "the human comedy." This attitude Robinson shared with his dearest enemy, the Church. I remember questioning a priest at the time Hitler's legions were tramping into Austria. "Oh, that will come out all right," he said, "things were really much worse in the times of Clovis." But that is obviously not the way to understand history, and certainly not the way to do anything about it. That is not the philosophy of history: that is just plain philosophy! There are times when even a philosopher of history would do well to take time off from his tragic posturing, and be "philosophical."

That is the way to "see" and to "accept" history; it is not the way to "understand" it. History is understood at 11:55 P.M.—"it is later than you think." That is, it is understood in terms of an imminent crisis. Even when we are in the midst of a present crisis, with its intolerable tensions, we understand the crisis in which we are acting in terms of a future more decisive crisis. We understood what was going on in Asia, we said, not as the mere conflict between Japan and the Western powers that was actually taking place, but in terms of the prediction, "The day of the white man in Asia is over." We understand the present Suez crisis in terms of the Russian control of the entire Arab world. We may not be "right" in our "understanding." We are never fully conscious of what later turn out to have been the "world-historical problems." But the point is, that is the way we *do* understand our history: we understand even our own present crises and conflicts in terms of a future crisis.

This is certainly true of the more elaborated "philosophies of history." They are always worked out at the eleventh hour, and provoked by some acute tension. We understand the fall of Rome to the Goths, with Augustine, in terms of the defeat of the Earthly City. We understand the corruption of Prussia, with Spengler, in terms of the decay of Faustian culture. We understand the French Revolution, with Condorcet, in terms of the final conflict between enlightenment and superstition. We understand the crises of capitalism, with Marx, in terms of the class struggle that will finally usher in the classless society. Is there any major philosophy of history that does not follow such a pattern? Is there any that is not, in this sense, "tragic"? The cyclical, the linear, the evolutionary ways of understanding history we do not today judge to be philosophies of history at all. They are "unrealistic," we say; they have not seen the real problems.

Historical knowledge of the past not only reveals how the tensions and problems came about; it explains the present by serving as an instrument of analysis. Problems seemingly unrelated in the present are unified in the light of their histories. Institutions that are "historically definable natures" are unified in the light of the problems they have generated. But historical knowledge is not only an instrument for analysing problems. It is also a tool for analysing the materials and resources with which we can face them. And like all understanding of means, this involves the evaluation of those means, for which history furnishes much, if not all, the necessary data.

In general, in the analysis of present materials historical knowledge reveals the genesis of what has some function or use, by taking us to the problematic situation in which it was worked out. Historical continuity alone will suffice to explain the presence in the present only of what has no use, and has survived by the sheer persistence of habit. History explains the toughness of what once had a use, and is now refractory to a changed function, generating a new tension: the obstacles or "deflecting forces." Our science explains the success of the active forces, why new ideas and techniques enable men to do what they do. History explains the conditioning forces, why we find limits set to the possibilities of our materials, why it takes so long to bend them to new uses. And history is a liberating and emancipating device, a potent intellectual technique of "political education," modifying those limits. It has always been uniformly so used, by an Einstein, or a Dewey, by any new program or movement. It can "show up" the past, and reveal the persisting deflecting forces for what they are. It discloses what they were designed to do, their original function, and focuses attention on any change in function demanded. It destroys "unreal issues" and "academic problems," which because they are no longer performing their earlier function have been perverted and prostituted by vested interests. But it condemns nothing that is not clearly damnable. The history of materials is not itself an evaluation: nothing is good or bad today merely because it has been. But it can make clear that fresh evaluation is necessary; and it provides many, though not all, the data necessary for that fresh appraisal.

But it were well not to forget, as Santayana says, that the function of history is to lend materials to poetry as well as to politics: "A good book of history is one that helps the statesman to formulate and to carry out his plans, or that helps the tragic poet to conceive what is most glorious in human destiny."[7] We might add, the comic poet as well, for history in general, and the history of ideas in particular, reveals just as much "the human comedy" as the human tragedy. History is understood for enjoyment as well as for use, for the visions and achievements it discloses as well as for its record of problem-solving and historical decision—for what the Father of History called "its great and wonderful deeds."

That revelation of achievement may well be the most significant gift of the past. Even today history appeals to men primarily as poetry, as a revelation of human nature: witness the present vogue for biogra-

[7] George Santayana, "History," in *Reason in Science* (New York, 1905), p. 66.

phy, expelled from our critical histories. For it is after all men with whose histories men are primarily concerned.

The philosopher is not merely the statesman of ideas, he is also the poet of the mind. And his great imaginative achievements—the dialectic of a Plotinus or a Hegel, the architecture of a Thomas or a Spinoza, the symbolic logician's world of pure form—exert an eternal appeal quite apart from any use they may find in our problem-solving. It is no accident that the major philosophers, though they start as statesmen or even as politicians of ideas, have ended as poets—such imaginative vision is indeed necessary to their majority. The great philosophies of history, like those of Saint Augustine or of Karl Marx, whatever incidental practical utility they may offer as instruments of analysis and as dynamic drives, surely find their most enduring value as poetry and not as politics—not even as the politics of salvation. I am even prepared to assert that the ultimate "dynamic" in history is just such vision; that the most powerful technique for getting men to act and believe together in new ways is a vision of God, a revolutionary idea. The effects, however, are so uniformly bad, that I am inclined to attribute this unfortunate fact about human nature to original sin. The vision of the great philosophies of history has about it much of the demonic!

It may well be true that the ultimate value of historical knowledge is the vision of man's history itself—the true *θεωρία* of history: of man as ever engaged in conflicts and insistent problems, each new one, though at the time it seem a crisis in the universe, but one more incident in a long series, with an endless chain yet to come—that *θεωρία* that makes comedy more ultimate than tragedy, and takes mankind beyond the tragedies of men.

But though visions be of transcendent importance, and to view the past as the record of human vision may well be the most significant way of regarding it, as it is certainly the major source of its undying appeal—it is not by vision that visions are understood. And whether the materials of our past are to be used as means in our problems, or, more significantly, to be enjoyed as works of art, they are to be understood in the same way: in the light of their histories, of the past problems that led men to create them and leave them for our ends.

PART II

Toward the Theory of Nature

CHAPTER 5

The Nature of Metaphysics: Its Function, Criteria, and Method

IN SPEAKING OF METAPHYSICS, I am not referring primarily to that subject-matter which for over a generation now has formed the stock in trade of "courses" in "metaphysics" given in American colleges. In the Report on *Philosophy in American Education,* Brand Blanshard and C. J. Ducasse have given an adequate account of what such courses have normally contained. They deal, we are told, first, with the problem of the *nature* of things, which Messrs. Blanshard and Ducasse break down into the questions:

> Are the countless different kinds of existing things really different, as they seem, or are they reducible to a smaller number—to ninety-two, or four, or two, or one? If to two, as commonly believed, how are these two related? If to one, which is fundamental? Is consciousness a by-product of matter in motion, or even perhaps identical with it? Or are the properties of material things merely appearances of and to mind? [1]

Secondly, the authors explain, these courses deal with the problem of the *structure* of the world—is it a litter of loose ends, or a single rational whole? Is it determined, or does it contain freedom? Is the truth theism, pantheism, or naturalism?

This account in the Report makes clear that the standard course in

---

The first three sections of this paper were read at a symposium at the meeting of the Eastern Division of the American Philosophical Association at Sarah Lawrence College, February 22, 1946, and printed in the *Journal of Philosophy,* XLIII (1946), 401–12. Section IV contains material from "On Being Rejected," *Journal of Philosophy,* L (1953), 797–805.

[1] *Philosophy in American Education,* by Brand Blanshard and others (New York, 1946), pp. 228–29.

"metaphysics" still reflects the assumptions and interests of the idealists of the last generation. It is still focused upon the "mind-body problem" inherited from Descartes, and upon the theological issues growing out of the religious inspiration of that idealism. This type of course took form in the 'nineties; and many a stalwart teacher has put in a lifetime examining and criticising the answers given to these problems by the traditional nineteenth-century "isms"—idealism, materialism, dualism, pragmatism, and the rest. In the interests of pedagogy, the differences between these "isms," springing out of their varying problems and insights, were soon sharpened into oppositions and antagonisms.

Today probably nearly all of those giving such a standard course in "metaphysics" have broken with that earlier idealism. But this teaching device still continues to determine the problems they regard as central and "metaphysical." And it is not surprising that it should have led some extremely able and candid minds, like Mr. Pepper in his *World Hypotheses*[2] or Mr. Sheldon in his *Process and Polarity*,[3] to come out with a cluster of four—or six—mutually irrefutable "metaphysical" positions. This conclusion, however irenic in intent, or however inadequate intellectually, seems really a tribute to their own expository skill and their powers of self-persuasion. But it is equally natural that most of the younger teachers of philosophy, for whom the nineteenth-century mind-body problem has never been the central concern of philosophic inquiry, should prefer to turn to issues that are today in the forefront of investigation and controversy. For at least fifty years now the assumptions on which were based the problems and the "isms" that were at the center of debate in the 'nineties have been carefully analysed and clarified. The outcome of this patient and acute analysis has been to transform those problems and to reconstruct those "positions." If "metaphysics" be limited to the continuing discussion of the issues growing out of nineteenth-century intellectual conflicts, with no awareness of the great advance in our scientific knowledge and of the progress of philosophic criticism, then, say many today, they will have none of it.

Some of these older questions are indeed genuinely metaphysical,

[2] Stephen C. Pepper, *World Hypotheses* (Berkeley, 1942).
[3] Wilmon H. Sheldon, *Process and Polarity* (New York, 1944).

though their terms have today been transformed. But the critics are right: this traditional enterprise surely fails to exhaust metaphysics. Metaphysics hardly centers upon the mind-body problem. It need not set out by accepting the purely gratuitous and historically conditioned assumptions which in Cartesian and Newtonian science generated that problem—assumptions which any sound metaphysical criticism would in fact reveal to be untenable. Nor is metaphysics a never-ending debate between rival world-hypotheses. In the light of its long history, metaphysics is rather a specific scientific inquiry, with a definite field and subject-matter of its own, a science that like any other is cumulative and progressive, a science that has in fact during the past half-century made remarkable progress. Metaphysics is the science of existence as existence.

I trust that I hardly need add that it is distinctly *not* the science of *Existenz*. Whatever the meaning of that Teutonic term, whose aggressions for a time after World War II seemed to be succeeding where Hitler's panzers ultimately failed—and I am hardly sufficiently versed in the toils of "existential subjectivity" to be entirely clear as to its precise significance—it seems to be the exact opposite of the public "existence" which metaphysics explores.[4]

[4] On further study, and in part as a result of the disgust and "nausea" produced in my mind by the pretty arid Wasteland in which English "philosophical analysis" seems to have been wandering of late, among recent philosophies of experience I have been impressed by the suggestiveness and value of certain of the ideas to be found in the "existential ontology" of Heidegger himself, which I have found most intelligibly set forth in English by Paul Tillich. I find very congenial its basic metaphysical framework—its naturalistic inclusion of man in Being, its "self-world" polarity, and its consequent position that all human experiences have ontological implications—that they are all what Dewey calls "transactions" of man cooperating with the rest of things, which point to genuine traits of the world in which man finds himself.

Of course, I should want to free this existential ontology from the absurd limitations of the peculiar experiences its German and French spokesmen have taken as fundamental, and focused their attention upon. To an American, concentration upon these particular experiences has been clearly conditioned by the Continental "crisis-situation"—aided and abetted by that pathological Romanticist, Kierkegaard. The Germans have found *Angst*—the "ontological anxiety of finitude," or in English the dread of death; the French have discovered "nausea." When I once asked Mr. Tillich about the relation between the two, he explained: "Nausea produces Anxiety." That answer seemed to me very odd, since for me it has always been just the other way round. I am not now, and never have been, an "existentialist." If I ever do become one, it will be

I

In the Western tradition there have been three different philosophical enterprises that have been called "metaphysics." These three types of inquiry are in fact quite distinct, though they have often been combined and confused. They spring from the three great Greek thinkers, Aristotle, Plato, and Plotinus, respectively.

There is a science [says Aristotle] which investigates existence as existence, and whatever belongs to existence as such. It is identified with none of the sciences which are defined less generally. For none of these professes to consider existence as existence, but each, restricting itself to some aspect of it, investigates the general aspect only incidentally, as do the mathematical sciences.[5]

This science Aristotle himself called "First Philosophy." His earliest editor, Andronikos of Rhodes, placing the texts that dealt with it after the books on physics, called the collection *τὰ μετὰ τὰ φυσικά*, that is, "the volume after the Physics" in the order of his edition—"Volume VIII" in our standard Oxford translation. "Volume VIII," "Eightness," or First Philosophy, disregards the diversities of things, and examines their most comprehensive and general characters. It analyses the "generic traits" manifested by existences of any kind, the distinctions sure to turn up in any universe of discourse drawn from existence—those traits exhibited in any *οὐσίαι* or existential subject-matter,[6] the

only when I have succeeded in knocking the Kierkegaard—the "Anxiety" and "nausea"—out of existential ontology. It is this element—*Das Nichts nichtet,* the preoccupation with death—that was the red rag that drove some of our saner German friends to a positivism *in extremis,* and that has made the gospel of existentialism so far primarily a theological apologetic for the desperate faith of despairing men.

[5] *Metaphysics* 1003a.

[6] I emphasize "existential subject-matter" to avoid the misinterpretation that this statement of the subject-matter of metaphysical inquiry—in which I am of course paraphrasing and combining Woodbridge and Dewey—applies not only to "existences of any kind," but also to such *non-existential* subject-matters as mathematics, logic, and the theory of numbers. These formal sciences are *not* concerned with existential subject-matter—as is religion, for example. They are concerned rather with "abstractions" from existential subject-matter, that is, from subject-matters encountered non-reflectively as well as reflectively, or in thinking. Their subject-matters are not "*οὐσίαι* in the first and best sense," "Primary *οὐσίαι*," as the *Categories* puts it (*Cat.* 1b). The subject-matters of

fundamental and pervasive distinctions in terms of which any existential subject-matter may be understood, as they are found within any such subject-matter. This science of metaphysics is thus a special interest, not a super-science dictating to the others. It is one science among many other sciences, distinguished from the rest not by its method of empirical observation and generalization, which it shares with them, but by its own specific subject-matter. The others can get on happily without it, though it can scarcely get on very well or very far without them.

This Aristotelian inquiry into the ultimate distinctions involved in existence as existence, coming down to present-day empirical naturalists, has always, with clear historical right to the term, been called "metaphysics." In the eighteenth century it received, at the hands of the tidy Christian Wolff, the alternative name of "ontology." But Platonists, in the light of Plato's vision of a totality of knowledge integrated in the "Idea of the Good," and convinced that the all-pervasive trait of "what is" is its unity, have again and again endeavored to unify all scientific knowledge into a single all-embracing system dependent upon a set of organizing "principles of Being." Identifying this enterprise of their own, which Plato called "dialectic," with Aristotle's "science of existence as existence," they have appropriated the term "metaphysics" to designate their science of Being, Totality, or the Whole. This Platonic "metaphysics" or enterprise of "dialectic" unification has taken many forms, as different as those of Thomas—who on this as on most fundamental metaphysical issues is a Platonist and not an Aristotelian—of Descartes, Spinoza, Fichte, Hegel, Herbert Spencer, Whitehead and Russell's *Principia Mathematica,* and of our contemporary apostles of the Unity of Science, the logical positivists.

Feeding on the steady unification actually achieved in our scientific knowledge, such Platonists have not only, like Plato himself, pro-

these "formal sciences"—which I should not myself consider to be "sciences" at all, but rather, elaborate "connectives"—are what the *Categories* calls "οὐσίαι in the secondary sense," and what the "Logic of the Moderns" in the fourteenth century called "second intentions." To them applies the ultimate metaphysical distinction between Subject-matter and its Structure, but not that between Powers and their Operation—for to such abstractions from natural processes the ontological category of "Time" is of course irrelevant. On these fundamental metaphysical issues I follow in general the Aristotelian position. Most present-day nominalists seem to agree with the Platonic position on these matters.

claimed the eventual unity of knowledge as an ideal; they have often thought they have actually reached such a set of unifying principles. More empirical thinkers have judged this claim premature and presumptuous, and have pointed to the mythical means by which the supposed unity of knowledge was actually achieved. The claim to have found unity when in fact there was none has often brought the Aristotelian "science of existence," which has never sought such unity but has been judged guilty by association with the Platonic enterprise, into disrepute.

Thirdly, this search for "the Whole" has passed over—historically, in Plotinus—into the search for "True Being," for "the Real." The unity of the world understood has been set over against the diversity of the world initially encountered, as the "True Being" or "Reality" on which everything else depends. "The Real" thus becomes the object of a search, and is not to be found on the universe's sleeve. When found, it condemns many things which had originally been taken as "real" to the class of "mere appearance." Since "the Real" is not on the surface of experience, the search for "Reality" involves the attempt to find an independent Being upon which mere encountered Nature depends. And since the distinction between Appearance and Reality, or Being, is a distinction of value, "the Real" becomes the Good, and as the source of all Being and Goodness in the world is identified with "the Divine" or God. For the Plotinian, as for the modern philosophical idealist, "metaphysics" thus becomes rational theology, and demonstrates the existence of a Being not to be found by the other sciences. It is this third Plotinian enterprise, vigorously pursued by the post-Kantian idealists, which has brought all enterprises known as "metaphysics" into greatest disrepute. Empiricists cannot find any such "Being" or "Reality" in experience, pragmatists and positivists deem the whole conception of a "quest for Being" or "Reality" "meaningless." [7]

[7] Woodbridge has a pertinent and illuminating comment on the idealist's "quest for Being": "When we attempt to describe the realm of being comprehensively, that is, when we attempt to tell what it is that we think about, language takes on a constitution marked by degrees of generality. 'Being' is our most general term and quite logically so. For, when we ask in the most general way what anything is and expect the most general answer possible, we can do nothing but translate that question into the indicative form of speech and say that anything is what it is. That is, it is 'isness.' But this expression is barbarous. We use instead the participle 'being,' transforming it

It is the Aristotelian inquiry into the generic traits of existence, and the ultimate distinctions in existential subject-matters, that together with other empirical naturalists I would seek to maintain, not the search for Unity of the Platonist or the search for "the Whole" or "the Real" or "Being" which constitutes "metaphysics" for the philosophic idealist, or the existentialist, and is in fact rational theology. I have no quarrel with rational or philosophical theology; and I am certainly far from suggesting that a wise philosophy should confine itself to the subject-matter of metaphysics, and refuse to go on to the many other critical enterprises that, in addition to the science of metaphysics, together constitute philosophy. And among these critical enterprises an adequate philosophy would have to include philosophical theology. But if it does, it should know clearly just what it is doing. Rational or philosophical theology is not metaphysics—though it might well learn much from that sober discipline. Metaphysics, in its first and proper sense as the science of existence, has nothing to say about "God" or "the Real" or "the universe as a Whole" as the ultimate context or implication of existence. But it has much to say about the way such myths function in the particular contexts of human living—about *any* "God," about *any* "universe as a Whole." For such unifying myths are one fundamental type of existence, one ultimate way of functioning, and to function as a myth, or "mythically," is one of the fundamental ways in which existence is discovered to function.

Metaphysics, in fact, has no particularly close connection with religion which it does not have with any other human cooperation with the rest of things. To be sure, in understanding what is, metaphysics cannot arrive at any valid conclusion which would leave the fact of religion

---

into a noun. Aristotle long ago gave the classical analysis of this trick of speech. And a trick of speech it is so evidently that it seems strange that anyone—but there have been many—should find the term 'being' a source of knowledge and inspiration. It is so clearly the expression of our attempt to speak most generally, that we ought not to suppose that by the use of it we speak most significantly. Here is where a great illusion arises. A term potent enough to gather under its wings all objects of all thought arouses the penchant for magic in us. We begin to say that the objects of thought *have* Being, that Being necessarily is, that without Being nothing can be or be conceived, that to know Being is to know fully and completely, and that to rest in Being is to rest peacefully. All this is true enough, participially, but its value, after all, is only that of linguistic rhapsody." (F. J. E. Woodbridge, *The Realm of Mind* [New York, 1926], pp. 33–34.)

unintelligible. Like every other activity of men in their world—botany, art, physics, politics, and all the rest—religion is part of the subject-matter of existence which metaphysics must understand. All of them, and everything else we can discover in the world, afford evidence as to the nature of existence. But to mix up religion with metaphysics, or to identify either with rational theology, is to confuse metaphysics and to do a marked disservice to religion itself. Both important human activities can fulfill their very different functions in human living all the better the more clearly they are distinguished. Religion tells us nothing about the nature of existence, and metaphysics tell us nothing in particular about the enjoyment of God.

Having drawn this sharp distinction, which it is well for both the metaphysician and the philosophical theologian to keep clearly in mind, I realize that this is not a wholly adequate statement of the relation between metaphysics and religion. But it is difficult to formulate briefly, without the possibility of misunderstanding, what I feel should be said further. I can try to put it: without some sense of the religious dimension of man's experience in Nature, and with the rest of Nature, it seems to be very hard for metaphysical inquiry to be adequately imaginative and comprehensive. I have been led to this observation by reflection upon those contemporary philosophical movements in which any sense of this "religious dimension" of human experience is notoriously lacking. For present purposes I should be willing to accept provisionally Santayana's formulation of what I am calling the "religious dimension" of man's experience and of existence itself, as consisting of piety and spirituality—piety being taken with Santayana as "respect for the sources of our being," and spirituality as "devotion to ideal ends."[8] This sense of a religious dimension of life is expressed by John Dewey, and by Bertrand Russell—at times. So far as I have ever found, it has not been expressed by G. E. Moore, or by most of the logical positivists.

A sound metaphysics, of course, would have to give different answers to the questions traditionally raised by this "religious dimension" of experience than those traditionally given—by any philosophical theology with which I am familiar. But it would consider the questions

[8] George Santayana, *Reason in Religion* (New York, 1905), Chapters X and XI.

seriously, and give some answers—even if the answers, like those of Hume, turned out to be negative. Not to consider these questions raised by this important aspect of man's experience of the world, and to have no answers at all, is what makes metaphysics—and philosophy in general—thin, meager, and barren.[9] This is to say nothing of the practical dangers involved in such a disregard of a fundamental aspect of human living. To have no intellectually responsible concern with the intellectual issues presented by the religious dimension of experience is, in these days, to leave oneself wide open to a wholly inadequate and uncriticised form of religion. Still more, it is to leave thus exposed to temptation those who have the right to ask for philosophical criticism and guidance from us philosophers—if we conceive ourselves to have any social function at all.

A metaphysician who shares the experience of a particular religious tradition might well say, with Spinoza, that one of his major problems is to find what God really is—though I do not mean that many men today could possibly share Spinoza's quality of medieval piety. Such a metaphysician might even say, with Hegel, that among his other concerns is the attempt to state precisely what religion has always expressed in symbols—though no responsible metaphysician today could limit himself, as Hegel did, to a single religion and a single theological formulation.[10]

[9] This is why I personally have found the ontology of Paul Tillich so much more stimulating and suggestive than most of what passes as "philosophical analysis" today, though Mr. Tillich is ultimately a "Plotinian" addicted to the third type of "metaphysics" here distinguished, and his ontology is broadly a form of Romantic idealism—that is, in my judgment he gives the wrong answers.

[10] I have been impressed by the recent attempt of Walter T. Stace, in *Time and Eternity* (Princeton, 1952) and in *Religion and the Modern Mind* (Philadelphia, 1952), to combine a thoroughgoing naturalism in metaphysics with an emphasis on the religious dimension of experience. This hardheaded Englishman, matter-of-fact, downright, and clearheaded, served for twenty-two years in the British Civil Service in Ceylon, and rose to be mayor of Colombo. He was greatly impressed by Buddhism, and treats it most sympathetically in his philosophical poem, modeled on *Thus Spake Zarathustra, The Gate of Silence* (Boston, 1952), although as a Westerner he cannot accept its quietistic emphasis. Mr. Stace has no philosophical theology: he makes no attempt to bring his naturalistic metaphysics and his mystical awareness together, though he has expressed much sympathy for that of Paul Tillich. But he does furnish a suggestive recognition of what I have called the religious dimension of experience.

II

The Aristotelian inquiry into existence, springing directly from Plato's analysis of the meaning of "to be" in the *Sophist,* is clearly illustrated in the analysis of the central metaphysical distinctions in Books Z, H, and Θ of the *Metaphysics,* and in the analysis of the significance of metaphysical terms in Book Δ. Aristotle examines the pervasive traits that appear in every existential field of inquiry, and analyses the metaphysical distinctions in terms of which they are expressed, like form and material, power and its operation, structure and process, regularity and contingency, etc. Building on Plato's definition:

> Everything which possesses any power of any kind, either to produce a change in anything of any nature, or to be affected even in the least degree by any slightest cause, though it be only on one occasion, has real existence. For I set up as a definition to define "being" that it is nothing else than power.[11]—

Aristotle made existence or *οὐσία* fundamentally the operation of powers, that cooperation of powers that is "substance" or process (*κίνησις*). And I judge that the recent progress of metaphysical inquiry has brought about a return to the Aristotelian identification of *οὐσία* or existence with *κίνησις* or process, conceived as plural, contextual, operational, and objectively relative.

Such an analytic and empirical metaphysics does not find that existence forms a "Totality" or "Whole." Existence is always plural and determinate. In the light of the available evidence, Spinoza and Hegel were wrong and Hume and Kant were right: we can say nothing valid about "the Universe" as a whole or a totality, because we can never encounter, experience, act or feel toward, existence as a "Whole"—even in reflective experience. We can indeed talk significantly about "the universe" or existence in general. But when we do, we are talking distributively, about *any existence,* or existential subject-matter. We are not talking about some unified all-embracing Substance or Being or Reality or Whole. Existence can of course *become unified* in vision, as it is slowly approaching unification in discourse and knowledge. But this unification always involves the element of "myth." And existence,

[11] *Sophist* 247E.

while it seems to present no achieved unity, does involve an ascertainable continuity of means and mechanisms which inquiry can explore and bring toward some eventual unification, together with a radical disparity among the various diverse ends this continuity of means and mechanisms can achieve.[12]

Nor does empirical metaphysics agree with the "Plotinian" idealist in finding "the Real" at the end of a long search. For it, whatever is encountered in whatever way, in non-reflective as well as in reflective experience, is "real." "The Real," "Reality," it takes as one of those inclusive terms which designate total subject-matter—like "being" for Greek metaphysics, or "nature" for philosophical naturalists. In itself it can indicate no distinctions. It is the starting-point of inquiry, the total subject-matter within which significant distinctions are then found. There can thus be no intelligible "search for the real," no significant "quest for being." Reality and being are what the metaphysician sets out from, not that which he is seeking to find. To take "nature" as the inclusive term has the advantage that it is harder to convert into such a distinction of value.

Within the real we distinguish between the real as initially encountered and the real as analysed and understood—as the experienced world most completely interpreted. When we make a contrast between "Reality" and "Appearance," we are making a distinction of value and importance, not one of existence. "Reality" means either everything whatsoever—as we are here taking it—or else that a distinction of relative importance has been made. In any other than an evaluative sense, to say that only the Good is "real," only Matter is "real," only Mind is "real," only Energy is "real," is to express a prejudice refuted by a child's first thought or by every smallest grain of sand. No, everything encountered in any way is somehow real. The significant question is, not whether anything is "real" or not, but how and in what sense it is real, and how it is related to and functions among other reals. To take "the real" as in fundamental contrast to what appears to us, is to identify it with "the Good," and not with existence. Such identification seems to have resulted invariably in confusions and insoluble contradictions.

"The real" is, indeed, the object of search, in that, starting with the

[12] See Chapter 7, "Empirical Pluralism and Unifications of Nature."

real we initially encounter, we go on to try to find *more* that is likewise real. In reflective experience we seek the real as understood and interpreted, and this brings us to many "realities" we had not before been aware of. But however much *more* of "the real" we may thus be led to discover, that fact does not make what we started with any *less* real. It is simply not true to say with the idealist that "appearances" first taken as "real" have on further inquiry, which teaches us more about them, to be discarded as unfit for that office. The notion that the subject-matter with which metaphysical inquiry starts, the world as initially encountered or "denoted," can possibly be discarded or dismissed as "less real," as "mere appearance," in contrast with the further realities at which it arrives, though often presupposed in the interest of discovered scientific, moral, or religious "realities" which are found to possess great value, is to the Aristotelian or empirical metaphysician the cardinal metaphysical error, which makes any sound metaphysics impossible. Metaphysics originated in fact in Aristotle with the criticism of "the Platonists" for committing precisely this unforgivable metaphysical fallacy. And whenever men have fallen into it, in the supposed interest of science, of morality, or of religion, sound metaphysics has had to raise its voice in protest. The essential function of metaphysics is precisely to criticise such "abstractions." The primacy of the subject-matter is the first principle of any sound metaphysics.

In consequence, the empirical metaphysician always has "the real" or "being" in his grasp. For the real, or being, or nature, is what he starts with in his analysis. His inquiry brings more and more of reality and being and nature into his ken. But it does not and cannot invalidate one jot or tittle of the reality or being or nature with which he sets out.

For the Platonic tradition in metaphysics, the *function* of "metaphysics" is to provide principles for organizing all knowledge into a unified system. For the Plotinian tradition—for modern idealism—it is to discover new kinds of existence that initially are not known to be there. For the Aristotelian tradition, however, for metaphysics in its original sense—for empirical naturalism today—it is to criticise undue concentration on certain elements and factors discovered in the experienced world. Its function, that is, is critical: with Bradley, Whitehead, and Dewey in this present century, as well as with Aristotle, who so ably pointed out the undue concentration of the Platonists, it can be stated as "the criticism of abstractions." In Dewey's words, metaphysics is "the criticism of criticisms," "the ground-map of the province of criticism." [13]

For the Platonist, metaphysics has a distinctive *method* of its own: the dialectical analysis of presuppositions. For the Plotinian, its method is likewise *sui generis:* direct intellectual vision or Νοῦς, combined usually with a preparatory dialectic. For the empirical metaphysician, the method of metaphysics is no different from the ordinary experimental methods of observation and tested generalization employed in any existential science, and his conclusions share in the probable and corrigible character of the findings of all experimental science.

III

Metaphysics is thus closely related to but distinguished from certain other inquiries: the inquiry into knowledge, the inquiry into language, and the "philosophy of science." Since the eighteenth century, metaphysics has traditionally possessed two branches, ontology and epistemology. The latter term has covered a multitude of sins. If "epistemology" be taken as the wrestling with "the problem of knowledge" —if it seriously seeks to discover whether there is any such animal as "knowledge" or not—then it is doubtful whether this is a valid or even a meaningful inquiry. But if it be taken analytically—if it be the inquiry into the factors involved in knowing and the distinctions forced by that fact, and the further implications of the fact of knowledge—then there is a valid inquiry into knowing. Sometimes, as by Descartes and Locke, this inquiry into knowledge has been taken as a necessary *preface* to any inquiry into specific subject-matters. Sometimes, as in Kant and Eddington, it has become a *substitute* for inquiry into existence. Yet knowability or intelligibility is a trait of every object of inquiry, of every possible subject-matter—else it could not be inquired into or made known. What is involved in this trait? How is it to be analysed and understood? "Knowledge" is not the subject-matter of metaphysical inquiry, but the traits of the experienced world—the world reflectively experienced, the world inquired into and known.

The relation of metaphysical inquiry to the inquiry into language is similar. I should like to be able to say, the inquiry into "logic"—into λόγος or discourse, into teaching and communication, into putting

[13] John Dewey, *Experience and Nature* (New York, 1929), pp. 398, 413.

language to work. Just as knowledge is not the subject-matter of metaphysics, neither is language and discourse. Metaphysics is indeed "analytic," but not of terms and propositions and language alone, as in the recent fashion of English "philosophical analysis." Metaphysics is analytic of natural existence, laying bare those generic traits and distinctions which terms and propositions and discourse can formulate. It deals with existence formulated and expressed. "Terminism" as a preface to or a substitute for inquiry into existence has flourished recurrently, as it is flourishing today. Like atheism, it is the product of a little thought, when an initial naive or non-functional realism breaks down, and men realize that discourse is not identical with or in one-to-one correspondence with its subject-matter, but have not yet achieved a functional realism. With William of Ockham, it holds that metaphysical distinctions are made by, are introduced by, language. Or, like Kant or James Mill, it holds that all structure in the experienced world is created by the "understanding" or by language, and does not dwell in the wholly amorphous body of facts of pure particulars at all. Yet a logical or discursive character—"logiscibility" Dewey once called it—is a trait of every subject-matter, of every universe of discourse—else it were not a subject-matter or a universe of discourse at all. What is involved in this fact? How is it to be analysed? What traits of existence make possible the manifold operations of language and communication? What are the metaphysical implications of the fact of language?

Thus metaphysics is not identical with the "theory of knowledge," as something taken in isolation, with no reference to the object of knowledge, to what is known—it is not the same as "epistemology" in this sense. It is not identical with the "theory of language" taken in isolation, with no reference to the subject-matter of language, to what is expressed and communicated—it is not the same as "formal logic." But metaphysics does inquire into the implications of the fact of knowledge, of the existence of inquiry, discovery, and verification, of the determinate fact that we possess and practice successfully an art of knowing. It asks, what is involved in this fact—what are its distinctive traits, what are the intellectual instruments for dealing with it, what are its implications for the nature of the world that sustains it, for the nature of any existence that can be made an object of inquiry? Metaphysics does inquire into the fact of language, of the existence of expression and communication, of the art of talking. It asks what is involved in the fact of talking—what are its distinctive traits, what are the intellectual instruments for dealing with it, what are its implications for the nature of the world that sustains it, for the nature of any existence that can be expressed and communicated?

How, then, is metaphysical inquiry related to the "philosophy of science"? If the latter be an analysis of the fields, methods, concepts, and languages of the specific sciences, then it is what epistemology ought to be. But if the "philosophy of science" be an analysis of the implications of the fact of science, of what is involved in its discovery and formulation of structures and mechanisms, of invariant relations, then it is a metaphysical inquiry and analysis—into the character and implications of the enterprise of science. Such an inquiry is illustrated in much of Dewey's *Logic,* and much of his *Quest for Certainty,* as well as by his fundamental analysis of science in *Experience and Nature.* In this sense, the philosophy of science is a branch of metaphysics, which to be adequate would have to include it. It would also have to include the philosophy of mathematics, a similar analysis of the implications of the fact of mathematics—what it involves, how it is to be made intelligible, what it implies; and also the philosophy of history, taken as the analysis of the historical aspect of existence, and the concepts by which that aspect can be best understood.

But likewise, to be adequate, metaphysics would have to include also an analysis of other types of human experience besides those primarily cognitive. It would have to embrace the philosophy of art, conceived on the lines of Aristotle's analysis of art in the *Physics,* as contrasted with his analysis of poetry in isolation in the *Poetics*—or conceived on the lines of Dewey's analysis of art in Chapter IX of *Experience and Nature,* and in much of *Art as Experience.* It would have to include the philosophy of practice—I take it that *Experience and Nature* is a large-scale metaphysical analysis of practice. And it would have to include the philosophy of religion, conceived in analogous terms, as an analysis of what religion is, and what it implies about the world in which it is naturally generated among men.

These are all basic types of human activity, in response to the generic traits of existence. They all have metaphysical implications for the nature of the world that generates and sustains them. Each can be analysed "in itself," as selected, isolated, abstracted from its context in the experienced world. But each can also be seen and analysed as revealing the traits of existence that call it forth—each can be seen "in perspective," "in its context"—"in experience," say the philosophies of experience, that is, in the light of its function in the experienced world, which reveals what it does, and hence what it is. Such inquiries, leading to such "seeings in context," I should call, following Woodbridge, who taught me all the metaphysics I know, *θεωρίαι*, "Theories" or enterprises of metaphysical analysis: the "theory" of nature, the "theory" of science, the "theory" of history, the "theory" of mathematics, the "theory" of language, the "theory" of symbols, the "theory" of art, the "theory" of practice, the "theory" of religion, and so on.

The adjective formed from *θεωρία*, "theoretical"—which translated literally into Latin appears as "speculative"—meaning, leading to "theory" or intellectual vision of something in its context, thus means also, "empirical," appealing to the experienced world; "functional," appealing to the function in experience; "contextual," appealing to the function in its context. Hence as an adjective, "metaphysical" is equivalent to "empirical," "functional," and "contextual." It is close, I judge, to what Hegel meant by "dialectical": while the aim of a particular scientific inquiry is to "isolate" its subject-matter, the aim of a "dialectical analysis" for Hegelianism, including the present living version of left-wing Hegelianism, Marxism, is to discover the function of that subject-matter replaced in the context or situation in which it actually occurs and from which it was "isolated" for scientific purposes. But this usage for "dialectical," a term whose meanings have been long established in the Platonic and in the Aristotelian traditions, strikes me as perverse, and I cannot recommend it.

The proximate function of this kind of "intellectual seeing in perspective" or "in context" is "theoretical" or "speculative"—that is, it contributes to intelligibility, it gives an understanding of the subject-matter so seen and analysed. But *θεωρία*, intelligibility, itself has a function which determines its distinctive character. What constitutes "understanding" or "intelligibility" in any particular case is defined by the end or use for which it is sought. Anything is always "understood for" some determinate end. And the test of whether it is adequately understood—of whether the understanding is adequate for its determinate function—is whether it can serve as an effective means to that determinate end. The further function of θεωρία, of metaphysical understanding, is to serve as a method or instrument of criticism and clarification.

The metaphysical analysis of any specific subject-matter, therefore, is to be defined as a critical analysis of the distinctive traits of that subject-matter, of the intellectual instruments, the concepts and distinctions, for dealing with it, and of its implications for the nature of existence. I have already suggested an extensive program for investigation, involving all the characteristic activities and pursuits of man's cultural life in nature. This program I can recommend, in the confidence that to work upon it in any part will bring more substantial philosophical fruits than to engage in the rather fruitless discussion of many of the problems and issues which are in the forefront of the fads and fashions of the day.

IV

In conclusion, I should like to make a few further comments on method in metaphysics. This is really quite a simple matter, calling for no extended treatment. For from Woodbridge, who rightly regarded himself on this point as the spokesman of ancient tradition, I learned that metaphysics is distinguished from other inquiries by its subject-matter, not by its method. "In regarding metaphysics as the outcome of reflection on existence in general," he wrote in 1908, "and, consequently, as a department of natural knowledge, I have supposed that intelligent persons could undertake such reflection and accomplish something of interest and consequence, by following the ordinary experimental methods of observation and tested generalization." [14] This means, that on the

[14] F. J. E. Woodbridge, *Nature and Mind* (New York, 1937), p. 108. This conception of the method of metaphysics, clearly expressed in the lecture on "Metaphysics" of 1908, Woodbridge maintained consistently in all his subsequent writings and in many conversations on the subject. It is true that in the presidential address of 1903, "The Problem of Metaphysics," Woodbridge wrote: "Science asks for the laws of existence and discovers them by experiment. Metaphysics asks for the nature of reality and discovers it by definition" (*Nature and Mind*, pp. 40–41). By 1908 "reality" had disappeared from the definition of metaphysics for him, and with it the method of "definition." The

basis of what experience and insight we may be granted, we frame some metaphysical hypothesis, treat it as a leading principle, and proceed to explore its consequences. My own ideal of the most fruitful way in which to carry on this procedure has always been the example of my beloved teacher, Wendell T. Bush. He had a real genius for exploring novel ideas. Unlike our present-day nominalists, who want always to emphasize the specifically different meanings general ideas take on in every new context into which they can enter, Bush was interested in seeing how fruitful ideas continue to have some meaning in very diverse contexts. Without such an interest, metaphysical inquiry naturally has little attraction for a reflective mind.

The value of a leading principle clearly depends upon whither we are led, and the only test of a metaphysical distinction or concept consists in the illumination and clarification it can bring to a wide variety of subject-matters—ideally, if we are seeking complete generality, to any subject-matter.

Metaphysical discovery—or progress in metaphysical inquiry—depends on the finding of new ideas that can be so generalized with fruitful results. It seems quite futile to argue before the event whether such ideas can be discovered or not. The only test of whether they can be discovered is to discover them. That ideas capable of wide generalization have been found in the past, is beyond question. The Greeks were quite good at it, and to this circumstance they owe the inexhaustible fertility of their thought for philosophic reflection. In modern times, such ideas have arisen in some particular field of human experience, usually, but not always, in one of the sciences, and have then been generalized and explored with momentous intellectual results.

---

address of 1903 was written before he had begun to learn from Dewey, and on this as on many other points of metaphysics differs considerably from his later settled position.

Woodbridge once explained to me that though he would not then put it as he had in 1903, having come to think of metaphysics not as contrasted with the sciences, but as one science among many others, he had been thinking of definition in the sense of Aristotle's *Posterior Analytics,* where it is not the preliminary to but the outcome of inquiry. This is the view he continued to hold in *An Essay on Nature* (New York, 1940): "We are often asked to define our 'terms' before we use them, although as a matter of fact definitions do not come first, but last, and great pains are required in arriving at them" (p. 221). It is the view Woodbridge held after 1908 that seems sound to me.

Like all the other sciences, metaphysics has today passed beyond the stage where striking new discoveries are made by the unaided efforts of a single great thinker. Like the others, its inquiry has become cooperative, so that the ideas it explores are now drawn from the common climate of intellectual experience, and are pushed in the same general direction. Consider the complex of ideas associated with biological evolution—the importance of time, the relation between organism and environment, and the rest. These evolutionary ideas, together with many others in our present-day intellectual experience, have been explored and generalized in thinkers as superficially different but as essentially close in their novel metaphysical distinctions and concepts as Dewey, Whitehead, and Heidegger, to take but three.

Our recent philosophies of experience have in this manner made genuine and remarkable ontological discoveries, and there has been of late much progress in metaphysical inquiry. In pointing out this obvious fact, I am of course not unaware that such a statement fails to apply to England, where the metaphysical tradition has always been weak and for the moment seems almost to have expired completely. Fortunately, it has not died in Scotland, which in philosophy as in so much else, like good whisky, has always led the British Isles.

Now, this metaphysical generalization and exploration of new ideas has always provoked those who have been carrying it on to speak in new and unaccustomed ways. If they have not, like any other scientists, been driven to invent a new technical terminology, they have at least used the old familiar words with new meanings. They have always found that traditional and conventional language has so crystallized that it cannot adequately express the new distinctions or the new concepts: it thus puts cramping limitations on their exploration. Consider the three examples just mentioned, Dewey, Whitehead, and Heidegger; or consider the great pioneers in intellectual reorientation, like Hegel, Kant, or indeed Aristotle himself.

There is a view fashionable today, in England and among those American students of philosophy who, as a result of the almost total lack of any linguistic training in American secondary schools, find the reading of foreign languages very difficult, that wisdom in philosophy is to be sought in the correct conventional use of the English language. Whether this criterion has been applied to any other language, I am not sure—it might have suggestive results if directed toward the Greek! [15] When the substance of Chapter 9 of this book, in which the attempt is made to work out a theory of signs, was read several years ago before a philosophical group, it provoked in a distinguished visitor from Oxford, who has since become the historian of philosophical analysis, the sole critical comment: "When *I* think of a sign, I think of a wooden board hanging in front of a pub." I can really imagine no way better calculated than this reliance on accepted and conventional English usage, to shut yourself off from ever getting a new idea or thinking a fresh thought, or from ever being able to recognize one in anybody else.[16]

Now, philosophy in general, and metaphysical inquiry in particular, are indeed very intimately bound up with language, and with an awareness of the power of language as an instrument—and of the dangers which language like all power carries with it if misused. A major part of that power of language as an instrument of metaphysical inquiry lies not in the fact that language commits thought to old usages, but rather in the fact that language can itself be put to new uses. Language is in truth the most potent instrument of manipulation the mind of man has ever devised. Indeed, it comes very close to being the inventive and manipulative mind of man itself—of being what Aristotle called "the mind that makes all things," the so-called "active intellect."

Through language alone can man free himself from the tyranny of

[15] This view is especially perplexing when, as in a recent contribution to the *Journal of Philosophy,* it is strongly defended in a paper in which half a dozen words are consistently misspelled. One might have supposed that the protagonist of correct English usage as the ultimate arbiter of truth would at least know how to spell.

[16] Bertrand Russell, in his witty and devastating critique of "The Cult of 'Common Usage'" (*Portraits from Memory* [New York, 1956], pp. 166–72), writes: "Philosophy, as conceived by the school I am discussing, seems to me a trivial and uninteresting pursuit. To discuss endlessly what silly people mean when they say silly things may be amusing but can hardly be important. . . . These philosophers remind me of the shopkeeper of whom I once asked the shortest way to Winchester. He called to a man in the back premises: 'Gentleman wants to know the shortest way to Winchester.' 'Winchester?' an unseen voice replied. 'Aye.' 'Way to Winchester?' 'Aye.' 'Shortest way?' 'Aye.' 'Dunno.' He wanted to get the nature of the question clear, but took no interest in answering it. This is exactly what modern philosophy does for the earnest seeker after truth. Is it surprising that young people turn to other studies?"

Quotation used by permission of Simon and Schuster, Inc.

the actual, and explore what Morris Cohen liked to call the ranges of possibility. Through the art of language man can manipulate the natural structures and relations he encounters, reconstruct them, and translate them into thought and knowledge. Through language man can lift himself above animal existence, look after and before, and survey the world from innumerable fresh perspectives. It is language alone that makes possible that human power we have come to call "imagination"—naming it, strangely enough, after a much humbler though practically indispensable function—the "intellectual imagination" that enables us to extend and sharpen our intellectual vision and see familiar things in new ways. Language is indeed a mighty god, and such is the sweetness and the glory of being a "rational" animal—an animal endowed with the power of *ratio,* with λόγος, with language!

All the more, then, in metaphysical inquiry, can language free us from the tyranny of having to construe the world crystallized in the forms so essential to practice, and so bound down to it. It can free us from bondage to the metaphysics enshrined in ordinary language, developed to serve well the immediate needs of daily living, the metaphysics of "common sense." Through a suitable manipulation of language, we can talk, fortunately, not in the old familiar ways, but in new ways—in ways that will permit and encourage us to explore new ideas, to push them, to generalize them and apply them in novel situations, in new fields and new subject-matters, that will make us see those fields and subject-matters in a new light, and discern relations and structures we had not before been aware of.

With a proper understanding indeed, of language, its nature, its manifold functions, and its status in existence, I would even be willing to define metaphysical inquiry as just such a linguistic manipulation and generalization of ideas, in the light of a factual analysis of concrete subject-matters. This, at least, is the "speculative" function of metaphysics, its "theoretical" function, in the proper and precise sense of "leading to *θεωρία*," to the seeing of things in their widest range of relationships. And this, I take it, is also what we mean in general by the "hypothetico-deductive experimental method" of the sciences. It is what Woodbridge means by "the ordinary methods of observation and tested generalization," which metaphysics shares with all the other sciences.

The critical function of metaphysics may well be something else again

—though I think myself that it is intimately bound up with this *θεωρία*, this synoptic vision. Here our British friends today may be on the right track. No doubt I fail to understand their enterprise. But I trust I have made clear why I have found so little stimulus for my own thinking in what they seem to me to be trying to do, and why their method of doing it strikes me as indeed brilliant—brilliantly wrongheaded and perverse. Our paths may hence cross from time to time, but they do not run parallel. In any event, I have here set forth the method employed in the following five attempts at metaphysical analysis.

CHAPTER 6

Substance as a Cooperation of Processes: A Metaphysical Analysis

SOME YEARS AGO, in accordance with the philosophical program set forth on pages 135–37, in the preceding chapter, I undertook an investigation I call "the theory of history," borrowing the general notion and the phrase from Frederick J. E. Woodbridge. This I take to be a critical examination of those traits of existent things that are called "historical," and of the distinctions and concepts in terms of which this historical aspect of existence may be found intelligible. "The theory of history" I regard as a branch of metaphysics, or, as I prefer, again following Woodbridge, as an enterprise of "metaphysical analysis." Some of the fruits of this analysis of history are contained in the first Part of this volume. While continuing to carry on this inquiry, I undertook also a similar metaphysical analysis of language and communication. In pursuing these two analyses, I found myself forced to formulate a set of more general metaphysical distinctions exhibited in these two subject-matters, but not confined to them. These distinctions I have been led to elaborate, because I have found them helpful in clarifying the analysis of various other subject-matters, including art and religion, and social and cultural institutionalized activities in general—the basic types of human activity called forth in man in response to the generic traits of existence. All these human enterprises in our world have metaphysical implications for the nature of the world that generates and sustains them. Such a metaphysical apparatus I of course view functionally, as an instrument of criticism and analysis. I have in fact found it to serve as such, and I shall try to illustrate how it does so.

Some portions of this chapter appeared in *The Review of Metaphysics,* X (1957), 580–601, under the title, "Substance as Process."

I

To avoid all doubt, let me make it clear that I am taking metaphysics as both Dewey and Woodbridge, following Aristotle, took it, and as I have attempted to set forth in the previous chapter: as the investigation of existence as existence, an inquiry distinguished from other inquiries by a subject-matter of its own, the general characters and the ultimate distinctions illustrated and exhibited in each specific and determinate kind of existence and existential subject-matter. This inquiry into existence taken generically and distributively was rebaptized in the eighteenth century as "ontology." I have no particular love for that term, especially in its present use by existentialists like Heidegger, and prefer, especially in this day and generation, to insist shamelessly and maliciously on the traditional designation. But it may contribute to a clarification to say that I am definitely limiting metaphysics to such an "ontological" inquiry.

Likewise, following that Aristotelian tradition, I take the method of metaphysical inquiry to be "analytical." But I do not agree with a recent fashion, that it is analytical of "terms" and language alone—however necessary and fundamental such a semantic analysis may be. Metaphysical inquiry is analytical of natural existence: it lays bare those generic traits and distinctions which terms can *formulate*. "Terminism," as the necessary preface to, or as an adequate substitute for, inquiry into existence, has flourished recurrently, as it is flourishing today on English soil. Such terminism, whether of the Ockhamites in the fourteenth century, or of the Oxford linguistic analysts of the twentieth, is, like atheism, the product of only a little thought. It arises whenever an initial naive realism breaks down through the discovery that discourse is neither identical with nor in one-to-one correspondence with its subject-matter, and when in their disillusionment with such a non-functional realism men have not yet managed to achieve a genuinely functional realism.

Moreover, metaphysics is "analytic" in the further sense that it seeks to disclose the traits of existence and to trace their implications: it can neither reduce everything to a character which has no intelligible opposite, like "mind" or "matter," nor explain why existence displays the characters it does. Existence can neither be explained nor explained away.

Metaphysical reflection on the world as intellectually experienced does indeed start with existence formulated and expressed in discourse. But it soon leads beyond that linguistic formulation to the subject-matter itself, to the world as "directly" or "immediately" experienced, to the context in which reflective experience takes place. Man's primary intellectual experience is indeed linguistic: we start reflection with the world already formulated, already sorted out into the categories of our institutionalized linguistic habits. It is the merit of "logical empiricism" and of English "linguistic analysis" to have recognized this basic fact of life. The trouble with these somewhat narrow schools is not their admirable analysis of linguistic data, but their "empiricism"—their rather naive and traditional views about non-linguistic data. Hence reflection on man's experience naturally approaches its context through language, through discourse. Discourse identifies its subject-matter, and formulates the distinctions which that subject-matter forces one to make. But man's intellectual experience is neither "primary" nor "ultimate." It is rather "mediate"; it has a setting in other processes, and a function in that setting. And its specific function there defines the function of linguistic formulation.

All this has been clearly revealed by our philosophies of experience, however muddled they may have been about the nature of "experience" itself. Metaphysics is in fact a cumulative inquiry, to which the recent analysis of man's non-reflective experience has contributed much. Philosophies of experience have taught most when they have tried to place the world stated and known in the context of the world experienced in other ways, in order to learn and state more. They have taught least when, professedly most empirical, and most positivistic, they have tried to stay as close as possible to the world immediately "given." There is a certain irony about the long and never-ending search for the "given," for what we supposedly start with, that is hardly dispelled by the shouts of triumph each time a new "given" is discovered. To seek to know what the world is like when it is not known, is after all intelligible only as a contribution to making the world better known. Whatever else the world may be when it is not known, it is at least not known.

This can be stated in the language of the philosophies of experience, that for inquiry "the immediate" is never "given," and that the appeal to "immediate experience" is never the starting-point or the first step in metaphysical inquiry. It is always an intermediate stage in the process of criticising reflective experience—of criticising the experienced world already formulated in some scheme of interpretation. The appeal to immediate or "direct" experience is an instrument of metaphysical criticism; it is in this sense that metaphysics has recently been defined as the "critique of abstractions." [1] The same point can be stated in the traditional language of metaphysics, the language of the philosophies of being, that we distinguish "substance" from "form," "essence," or "structure," not in the interest of discovering what in substance is not structure, what is "matter," but to reveal further structure.

We can start our metaphysical inquiry with any subject-matter, any field of inquiry, any reflective or linguistic experience. We find ourselves starting inevitably not with a "mere" subject-matter, but with a subject-matter about which something has already been formulated and expressed, not with a "mere" field of inquiry, but with a field of inquiry in which something has already been found out and discovered. It is worth dwelling on this fact of subject-matters formulated, of fields of inquiry in which discoveries have been and can be made. For it involves the distinction basic to all metaphysical inquiry, basic in that without in some fashion making it there could be no inquiry at all: the distinction between what is said, and what it is said about, between what is

[1] See Robert D. Mack, *The Appeal to Immediate Experience* (New York, 1945). This is the definition and the metaphysical method of Bradley, Dewey, Whitehead; of the Hegel upon whom they all draw; of the continental post-Hegelians, criticising the "intellectualism" of the Hegelian tradition in the light of "life" (the *Lebensphilosophie* of Nietzsche and Dilthey) or *Existenz* (Kierkegaard); of the phenomenologists, criticising the formalism of the Neo-Kantians (Husserl), and of the existentialists (Heidegger, Jaspers, Tillich); of Bergson, opposing experienced *durée* to "the 't' of physics," and of William James, opposing "immediate experience" to the "empiricism" of Mill; and of many other late nineteenth- and early twentieth-century philosophies of experience. See Paul Tillich, "Existential Philosophy," *Journal of the History of Ideas,* V (1944), 44–70, an excellent survey of the major recent "philosophies of experience" and their varying languages, and also a clear illustration of the cumulative character of metaphysical inquiry, and of its progress during the past century.

discovered, and what it is discovered in and about, between the conclusions arrived at, and what is being investigated, between interpretation and facts, between idea and object.

In the metaphysical tradition, this has been expressed as the distinction between "subject," what "underlies" all discourse and inquiry—τὸ ὑποκείμενον—and "attributes," what can be said to "belong" to that subject-matter, what can be "discovered" in that field of inquiry; as the distinction between "subject-matter" and its "structure," between οὐσία and εἶδος, between "substance" and "form." The very fact that this distinction can be expressed in so many ways and in so many contexts, that it can be stated equally in the language of the philosophy of being and the language of the philosophies of experience, and in the language of each particular philosophical tradition, is good evidence that they have all been talking of the same world, and expressing a distinction bound to turn up in any language and any universe of discourse. From their various starting-points, men have been led, by the same permanences of their experience of a common world, to recognize and formulate, each in his own particular philosophical language, certain common distinctions and traits; and these distinctions are translatable into other philosophical languages. This fact suggests not only the distinction between the *traits* formulated, and the *way* in which they are formulated and expressed, between what is translatable and translated, and the particular translation; of itself it leads to the further distinction, between what is said in every way, and the common world which forces men, through their experience of it in non-linguistic ways, to discriminate and distinguish, and compels them to employ discourse to formulate as distinctions those encountered discriminations.

In the traditional language of metaphysics, what must be accepted, worked with, inquired into, manipulated, transformed, and reconstructed in practice and in art, controlled and enjoyed—this is Οὐσία, "Substance," "primary existence." Οὐσία or Substance I thus take in its root meaning of "subject-matter." It means the facts encountered, the field inquired into, the subject-matter talked about, the forces worked with, the material manipulated, transformed, and reconstructed, the events controlled and enjoyed, the object of concern of all human activities.

No commitment as to the character or nature of Substance is made in distinguishing it from what is discovered, formulated and expressed in words and discourse, and grasped in knowledge, as the traits, characters, habits and ways of operating to which the subject-matter being worked with conforms, and which can be used to manipulate and alter it. This in traditional language is Εἶδος, "Form," "Structure."

In the different language of the philosophies of experience, "Substance" or "primary existence" is what is encountered in all types of experience, active, practical, aesthetic, religious, "immediate," "direct," *as well as* in reflective or linguistic experience; while "Form" or "Structure" is what is distinguished in reflective experience and formulated in discourse, including mathematical discourse. Structure is thus the "objective" of inquiry, of discourse, of knowledge and science, which all seize on these traits and ways of operating, on various types of Structure or Form.

Substance, starting with its root-meaning of "subject-matter," thus becomes for me, in the language of the philosophies of experience, the encountered "context" or "situation" within which reflective experience distinguishes Structure. It is what Aristotle calls "the confused mess" (*τὰ συγκεκυμένα*) which is clearly "first for us, within which we distinguish principles, causes and elements." [2] Dewey's term for *Οὐσία* or Substance in this sense is clearly "the Situation," conceived as a "universe of action," [3] and I have found it extremely suggestive to follow up this equating of Aristotle's term with Dewey's. For Aristotle's world of individual *οὐσίαι* or "substances," conceived concretely and *φυσικῶς* as determinate processes operating in a context, and Dewey's world of "specific situations" or "universes of action," conceived as interactions, or more precisely as "transactions," [4] are after all the same world. And I have found that Aristotle's analysis of Substance as the operation of powers, and Dewey's analysis of the Situation, mutually illuminate each

[2] *Physica* I 184a.

[3] One of the clearest and fullest of Dewey's many analyses of "the Situation" is to be found in his *Logic* (New York, 1938), pp. 66–69. Some of Dewey's terminology here is adopted and pushed further in these metaphysical papers, especially his notion of a "universe of experience," or a "universe of action," as the precondition of a universe of discourse.

[4] John Dewey and Arthur F. Bentley, *Knowing and the Known* (Boston, 1949), pp. 71–73.

other. Though one is expressed in the language of the philosophies of being, and the other in the language of the philosophies of experience, both are functional and contextual analyses.[5]

So this metaphysical analysis has led me to try to push a little further the behavioristic, operational, and contextual view of "being," "Substance," or "primary existence"—what might best be called the "functional realism"—that I have come to find in both Aristotle and John Dewey. In this and the following papers, I am attempting to restate Aristotle, with those modifications and additions suggested by the present state of metaphysical inquiry, and its recent rapid progress. I am trying to extend the Aristotelian analysis of "process" or κίνησις by applying Dewey's analysis of "the Situation," and other similar analyses found in our recent philosophies of experience. And, I may add, I have adopted some of the terminology of Woodbridge where it seemed appropriate. These genetic considerations have of course no bearing on the validity of this analysis: that depends on where the analysis gets. But they clarify why I am pushing in the direction I am, and why I am employing the terminology I do.

II

Substance is distinguished from Structure as the context within which Structure is found, as the situation in which knowing and inquiry are going on. But Substance is not to be contrasted with Structure, it is not to be set over against it. And it is not to be contrasted with the "encountering," with the inquiry into a field, the talking about a subject-matter, the working with forces, the manipulating, transforming, and reconstructing *of* materials, the controlling and enjoying *of* events. All these human activities, all these ways of encountering existence, all these types of "experience," take place *within* the context or situation in which Structure is distinguished—they are all carried on *within*

[5] Perhaps Whitehead's world of "actual occasions" belongs here too—though I have not myself found it so illuminating, for his analysis of an "actual occasion" is based on his analysis of "human experience," and that suffers from the limitations of his very British conception of "experience."

The conception of "the Field" is likewise relevant. "The Field" is being fruitfully employed today in many specific sciences, though it has been carried furthest in physics. This is a cardinal example of a concept arising in one of the sciences that can be fruitfully generalized. Given such a metaphysical generalization, it could then be said, that "Substance" is "the Field."

Substance, and not as external to it. Human experience in all its varieties I am thus taking as an "encountering," as an interaction between men and other factors *in* a context, situation, or universe of action. Or, as I prefer to put it, following Woodbridge, human experience is a "cooperation" between the behavior of men and the behavior of things, that takes place *within* Substance. "Experience" is thus not a relation between men and Substance; it is not an encountering of Substance by something standing outside Substance, and external to it. Experience is rather a *participating in* Substance, a cooperation of factors *in* Substance. The term "cooperation" is Woodbridge's; Dewey in 1949 introduced the term "transaction" to designate the same relation, defining "transaction" as: "not items or characteristics of organisms alone, nor items or characteristics of environment alone, but the activity that occurs of both together." [6]

Substance, then, the existing world, is what is encountered in all types of experience. And Substance *is* what it is encountered *as,* in all these ways: it is what it is "experienced *as,*" reflectively and non-reflectively. Substance may well be *more* than what it is encountered as, even in our best knowledge, in our highest religious and ethical vision, and in our most inspired artistic imagination—which are all fundamental ways of experiencing or encountering the world, all approaches to Substance. Substance doubtless *is* more—but it is at least all of that. This is the fundamental principle of all sound metaphysics, the primacy of the subject-matter encountered, which cannot be intelligibly called into question.[7]

Now, in most general terms, Substance is encountered as "activities" or "operations" taking place in various determinate ways—as acting and interacting with us and with other activities, as cooperating with us and with each other, as doing things to us, as something to which we

[6] Dewey and Bentley, *Knowing and the Known,* p. 71. It is for this reason that I have been impressed by the analogy to the conception of experience in the "existential ontology" of Heidegger. That also emphasizes the naturalistic inclusion of man in "Being," the "self-world polarity," and the consequence that all human experiences have ontological implications, that they are all "transactions" of man cooperating with the rest of things, which point to genuine traits of the world within which man finds himself. See p. 123, note 4.

[7] Spinoza held that God or Nature or Substance has "infinite attributes," though man encounters only two. He should have said, "May have an indefinite number of others." But then, he knew all about God.

do things in return. In taking human experience as an "encountering," as an active interaction or transaction or cooperation between man's activities and other activities in his world, I am of course following all our best knowledge in biology, psychology, anthropology, etc. I am rejecting the intellectualism that restricts "experience" to cognitive experience, and also the view that makes any type of experience—even cognitive experience—wholly passive—both the intellectual vision of the Greeks (Νοῦς), and the physical vision of modern empiricists. I am also following the main emphasis in the many careful analyses of "experience" from the "inside," the many phenomenological analyses made by the philosophies of experience from Kant to James, Dewey, and Heidegger. These all point to the *active* character of the many types of experience in which cognitive experience has its setting. They point also to the active, cooperative character of cognitive experience itself, to knowing as an *active interpretation* of materials, as an art or τέχνη. Finally, I am following the Greeks—Plato and Aristotle—for whom experience is a cooperation of the powers of man with the powers of nature, most adequately expressed as τέχνη, "art," the active manipulation of natural materials, which "in a sense imitates and in a sense carries further what natural processes do,"[8] so that, with due regard for the absence of any intelligence, any conscious intent or "purpose" in natural processes, "art" can serve as the best illustration of all processes. Since Substance is encountered as a cooperation or interaction of activities or processes, Substance is at least that.

Again, when in reflective and linguistic experience we state what any determinate substance is, when we formulate what any specific subject-matter is, its τὶ ἐστι, as contrasted with grasping and stating any of its various traits and properties, we state what it does, its behavior and operations, its determinate way of acting and interacting. We state what Aristotle called its φύσις or "nature," and what the moderns have called the "laws governing its action," or, more precisely, "the laws 'formulating' its action, and 'illustrated by' and in that action." When we ask, What is motion? What is electricity? What is light? What is energy? the statement is always a formulation of how it "works," acts, cooperates, or behaves.

Substance is accordingly both directly encountered, and stated or

[8] *Physica* II 199a.

known, *as* its behavior and operations. And thus Substance can be said to *be* its behavior and operations. Substance is a set of activities taking place in specific ways, of "activities exhibiting structure," as Woodbridge puts it. Thus in the present state of metaphysical inquiry, we have arrived at an ontological "behaviorism" or "operationalism." Or rather, we have returned to the behaviorism and operationalism of Aristotle, for whom likewise any *οὐσία*, any substance, is what it does, is its behavior, is the operation or "putting to work" of its powers, the *ἐνέργεια* of its *δυνάμεις*, the actualization of its potentialities. Substance is *κίνησις* or *μεταβολή*, "motion" or "activity" in accordance with a specific *φύσις* or "nature"—with a specific way of acting and being acted upon, a specific way of cooperating with other *κινήσεις* or processes.

In a word, Substance is what we today call "process," and what Aristotle called *κίνησις*, analysing it as: *ἡ τοῦ δυνάμει ὄντος ἐντελέχεια, ᾗ τοιοῦτον*. More precisely, Substance is encountered and known as a complex of interacting and cooperating processes, each exhibiting its own determinate ways of cooperating, or Structure.

This behavioristic and operational way of formulating the nature of "primary existence," which is an ontological, not a "psychological," behaviorism and operationalism, in that it applies to the behavior and operation of whatever is encountered, and not to human behavior and operations alone, this "contextual" view which I like to call a "functional realism," represents the present state of metaphysical inquiry. For this view I can of course claim no originality; nor would I if I could. It is not my bright idea, but is rather the conclusion of all responsible metaphysicians today, which I am proposing, not to defend, but to illustrate and explore, and to try to push a little further.[9]

[9] Of course, I am aware that there are some persons, even in these days, calling themselves "metaphysicians," who are not responsible. But I doubt whether they are really metaphysicians.

I repeat, I am merely restating Aristotle, and could cite chapter and verse where everything I have said is at least implicit—though sometimes it is very implicit. And I admit there are some things in Aristotle, like the Unmoved Mover and the Active Intellect, that are myths—Platonic myths. But, as we shall see, myths have a very important ontological status in Substance. For the general interpretation of Aristotle here assumed, see my forthcoming volume, *Aristotle: Philosopher of Discourse and Process.*

In metaphysics I am very glad to be wholly orthodox—or at least "neo-

Hence it seems preferable not to say, in the present fashion of our philosophies of experience, that Substance is "events." "Event" is usually taken in a positivistic or phenomenalistic sense: and as such, "events" are clearly not Substance, not what we encounter, but a way of talking about Substance, about what we encounter. An "event" is the product of an intellectual analysis of Substance. But Substance is not a way of talking, not the product of analysis: but what we encounter, what we bump into. Again, we are said to "observe" events; but we do not "observe" Substance, we encounter its processes, we interact with them, cooperate with them. Events are said to "occur," to "take place," to "come to pass." They do not "act" or "do" things, they do not interact and cooperate. But processes act, do things, interact and cooperate: they exhibit "powers." And powers are fundamental in what we encounter. "Events observed" possess and exhibit a purely formal structure, a mathematical structure, that can be expressed in a formula, in which they figure as the particular values of variables. But "processes encountered" exhibit a "functional structure" also, a structure of means and ends, of powers and their operation.

Substance is not encountered most revealingly—and certainly not exclusively—in vision, or in sensation, or in perception in general. Substance is encountered in acting and being acted upon, in making and doing, in manipulation and experimentation, in τέχνη, art. Sensationalism in any of its various forms—in subjectivism, the "sense data" of Russell, the "intuition of essences" of Santayana, for whom "nothing given exists"; in the presentative realism of Hume, Samuel Alexander, or the American Neorealists, or in the relational realism of Whitehead—is a wholly inadequate account of the way in which Substance is encountered, a sheer misconstruing of immediate, direct, or non-reflective experience. Substance is encountered primarily as a universe of action, not as a universe of vision, or as the visible world. I fear that on this point Woodbridge was wrong.[10] Even sensation itself is of course not passive; sensing is an activity, a process, an inter-

orthodox," which I confess is not always quite the same thing. The art of philosophy, indeed, can well afford to cherish some claim to originality, for philosophic criticism and vision are always dealing with new forms of experience and with fresh and novel intellectual problems. But the science of metaphysics cannot properly claim to be original: it must aim rather to be sound.

[10] F. J. E. Woodbridge, *An Essay on Nature* (New York, 1940), Chapter II.

action, a transaction, a cooperation of powers. It is not a mere intuiting of "sensa" or "sense data."

The witness of the classic tradition can of course be claimed for the recognition that Substance is active, productive, "dynamic," the locus of powers. Aristotle's "dynamism" is familiar: οὐσία is fundamentally the ἐνέργεια, the "setting to work," or the "operation," of δυνάμεις, powers. But Plato also says: "Being is nothing else than power (δύναμις). Everything which possesses any power of any kind, either to act upon anything in any way or to be acted upon in any way, even if it be on only a single occasion, *really is*."[11]

III

I have been speaking of Substance as the encountered context within which reflective experience distinguishes Structure. But Substance is more than mere "context in general"; Substance is always specific and determinate. It is always encountered by men in *a specific* transaction, *a specific* cooperation. We never encounter Substance "in general," subject-matter "in general."

The specific encountering or cooperation selects its own "relevant field" or "context" of interaction, and thus delimits the boundaries of that particular "universe of action," of that particular Substance. What and how much of nature's processes and structures is relevant, what interactions and relations have to be taken into account in determining the limits of "that particular substance," is dependent on the specific interactions generated in that particular encountering itself, on the particular "direction" taken by the cooperating processes that constitute that substance. Speaking humanly, with an emphasis on the human cooperation in the particular substance or situation, what is relevant to that particular substance or situation is dependent on the "end-in-view"—on the particular problems that are generated by that particular cooperation—which may vary of course, from some immediate practical action, like jumping from the path of an oncoming car, to saving your soul, or pursuing metaphysical inquiry. In any case, the particular "direction" or "end" generated by the specific encountering selects its own relevant "field" or "context." What precise processes and structures are actually relevant in any particular case is

[11] *Sophist* 247.

always a finding, a discovery: it cannot be determined in advance. In this sense, in which the boundaries of any particular "substance" or "situation" are always a matter for inquiry, Substance is encountered, not as "determinate" to begin with, but rather as "determinable": the particular substance or situation *becomes* determinate in the further cooperation of the processes involved.

This "self-delimitation" of any particular substance or situation is an additional reason why Substance is not "events." What constitutes a particular "event" has always to be determined from a perspective external to that event: an "event" has to be "selected" from the continuity of natural processes by an "observer" outside it. In contrast, a "substance" or "situation" that is a complex of processes is self-selecting and self-determining. Whitehead, for instance, in his early "philosophy of nature," finds "an event" to be "the whole of Nature through a duration"; and he faces a major problem, of somehow selecting and delimiting any particular "event." He later gets warmer, when he speaks of "an actual occasion" as a "superject of informed value." He seems to be trying to say, that an "event" or an "actual occasion" is delimited by its consummation. At least, he *could* mean that; and he clearly *ought* to.

The language of the philosophies of experience expresses this specific character of Substance by saying, we always encounter in experience "a specific situation," a particular "universe of experience and action." The language of the philosophies of being puts the point, by saying, Substance is always determinate process, is always a specific complex of cooperating processes.

Moreover, Substance is not only "concrete" and "particular": it is also "dynamic." It is shot through with "directions," "ends," "powers now coming into operation," "vectors"—it is full of tensions and pressures. Substance or the Situation exhibits a great variety of functional and teleological structures, of relations between means and ends, between powers and their operatings. Substance is full of "necessary fors," "good fors," "bad fors," in terms of which its various factors can be "evaluated." In other words, just because it is literally teeming with directions and ends, because it exhibits so much natural teleology, Substance is shot through and through with "values."

This means, negatively, that Substance cannot be taken as a "flux."

The notion that Nature and Time constitute a "flux" is one of the most perplexing construings of what is encountered ever perpetrated. It is even worse than to construe Substance as "events"; for "event" at least means "e-ventus," outcome, and a functional order can be recognized in "events." Obviously, if Nature be reduced to a flux, then everything of significance and importance will "transcend Nature," and lie "above Nature"—men and history and human life. Nature will then be indeed "one-dimensional"—though strictly speaking I doubt whether a flux could possess even a single dimension. The "flux of Nature and Time" will then be "meaningless" in itself, and will have to be "given a meaning" from "outside" or from "above"—though just *how* would seem an insoluble problem. What "meaning" could a "flux" be given, except as "something to escape from"? or perhaps with Santayana, as the scene of the transitory embodiment of eternal essences? I suspect that this is just why supernaturalists like Santayana or Reinhold Niebuhr try to reduce Nature to a "flux." For one so concerned as Niebuhr to emphasize the historical character of existence, this does indeed seem rather surprising: for it appears to place him rather with the "eternalistic" and "mystical" philosophers. But this again, I fear, is only one of those radical confusions that Niebuhr's metaphysics seems to produce in my mind.

No, Nature cannot be taken as a flux, Time is not a flux. Substance, existence, is shot through with "importances for," with "significances for," with "meanings for"—"for" the directions and ends it itself generates.

It is significant that even our most abstract analysis of Nature, that which arrives at the greatest degree of "isolation" from the concrete fullness of Substance encountered, the one worked out in the physical sciences, has not come to any ultimate "flux." It arrives, not at a "succession of the motions of atoms," but rather at a "field of radiant energy," a field full of tensions and directions and vectors. And this suggests that the very notion of a "flux of Nature" is mere antiquated science—that it is, as Whitehead has pointed out, the end-product of Newtonian disconnectedness, most clearly expressed in Hume's flux of impressions.

In contrast, as against such a "flux," the philosophy of *Existenz* seems to stand on much firmer ground. In what is directly encountered it finds *Sorge, Angst,* and *Zeitlichkeit*. It recognizes that Being is "dynamic," full of tensions and directions; and surely this finding is right. Unfortunately, *Existenzphilosophie* seeks these metaphysical characters of Substance, with typical German perversity, in "the Subject," in the "Soul," in "Existential Subjectivity."

Substance, then, is always encountered as specific and determinable, and this means, as "relative"—relative to the direction or end the encountering generates. The field, situation, or context can be extended indefinitely, but we never reach or encounter any "ultimate" field or context. We arrive only at a field or context that is "ultimate for" that particular Substance or Situation. Substance is ineradicably plural.[12] We encounter many substances, many situations, and though they are interconnected and interpenetrate each other, they never in our experience become wholly unified.

IV

We have been emphasizing the distinction between what is encountered and what can be formulated in discourse, between Substance and Structure, between operations and their ways, not to try to find out what Substance would be like if it had no discoverable and formulable Structure—if it were "pure matter"; or what operations would be like if they did nothing in particular, and were wholly indeterminate—if they were "pure activity"; or what powers would be like if they could do anything whatever—if they were "pure potentiality," "pure creativity," and could, like Santayana's restless matter, embody any essence whatever. Metaphysics is content to leave to God the creation of such a *materia prima*. He would have to create it, for even God could not discover it in this world. Human creators, theologians or evolutionists, trying to recreate the world as God and Evolution have created it, never stumble upon such a structureless matter, for they always know what is to come. They know that darkness was upon the face of the deep, for they know that God said, Let there be light. What would darkness be like, were there no light to come? A far sounder theology tells us, In the beginning was the Word—Structure—

[12] For some of the further metaphysical implications of the ontological pluralism here being explored, see Chapter 7, "Empirical Pluralism and Unifications of Nature."

for without Structure nothing could begin. Kantian creators, trying to reconstruct "experience" out of a "formless manifold" and a scheme of intelligibility, have likewise failed to discover a "pure matter"; for they know that their manifold "lends itself" to that scheme of intelligibility, and they know in detail the determinations to which it submits, the structure it can assume in actual "experience." What other knowledge of its structure could we ever hope to acquire? Pure matter, pure activity, pure immediacy, a manifold without any form or determinations whatsoever, are not only not discoverable; they could not possibly exist, they are quite literally "meaningless." For Structure is the basis of all meaning and signification. Without Structure nothing can either be or be conceived.

Yet there remains an inescapable difference between a symphony, and a score or phonograph record of the symphony. What they all possess in common is a single "structure," the structure of the symphony, expressed, we may say, in varying languages. What the score and the record both express is not coextensive: records being what they are, are not perfect, they leave out a lot. If we ask what they leave out, we are taken to the mechanisms of translation—to the grammar and the categories, we may put it, of the recorder, what it can reproduce, *its* structure. The score in turn leaves out everything that distinguishes the symphony as an activity, a process—the reading of the conductor, the playing of the orchestra, the particular way they "interpret" it, we say—that is, the distinctive structure involved in any particular rendition. And both score and record leave out the sound produced and heard, which takes us to the mechanisms of production and transmission, the physiological mechanisms of the auditors, etc.—their ways of cooperating in the symphony heard, which includes them all. The sounds heard form a third language, expressing the same structure of the symphony expressed also in the score, and in the record, but with a further auditory structure of their own, a structure which likewise leaves out much, in most cases.

Whenever we ask, what is it that is not expressed in any any of these languages, what is not revealed as structure, we are led back to the symphony itself, to the subject-matter, to the Situation, to Substance. But we do not emerge with "matter"—we emerge with additional structures. For we have in each case found further structures involved in the complex of processes that cooperate in the symphony. We have been led to analyse the complex of processes there discovered into the specific cooperating processes involved, each with its own complex structure or distinctive way of operating. We have found the writing of the symphony, the playing of the symphony, the recording of the symphony, the transmitting of the symphony, the reproducing of the symphony, the hearing of the symphony. And these are all involved in and related to each other in complex ways that can be explored.

Common to all these various expressions in differing languages—the symphony written, the symphony played, the symphony recorded, the symphony reproduced, the symphony heard—is something that has made it possible to say, it is the same symphony that is expressed in each language—something that makes it "that symphony" and not some other symphony. There is a distinctive structure, in terms of which that symphony is identified, no matter what the language in which it is expressed, without which it could neither be that symphony, nor be conceived as that symphony, nor expressed in any language as that symphony. This distinctive structure is "the structure of that symphony." And this structure, though expressed in various languages and embodied in various "materials"—in ink-marks on paper, in grooves in plastic, in the vibrations of air produced by various instruments, in audio-frequency modulations in an electric current, in a temporal sequence of complex auditory sensations—is not to be identified with the structure of any of those "matters." It is not the structure of the marks on paper, nor the structure of the grooves in plastic, nor the structure of sensations. It is rather the structure of "the symphony," to which all these expressions must conform, to which the material of the various mechanisms must conform, to which the operations of writing, playing, recording, transmitting, reproducing, hearing, etc., must all conform. It is the "Form," the λόγος or "formula," the "formal cause" of the symphony, in Aristotle's language. In Spinoza's, it is the "idea" of the symphony, conceived under various "attributes." It is what "makes" the symphony *"that* symphony," τὸ τί ἦν εἶναι of that symphony, its "intelligibility" or intelligible aspect. It is what we "grasp" intellectually, "recognize as," "understand by," "know as," "mean by," that symphony. It is an ultimate fact about the symphony. There can, I take it, be no question about this: it is non-controversial.

Yet this "structure of the symphony," though it is that by which we *identify* that symphony, is *not identical with* that symphony. It is not what we hear when we hear "that symphony." When we hear the symphony, we do not hear the structure, but music "conforming to" that structure. We do not play the structure, but the sounds our instruments can produce "in conformity with" that structure. We do not "make" the structure, but marks on paper, grooves in a record, "illustrating" or "embodying" that structure. The hearing, the playing, the making, all conform to that structure, but they themselves are not that structure. They are certainly not structure alone. They are activities, operations, behaviors, which "exhibit" a particular structure, "illustrate" a structure, are "instances" of a structure, "display," "possess," or "have" a structure, and are identified by their structure, but are not to be identified with their structure alone. They are not structure, but processes. Processes are activities "conforming to" a structure, "understood" in terms of a structure, but not identical with that structure. They are experienced reflectively, or understood, in terms of their structure. But they are experienced in other ways: they are played and heard, as activities exhibiting structure. They are never experienced as activities without structure—though I am not too sure about some concertgoers.

The symphony is not identical with its structure, it is a process with that structure. And this leads to a further distinction, fundamental in all activity and process. We have found many symphonies; but they seem to fall into two classes. There is first the symphony played, and the symphony heard; and there is secondly the symphony written and recorded. Which is "the symphony"? the playing and the hearing, or the score and the record? What is "the symphony"? We are asking Aristotle's question: "What is a substance?" τὶ ἐστι οὐσία;

The answer is, clearly both classes are, but in different senses. The first two are activities and operations, the second two are something that is not activity and operation. The score and the record are δυνάμεις, "powers." Both are "the symphony," in an appropriate context. When we want to buy "the symphony" to study and enjoy, we want to buy a score, or a record, not an orchestra. But the score and the record are not the symphony merely because they are expressions of the same structure. When we play them, they *become* the symphony, and we understand them as what can be so played. We do not really understand them in other terms, as paper with marks, as plastic with grooves. They are that, to be sure: those things can be truly said of them, those are their properties, their own distinctive structures, quite apart from their cooperation in "the symphony." But we don't understand them unless we know what they can do, what their function is. Being the products of art and intelligence, that is what they were made for. They have, to be sure, many other powers: we can light the fire with the score, or throw the record at the cat. But those powers are not essential to what they are. And we can hardly be said to understand them if that is all we know what to do with them. We don't understand them adequately unless we know their use as mechanisms for producing the symphony. And "the symphony" is not really understood if we take it only as a score or a record, as a "power." It is fully understood only as an operation.

I have been using "the symphony" as an instance of an *οὐσία*, a substance, one that is indisputably encountered, something clearly found in our world, and indisputably "real." There is no question that we do find such symphonies; the existence of such substances is non-controversial. We first found "the structure of the symphony," its "essence" or "idea," which identifies it as that symphony. This structure I shall call the "formal structure" of the symphony. If we ask, what makes *that* symphony *a* symphony, we should have to inquire further into that formal structure, into what it is to be a symphony rather than a concerto or a sonata; and the answer would be in terms of traits and characteristics of that formal structure. But when we went on to consider the symphony not merely as identified and expressed in terms of its formal structure, but as a process—as music played and heard conforming to that structure, as cooperating processes exhibiting that structure—we were led to a further structure of a different type—a structure of powers and their operating, of the record and the score and the symphony played, of the symphony played and the symphony heard—a structure of means and ends. This second type of structure

I shall call "functional structure," using the term "functional" to designate the relation between powers and their operations, the relation between means and ends.[13]

The "functional structure" of the symphony is the relation between the symphony as a process or operation and the means, mechanisms, or powers which cooperate to bring about the symphony as their eventuation. And this functional structure leads us to further structures of the various powers or means involved in the cooperating processes that *are* the symphony—of the score, the orchestra, the recorder, the reproducer, etc. Each of these mechanisms or powers has a "formal structure" of its own, and a "functional structure" of its distinctive way of operating. In other words, in the symphony, as in any complex process or substance, there are discoverable various structures of different types, variously related to each other.

Thus any analysis of process takes us to various structures of differing types. In the process of "house-building," for instance, we find first the formal structure of the house itself, the order and arrangement of its constituent parts or elements, its "constitution" or make-up. We find the functional structures of the materials or powers involved, what they can do in relation to other things, the ways in which they can cooperate and interact, their functional structure as means to the end of the completed house. We find that these means or materials also exhibit a formal structure of their own, in the constitutive sense, a particular way in which they are put together, as contrasted with the way in which they operate and behave. This may be called an "inherent" structure, in addition to their functional structure *as* means or materials *for* the house. Thirdly, we find a structure of the en-

[13] As to this terminology: I am rather arbitrarily selecting the adjective "functional" to designate the metaphysical distinction and relation between powers and their operations or functionings. "Function" and "operation" are one word in Greek: ἔργον. Aristotle's ἐνέργεια means literally "putting to work," for which the Latin equivalent is "operation." ἔργον means "function," ἐνέργεια means "functioning."

I am using the adjective "teleological" to designate the metaphysical distinction and relation between means and ends, or τέλη. The relation between "functional" and "teleological" is the relation between the power-operation relation, and the means-ends relation. Obviously, the two relations and distinctions arise in two different contexts. But so far, it has not been necessary to emphasize the distinction between the two relations, and they are here used as equivalent.

vironment or field of house-building, a structure formulated in the laws of mechanics and gravitation, making possible the construction of the house. This structure of the environment is the functional structure of the way the environment cooperates with the materials employed to make the construction of the house possible. And we find a functional structure of the process of constructing itself, of the working with these powers of the materials and powers of the environment.

The major distinction I wish to press here is that between *formal structure* and *functional structure,* between "the way things are put together" and "the way they behave," between the constitutive structure *of* mechanisms and means, and the structure of their *functioning as* means and materials *for* a determinate process. The formal structure is an internal structure, their constitution or make-up; it is invariant through a range of different contexts. The functional structure is the structure of their way of cooperating in a specific context, their way of interacting in a particular situation. The first structure is "inherent," self-contained, ἁπλῶς, in isolation from that particular process. The second structure is "relative" to the process and its field, to that situation: it is a "function" of that context and its complex cooperation of powers.

This, I take it, is the basis of Locke's distinction between the "primary qualities" of bodily substances, and the "secondary" and "tertiary qualities" of such substances. In Locke's formulation, this of course had nothing to do with the distinction between "the Objective" and "the Subjective," but was rather between "the internal texture of the parts" of bodies, and "their powers to produce changes in other things" —that is, between the "intrinsic" and the "relational" properties of bodies.[14] Locke's mistake—and Newton's, whom he here as so often reflects—was to make the distinction absolute, instead of making it relative and functional, that is, making it a distinction itself arising in a determinate universe of action or context. That is, "intrinsic properties" or formal structure are intrinsic and formal *for* some particular context or situation. So taken, the distinction between "intrinsic" or "formal" and "relational" or "functional" structure is funda-

[14] See John Dewey, "Substance, Power, and Quality in Locke," in *Freedom and Experience,* ed. Sidney Hook and M. R. Konvitz (Ithaca, 1947), pp. 205–21.

mental to any analysis of Substance as a complex of processes. It is the distinction between what is a "function of," or "dependent upon," that particular cooperation or context, and what is "independent of" that cooperation—what can be analysed in isolation from that determinate context.

Newtonian and Lockean "primary qualities" or formal structure are clearly not independent of all contexts, or isolable from every field or situation: it was the error of Newton and Locke to think that they are. This formal structure selects its own field or relevant context, namely, those conditions necessary for wood, for instance, to be wood—a certain range of temperature, a certain humidity, a certain gravitational field, etc. Thus wood would not be wood on the sun. We can say, a certain "universe" is necessary for wood to be wood. This "universe of wood" is not "the universe," but a determinate universe, that is, a universe including all those powers whose cooperation is involved in establishing the conditions under which wood can be wood. Now, to this "universe of wood" the specific conditions of the "universe of house-building" are irrelevant. Hence, the formal or inherent structure of wood is relative to this "universe of wood." It is ultimately what wood can *do* in the context of physico-chemical analysis, the functional structure of wood in that context. But this "formal" or "internal" structure of wood is "absolute" *for* house-building: there it is just "given," and has to be accepted. "Absoluteness," "being ἁπλῶς," "isolability," is always a relative and functional distinction in a determinate context or process: it means "absolute *for,*" or "independent *of,*" that specific context. It can never mean, "for" or "of" all contexts whatsoever. There is, as we have seen, no "ultimate substance" or "ultimate context"; there is no "absolute" or "unconditioned" *überhaupt*.

This "internal" or "formal" structure of the means and materials of processes—the way in which they are put together—is ultimately "physico-chemical." This I take to be a definition of the subject-matter of physico-chemical inquiry: namely, those structures of means and materials that are *not* functions of any particular "universe of action" or "complex of processes," but are rather involved in all natural processes and actions, making possible their operation, and at the same time setting limits to what they can do—structures to be used and conformed to by men in their practical and artistic activities.

Their isolability from any particular context makes a knowledge of them of the widest instrumental value in all contexts. I find Dewey in 1941 stating a very similar definition: "Physical subject-matter consists of the conditions of *possible* experiences, in their status *as* possible."[15] I take Dewey's "experiences" as here equivalent, in his language of the philosophies of experience, to my "processes," in the language of the philosophies of being.

This distinction between the "formal structure," the constitution and make-up, and the "functional structure" of powers and means, their ways of cooperating in the specific situation, is well illustrated in the old distinction between the "human frame" and "human nature"—as in David Hartley's *magnum opus* in the eighteenth century.[16] The "human frame" is set by heredity, while "human nature" is the functioning of man's powers in a particular social context, a determinate cooperation with that context. Man's "frame" is independent of that particular social context, man's "nature" is a function of that context. And here too the distinction is clearly ultimately relative. For the "frame" of man, his hereditary powers, is itself a functioning of the human genes in a certain biological environment. The genes set limits; but what those limits are is revealed only in the specific functioning of the genes.

V

Adopting this convenient way of referring to "formal structure" and "functional structure," let us now examine the relations between the "frame" and the "nature" in general. We find that:

1) The "frame"—formal structure—is not a "function of," is not "dependent upon," is not "defined in terms of," the specific situation or cooperation of processes, the determinate context, in which the discrimination between "frame" and "nature" is encountered. The "frame" is isolable from that context, and with reference to it is "invariant"—though it is not isolable from all contexts whatsoever. Wood is wood, it preserves the same frame, whether we are using it to build a house, a fire, or a raft; though different powers and properties of

[15] John Dewey, "The Objectivism-Subjectivism of Modern Philosophy," in *Problems of Men* (New York, 1946), p. 320.

[16] David Hartley, *Observations on Man, His Frame, His Duty, and His Expectations* (London, 1749).

wood, dependent on that frame, are called into play in each case—rigidity for the house, combustibility in air for the fire, buoyancy in water for the raft. But wood preserves that same frame only in the "universe of wood"—that context which includes all the powers whose cooperation is involved in establishing the conditions under which wood can remain wood.

2) Knowledge of the "frame" does not depend on the way it co-operates in the specific situation in which it is encountered and distinguished. Such knowledge is discovered through analysis and manipulation of the thing in a more generalized context. In the case of wood, it is gained through the analysis of its behavior, and of the behavior of its constituent factors or elements, in the context of physico-chemical analysis, the "widest" context of the wood's behavior, the one most "independent of" or "isolated from" the contingencies of particular "universes of actions" like house-building, raft-building, or fire-building.

3) The "nature" of anything *is* a "function of" that context in which we distinguish it from the thing's "frame." A thing's "nature" or functional structure is its powers to interact in specific ways with other things. That "nature" involves its determinate way of cooperating with the other powers present in that situation, which is one of the powers that go to make up its "nature."

4) Knowledge of the "nature" or functional structure of anything *does* depend on knowledge of that determinate way of cooperating, on knowledge of the specific power there revealed—though that "nature" is far from being exhausted in that specific power. The generalized formulation of these "powers" that make up the "nature" of anything—of the thing's functional structure—will state the thing's "properties," its characteristic ways of interacting or cooperating under specified conditions—such properties as the tensile strength of wood, its degree of compressibility, its specific gravity, etc. It is the aim of science to arrive at such properties or generalized powers, and to formulate them precisely.

5) The way things behave is dependent on the way they are put together. Without that specific frame or constitutive structure, that behavior does not occur. Such a frame is the necessary condition of that behavior. The behavior is a "function of" the frame. The way things

behave is *also* "dependent on," a "function of," the situation or cooperation in which they behave in that particular way: the situation or context is *also* a necessary condition of that behavior.

6) Knowledge of the way things behave—of their functional structure—is *not* dependent on knowledge of their frame, the way they are put together. The former knowledge is normally gained first, while the latter usually requires a long search and inquiry. Indeed, as Woodbridge puts it, "the completest analysis of the way they are put together [of their frame] affords no indication whatever of their consequent behavior." [17]

How things *will* behave, what they can do and what they cannot do, their powers and their limits, cannot be discovered by analysing the way they are put together, their frame, apart from their functioning in some determinate process. The formal structure of mechanisms does indeed set "limits" to how they can behave, it "determines" their behavior, it sets "boundaries" within which their operations are confined, and to which they must conform.[18] But these limits, boundaries, or "determinations" are not discoverable in the formal structure or frame of mechanisms—in those mechanisms analysed in isolation from their functioning *as* mechanisms: they are not known when that formal structure has been ascertained.

The powers of mechanisms or means are powers of interacting and cooperating with other factors *in* a determinate situation: they are always relative *to* that situation. Powers are never revealed except in a field or situation, in a complex of processes. Strictly, they are always powers *in* and *of* the whole situation, in and of the entire cooperation of processes; they are not powers of the particular mechanism alone. Limits also depend on the formal structure of the mechanism: they are a function of that structure. Without that structure, they would not be what they are: that structure is a necessary condition of those limits,

[17] F. J. E. Woodbridge, "Behaviour," in *Nature and Mind* (New York, 1937) p. 183. "Hume's analysis of cause and effect and necessary connection, in spite of its metaphysical, psychological and historical limitations, ought to convince anyone that, while specific behaviour may habitually be inferred from specific structure, there is nothing discoverable in that structure to warrant that inference." Woodbridge here uses "structure" for what I have distinguished as "formal structure," or frame. This Humian position will be qualified a little later.

[18] I take "determination" and "determinism" very literally as a setting of "termini" or boundaries and limits.

it is one of the factors that cooperate to determine those limits. But the precise limits the frame of a mechanism imposes on its operations are revealed only when it is functioning *as* a mechanism *in* a determinate situation or process: they are never revealed independently of a situation.

That is, the formal structure of a mechanism is *only one* of the factors that interact to determine how that mechanism will operate in any specific process. For the operation of a power is always a cooperation with other powers, each with its own frame or formal structure contributing limits of its own to the cooperation. That is, the operation of powers and the determination of limits is a complex function of the formal structures of all the cooperating factors. The limits set by the structure of any one factor are limits of its functioning *in* that situation. Limits, like powers, belong to the whole situation, and not to the single factor apart from that situation: they belong to the specific cooperation. They are the powers and limits *of* a mechanism *with* that structure *in* that situation; they are never powers or limits "in general."

This is why an examination of the frame or constitutive structure of a mechanism apart from its functioning *as* a mechanism never reveals its powers—how it can act—or its limits and determinations—at what point it must stop short. For those powers and limits do not belong to the frame apart from its functioning in a determinate situation: powers and limits are basically relational, not "absolute" or "inherent." They have their locus, not in anything taken in isolation, but always in a specific cooperation with other powers.

This is the reason why some measure of control is necessary for discovering what the powers and limits are. For the manipulation of other factors in the situation, and their differential alteration—experimentation, in other words—reveal new powers and new limits. This is the source of the enormous fertility of a genuinely *experimental* science in increasing our knowledge, as against a science that is merely "empirical," and limited to observation and description alone. "Experimentation" means picking factors apart and putting them together again in new combinations, producing new situations never encountered before, never encounterable without active manipulation, thus revealing powers and limits never encountered or encounterable without such an active manipulation and art of experimentation. "Experience" tells us how things *have* behaved, and how they *do* behave. But only experimentation can tell us how they *can* behave. Since science aims to discover how things *can* behave, there can be no genuine science without control—without experimentation and manipulation.[19]

Every situation or process can be analysed into a plurality of interacting powers, each with its own interacting limits or determinations—as many powers and limits as can be differentially altered. The complex determination that results from this plurality of powers operating within this plurality of limits is always itself "determinate"—it belongs to that specific cooperation, not to any universal system of determinations. Hence 1) "Determination" is always plural, not unified and monistic; it is always the product of a number of separate determinations, and additional determinations are always possible. 2) Determination is always "determinate," and never "total": it is always that specific outcome, that resultant pattern of cooperating. 3) There is no "ultimate" determination, no one factor that sets limits, antecedent to the cooperation, that cannot be altered by changes in the other factors in the cooperation. 4) Determination can be said to be "ultimate" only *for* a specific situation or cooperation, as the unique resultant of that cooperation. Every specific cooperation of powers and limits in an actual situation is "ultimately" that specific cooperation, with its own complex and determinate "determination." Every particular situation or cooperation is thus unique, and exhibits its own unique cooperation of powers and limits, its own "ultimate" determination. That is, every situation is a concrete, individual substance.[20] "Universal determinism," the fixed and rigid scheme of limits of Laplace,

[19] This fact has important implications for sciences like economics, or theology.

[20] This I think is what Whitehead means when he says: "Every actual entity [determinate situation], since it is what it is, is finally its own reason for what it omits." And again: "A temporal occasion . . . and God . . . satisfy Spinoza's definition of substance, that it is *causa sui*. To be *causa sui* means that the process of concrescence is its own reason for the decision in respect to the qualitative clothing of feelings. It is finally responsible for the decision." A. N. Whitehead, *Process and Reality* (New York, 1929), pp. 71, 135. Whitehead calls this the Principle of Concretion, or the Empirical Principle. I take it to mean that all determination is plural and determinate; the precise limits set are in each case a unique discovery.

is "meaningless." There is no ultimate and monistic total limit or determination set antecedent to the process or situation. "Limits" are always plural, and hence manipulable: additional determinations can always be added to any specific situation.

Human freedom is the power to add additional determinations to the situations in which it functions. Spinoza and Kant were right: freedom involves a greater determination than human bondage, which is mere partial determination. Freedom is the power to add determination by "reason" or intelligence. Spinoza and Kant went wrong, however, in making freedom "complete" determination by reason. That is not human freedom, but Divine freedom, appropriate to God's will, not man's, which never enjoys "perfect" freedom, but rather, specific and determinate freedoms, and always within narrow limits.

This is the basis of human power, the power of art, *τέχνη*, to reveal new powers and new limits in instruments and in materials. And I mean not merely physical instruments and materials, the basis of art and technology in the narrower sense—the metaphysical implication of the fact of art and technology. It is exemplified also in the instrument of intelligence and the materials of human nature: in man's social arts and techniques. There is no ultimate antecedent determination or limit set to the power of intelligence to manipulate human nature. Such fixed and rigid limits set to human powers—to "human nature"—by the human "frame," like "the impulse to power and domination," so popular nowadays, or "sin" unified, made total, antecedently rigid and inflexible as "pride," are not only the denial in practice of all the manipulability secured through analysing the structures of the plural factors that combine to make human nature operate as it does under determinate historical conditions. They remain in the realm of a mere labeling of the specific resultant, with what human nature *does* in a certain situation, without going on to discover *how* it does it, in the interest of a manipulation that would reveal what human nature *can* do with those specific limits altered. Thus "the impulse to power," "pride," and "sin," taken as universal inflexible limits, are not only unscientific in attitude, and method, since they refuse to inquire further; they are metaphysically unsound and naive.

The fact that the operation of powers and the determination of limits belong to the situation as a whole, and are a function of all the factors cooperating in it, might be illustrated in countless other ways. Thus in the perceptual situation, the actual colors belong to and have their locus in the visual situation as a whole. In that situation, grass has the power of functioning as green, and actually *becomes* green. It has that power in itself, when not seen; but in the absence of light, or of a seeing eye, that power does not operate. In the visual situation, the railway track converges in perspective, when the eye is seeing, or when a camera is reacting photographically. Again, in the linguistic situation, the mechanism of language, words and sentences, does not reveal its power of operating, that is, the "meaning" those words can convey, apart from a determinate situation of communication. The formal analysis of the structure of the mechanism of language, of syntax, reveals no operation, no "meaning," whatever. Meaning belongs not to the words or sentences taken by themselves, but to the sentences functioning in the complex cooperation that is the communicative situation, and that meaning alters if any of the other factors alter.

Or again, the processes of human behavior in general, the subject-matter of psychology, belong, not to the organism alone—to that single mechanism of human behavior—but to the entire situation—to the organism functioning in its environment. Still better, these processes belong to the situation functioning "by means of" the organism, as well as by means of the many other mechanisms of human behavior involved in the situation. In other words, the subject-matter of psychology is not the behavior of the organism, but the behavior of "the Situation"—it is what Dewey came to call "transactions"[21]—as just suggested for the "perceptual situation" and the "communicative situation." This would be put more accurately by calling it "the situation functioning perceptually," or "the situation functioning communicatively."

Such explicit expressions do not put the emphasis on certain "types" of experience—"perceptual experience," "linguistic experience," "cognitive experience," "aesthetic experience," "artistic experience," "moral experience," "religious experience," and the many others. On that approach lurk all the pitfalls: 1) of locating a unique kind of "experience" in each case; 2) of taking that experience "subjectively"; 3) of focusing only upon the reactions or activities of the organism, and con-

[21] See Dewey and Bentley, *Knowing and the Known,* pp. 71, 73.

fining "psychology" to the physiological analysis of but a single one even of the human mechanisms involved in human behavior, the body.

Such a formulation puts the emphasis rather on certain ways of functioning, that involve a complex organization and interaction of factors. 1) These factors may all, on occasion, in another situation, function in a different way. That is, it is not the factors, but the way of functioning, that is distinctive and unique. 2) Most of these factors are not "in" the organism—certainly not "inside the skin"—and hence inaccessible, but are spread out in the situation, and hence accessible, and amenable to manipulation, with all its fruits of analysis, knowledge, and perhaps of control. 3) Most of these factors of human behavior are not subjective, or private, but are "objectively" there in the situation and publicly accessible, or at least social. That is, "moral experience," or "religious experience," are far from being "private" or "subjective"—though no doubt, like all forms of experience, they involve a "private" or "subjective" pole. 4) Indeed, I suspect that "the subjective" is not a distinct "type" of experience, not a distinctive kind of "psychological" material, a unique kind of factor, but is itself a certain way of functioning in the situation.

Hence the student of human behavior would do well not to take as his subject-matter "aesthetic experience," or "artistic experience," or "religious experience," for example, but rather the behavior of "the aesthetic situation," "the artistic situation," or "the religious situation." Or still more explicitly, his subject-matter is "the situation functioning aesthetically," or "artistically," or "religiously." Such an approach I have found fruitful, especially for these ways of functioning.[22]

It helps to be explicit, on occasion at least, and to say, the subject-matter of psychology is the situation functioning in various ways by means of the organism, and by means of many other mechanisms, including the most characteristically human mechanisms involved in all human behavior and experience, the great systems of signs and symbols, like language, mathematics, art, and religion. This at least calls attention to the many non-subjective, public, and "extra-organic"

[22] For the beginnings of such an approach to "the situation functioning aesthetically," see Chapter 10, "Qualities, Qualification, and the Aesthetic Transaction." For a fuller development of this approach to cognitive behavior, see Chapter 8, "Ways of Construing Mind and Intelligibility."

mechanisms that are the necessary conditions of all human behavior above the purely animal level. It is indeed amazing that students of man should ever have convinced themselves that the mechanisms of human behavior are located exclusively within the skin of the organism, or within a private and subjective "mind," in view of the obvious fact, that everything that distinguishes man from the other animals is a common and social possession.

One point remains to be cleared up in connection with this analysis of the relation of "frame" or formal structure to "nature" or functional structure. It is the meaning and the interpretation of the Humian empirical principle quoted in Woodbridge's formulation on page 167, note 17. Woodbridge's most concise statement runs: "Analysis of [formal] structure reveals no reason for behaviour."[23] This is indeed too concise, and calls for some qualification. Neither Woodbridge nor I have any intention of denying—any more than Hume himself—the obvious fact that functional structure, the way things behave, is discovered, and can be generalized for a wide range of contexts. As Hume put it, "None but a fool or a madman will pretend to dispute the authority of experience." The position taken is what James called "radical empiricism," that relations or functional structures are directly encountered; this view is shared by Woodbridge in the passages quoted, and by Hume—at least when he is not consciously being malicious.

Now, the analysis of formal structure *does* reveal component factors —elements or processes—whose ways of behaving have been already ascertained, and which may well be relatively invariant through a wide range of combinations and contexts. Whenever we find such elementary processes, we may be pretty confident that they will continue to behave in the ascertained way, since they are relatively independent of the particular cooperations into which they enter. The principles of mechanics seem to be that kind of behaving. They formulate ways of acting very largely, in our ordinary experience at least, independent of the particular situation in which they are encountered. That is why, of all ways of behaving of means and materials, they were exactly formulated first, and why we have been so much more successful in inventing new machines than in inventing new seeds—to say

[23] Woodbridge, *Nature and Mind,* p. 191.

nothing of new forms of human behavior. We can predict the way in which stones, seeds, cats, and men will *fall,* since that depends not on any complex situation, but solely on their mass and the density of the medium.

More generally, physico-chemical behaviors are found to be involved in the frames of all means and materials entering into processes. Thus all the complex factors cooperating to produce the symphony, for instance, including men, always involve physico-chemical processes as essential factors. These ways, ascertained and formulated in physical science, are invariant through a range of contexts that can itself be discovered. These are more complex than the ways of molar masses, the ways of mechanics. But many of them have been discovered and formulated—such as chemical ways, and the behavior of the field of radiation. They constitute the body of physical science. Whenever processes of that type are found involved in complex cooperations, we can predict and count upon their behavior. They exhibit an invariant or constant operation as means and conditions in more complex cooperations of processes.

Such an analysis makes it possible to state what is wrong with any narrowly "phenomenalistic" or "positivistic" account of functional structure, like Hume's, which holds, "we must wait for experience with all matters of fact," and adds, that experience reports only an "observed succession" or "experienced union" of "impressions"—or "events." We can only "describe" and formulate the "observed course of nature"—the way things behave—and we must wait until we have seen that way.

This Humian position does hold that functional structure can be discovered, and generalized. Having discovered, by "repeated conjunction of impressions," that fire will burn wood under certain circumstances, we can infer that whenever those circumstances are repeated, burning will occur. But the position gives no account of the prediction of ways of behaving hitherto unobserved, like the prediction of Neptune, or of new elements in the periodic table, of which the history of science is full. It gives no account of the possibility of technological invention. Logically speaking, it has no intelligible function for hypotheses.

This positivistic account overlooks the fact that every complex process can be *analysed* into cooperating processes. And though that particular eventuation may be encountered for the first time, and may even be unique, considered as a unique cooperation of subordinate processes, the ways of behaving of those subordinate processes are not unique, and not limited to that particular cooperation. With the cumulative character of our scientific knowledge, such processes are for the most part not encountered for the first time, but have already been ascertained. Hence we can always tell a great deal about the way in which a novel, unobserved cooperation of processes will behave. In an isolated system, like the planets, we can predict with complete success: we know exactly how all the masses will cooperate. With familiar means and materials, in familiar contexts, as with mechanical inventions, we can be pretty successful. In more complex cases, we can make shrewd guesses, or hypotheses; we can at least delimit the area in which to look for the unexpected.

Conversely, when we can analyse a process whose way of behaving we have observed, into a cooperation of factors whose own ways of behaving we have also observed in other contexts, we have genuinely added to our "understanding" of the process: we have found "reasons" for its behaving the way it does. Its behavior is no longer a brute fact, unconnected with anything else: it has been found to be an instance or an illustration of ways of behaving displayed in other contexts and under other conditions. Thus the burning of wood illustrates the interaction of carbon and carbon compounds with oxygen; as the floating of wood in water illustrates the behavior of bodies of that specific gravity in liquids of that density. Hume is right, of course, in holding that that interaction and that behavior remain still "matters of fact" to be discovered: there is no "reason" why they should act as they do, even if their actions could be shown to be ultimately illustrations of the ways of behaving of the field of radiation—that would remain an ultimate matter of fact.

But on the specific point in question, Hume is wrong: the analysis of formal structure or frame does yield "reasons" for behavior—though those "reasons" continue to be functional structures, or ways of behaving, of which the behavior of the thing with a frame is an instance. That is, the distinction between formal and functional structure is a relative distinction in a specific context; and ultimately all structure is functional, the structure of ways of behaving. The narrowly positivistic position, which would rest with a mere description of what has been observed—in theory, if only dubiously in practice—denies that analysis can find "reasons"—that it can reveal cooperating processes whose behavior is known, and find the conditions under which what is observed takes place. But that is precisely the kind of "reasons" which analysis can furnish. Such a denial of analysis is like that of the Chinese gourmets of Charles Lamb, who, having observed that when a house burnt down it produced delicious roast pig, proceeded to burn down houses, with no thought of further analysis of this rather extravagant culinary process. Thus we may well call such a positivism "the roast pig view."

In general, there is here no denial of regularity, order, constant ways of behaving, functional structure. Surely there is as much as we can find: no limits can be set to its discovery. The value of finding it, for both intelligibility and control, is great. But we cannot use regularity found to deny other things found, as we are often tempted to do if we *start* with order and structure. We cannot infer contingency, novelty, individuality, from order: we cannot infer Substance from Structure.

VI

We are now in a position to put together some of the major distinctions that have emerged in our analysis of Substance as a cooperation of processes, and to state them as fundamental "Ways of Functioning" of "factors" in Substance or the Situation. We encounter things or factors functioning as:

Operations	(Verbs)	Ways of Operating	(Adverbs)
Powers	(Nouns)	Kinds of Power	(Adjectives)
Connectives	(Conjunctions)		

These are ontological distinctions: they are five "ways of functioning," and hence are five "ways of being." "To be" anything means to function, and hence to be, in one of these five ways. They might hence be called five "types" of being, except that this suggests that they form five different kinds of thing; and that in turn suggests that any one thing is determinately and always that specific kind of thing, and no other. I should accept the criticism directed against "fixed essences" in this sense. These are rather five different ways in which the same thing can function; there is nothing that can function in only one of these ways and no other, nothing that is always a single "type." Hence the difficulty is to find a term general enough to designate what it is that functions in these different ways. "Thing" in the broad sense of anything that can be determinately talked about, is possible. "Factor" is perhaps best, as it indicates the product of a factorial as opposed to a reductive analysis. "Entity" seems too limited—is "Structure" an "entity"?

Now, since these five "ways" are five different ways in which factors can be *said* to function, or *said* to be, they might be called five "predicables" or five "categories." These terms mean, in Latin and in Greek, "ways of saying," and indicate primarily a linguistic classification. Thus in Aristotle "categories" are different types of predicates. Traditionally, these terms have been associated with the view that categories are introduced by language, or, as in Kant, by the understanding, into a subject-matter in which they are not present before that introduction. Hence what it would mean to call them "categories" depends upon one's analysis of the relation between language and its subject-matter. In terms of the functional realism of the present analysis, there would be no objection to calling them "categories," since that position implies that ontologically, they are ways of functioning in Substance before they are formulated as ways of stating: they are definitely ontological or metaphysical categories.

"Operations," we have made clear, are what we encounter directly in Substance or the Situation. "Ways" are what we have been calling "structures," functional structures, as something discriminated in concrete operations and cooperations. "Kinds" are a different type of structure, a type not yet emphasized, though touched on when we asked, What is it that makes *the* symphony *a* symphony? "Powers" we have also found discriminated in encountered situations, in both action and understanding.

Because we have been approaching the subject-matter of metaphysics through linguistic experience, because we have been trying to state in general terms the ways in which things cooperate and function in

Substance encountered, and because these "ways," though discriminated in action, are then distinguished and formulated in discourse, and are, in fact, the basis of the manipulative art of language, these five main ways of functioning can also be designated by the grammatical terms applied to the formulations in discourse of those different ways. They can be distinguished as those normally expressed by "Verbs," "Adverbs," "Nouns," "Adjectives," and "Conjunctions." Besides being convenient, this terminology suggests, in addition to the encountered relations between these different ways of functioning, or structures, that we have so far been examining, certain further relations involved in man's cooperation with them through discourse; that is, it suggests how such ways of functioning can be "translated" linguistically from one to another, how they can be manipulated linguistically in general, and what that makes possible in the way of man's practical as well as linguistic cooperation with the powers of Substance.

Things "are" what they can "do"; and these doings, these operations, are "prior for us"—they are our *ratio cognoscendi;* though what things are "in the order of Nature"—their *ratio essendi*—is what they *can* do, their powers, rather than their observed operations. That is, what things can be said to be, is what they can be said to be able to do. But in our experience of the world, in Substance encountered, what "verbs" express is primary, and in the universe of action it is ultimate. We begin, determinately, with "verbs," with operations; and we end with "verbs," with action, with doing something, even if that doing be "contemplating" or "enjoying meanings." In between, in reflective or linguistic experience, which is thus "mediate" or "intermediate," we distinguish, as ways of functioning in the Situation, what can be designated by the other parts of speech. Thus operations, actions, doings, behavings, with all their discriminable traits and ways, are what we directly encounter in our "universes of action" or "fields of cooperating." They form the ultimate subject-matter to which our language and talking refer, the ultimate material it uses in practicing the arts of discourse, and the ultimate evidence by which our assertions are warranted. Operations or "verbs" are what is denoted in "empirical method."

But "verbs" or operations are not the "objective" or "object" of inquiry and knowledge. That objective is rather "adverbs" or ways: *how* operations take place, their functional structure. "Verbs" can be said to be the objective of the acting situation, in which knowing forms an intermediate stage: that objective is the producing of a new "verb" or operation. But the objective of inquiry is, *how* something is or can be done; and this objective includes both the functional structure of the process and the formal structure of the mechanisms and materials involved. The objective of the acting situation is, doing it, manipulating it, doing something with it.

Thus the objective of inquiry and knowing is a "how," an "adverb," the functional structure of "verbs" or "behavings." It is to distinguish operatings by their ways, by "adverbs." When stated in discourse, these ways become "kinds" of operation. And the objective of inquiry includes the further distinguishing of the "ways" of "adverbs" themselves —their "degree." Thus, in the simple case, when we start inquiring, we ask, *how fast* is that car coming? *how soon* will it get to the corner? *how quickly* can I stop? Since the discrimination is effected in a situation or universe of action, it is always comparative, an affair of more or less, of *how much more*. It is always relative to other ways of operating involved. *How much sooner* will that car get to the corner than I? *How much more quickly* can I turn than he? Taken as a means to the end imposed by the situation—in this case "avoiding a collision" —this "reflective" or "knowing" phase of the "acting situation" is ultimately concerned with "better" or "worse": not merely with "how?" nor even with "how much?" but with "how best" can the collision be avoided?

In the more complex cases, like those of scientific inquiry, we ask, which of the various hypotheses advanced can *best* satisfy the conditions of the inquiry? which can *best* accord with the experimental data? That is, which can *best* perform the function which a scientifically warranted statement of knowledge must perform? Thus the "ultimate" objective of inquiry and knowing, their ultimate *quaesita* in any situation, is not merely "how" something is done, and not even "how" to do it—but rather "how best" to do it.

This has many important consequences. First, it suggests that "evaluation," the determination of the "better" and the "worse" ways of acting, or "adverbs," is fundamental in every universe of action that has an intermediate stage of reflecting, inquiry, and knowing, and is not merely the operation of habit or impulse. "Values"—that is, what has been reflectively "evaluated," and is hence "valued" in cognitive experience—are an integral factor in every situation reflectively cooperated with, in every substance reflectively experienced. A "value" is therefore not a "noun," a thing, but a verbal adjective, a past participle, an "evaluated." What has been so evaluated then functions as a "comparative power," determined by an operation. Hence "values" are not "external to existence," they do not exist in a separate "realm," but are powers encountered in every substance, inherent in its functional structure of means and ends. "Evaluatableness," and hence "valuedness," is a power of every situation or substance.

Since "values" are thus means or mechanisms of the cooperation, they are not "subjective," nor are they "subjectively relative"—that is, indeterminately relative, "just relative," relative to the arbitrary preference of the valuer. They are *objectively relative,* determinately relative to Substance, to the encountered cooperation. Hence they are "functionally real," real in their actual functioning in the situation, "valuable for" its specific cooperation of powers. Since they are relative *to* the situation and its functional structures of means and ends, that relation can be objectively inquired into and determined.

Thus, far from being excluded from scientific or experimental treatment, or from being even irrelevant to scientific inquiry, "evaluation" is as amenable to the employment of scientific methods as any other process of inquiry into Substance. Indeed, scientific inquiry is itself precisely a process of evaluation, of "how best" to do something. It is especially so when it is an inquiry into "how best" to assert and formulate some natural structure so that that formulation, that precisely stated scientific knowledge, that "warranted assertion," will serve best as an instrument in the widest possible range of universes of action—when it is, as we say, "most theoretical," and *therefore* most practical. Indeed, scientific method is most impressive as a process of evaluation when it succeeds in formulating the most adequate scientific theory—what is usually said to be "theoretical" or "pure" truth.

Thus "intelligibility" and "evaluatability"—or, if we prefer not to use that portmanteau word, "value"—are not opposed, or even separate but compatible, powers of Substance. They are the same identical power. Or, stated in terms of the operation of this power, "understanding" and "evaluating" are identical processes. We best "understand" anything when we know best how to deal with it—what it is good for, and how to use it for that end.[24]

The ultimate objective of the process of knowing or evaluation is thus the comparative of an adverb, "better": which way of doing something is "better" than all the others? It is not the superlative: which way is "best?" "Best" can mean only, "best under specified conditions," "best in a given context," "best for that situation"—and this means, "better than the other possibilities." "Platonism" in dealing with values, the contention that we cannot know what is "better than" anything else unless we have a prior knowledge of what is "best," has no supporting evidence, and is contradicted by our constant experience. This is equivalent to holding that we cannot know whether one line is "longer" than another unless we know first the "longest" line. What is "best" absolutely—ἁπλῶς, *simpliciter*—is, like all superlatives and ultimates, a "myth." It has the genuine values of a myth, but it is not objectively determinable. It could only mean, "best in the ultimate context." But, as we have seen, there is no discoverable ultimate context. The ultimate "better than," and hence the "best" for any determinate situation, which is consequently the ultimate objective for human inquiry and science, is, How can mankind best live? This objective is "ultimate for" man's resources, the natural and social materials, the knowledge available as powers at any given time. It is not, How can mankind live best, absolutely?—in Heaven, or in the Perfect City, with all limitations, and hence all powers, removed. This is again a "myth," or a Kantian "regulative idea." As Hegel pointed out, such Utopian or millennial myths are notoriously limited by, and relative to, the powers and resources of the specific culture that produced them: "Plato's Republic is in essence nothing but an interpretation of the nature of Greek ethical life."[25] Today the question might be phrased, How can mankind best live with

[24] Woodbridge puts it: "If we ask, as we are sometimes tempted to do, what is the ultimate reason for the existence of things, the only intelligible answer we can give is something like this: things exist to be controlled for ends through the discovery of their structure." "Behaviour," in *Nature and Mind,* pp. 191–92.

[25] Hegel, *Philosophy of Right,* tr. T. M. Knox (Oxford, 1942), p. 10.

the power of the scientific method?—a power possessed by no previous culture, bringing with it new powers in detail, and setting new limits, wholly novel opportunities and responsibilities.

This ultimate objective of inquiry, how best to do anything, as it becomes unified, comes to be, how best to do everything that has to be done in living. But the proximate objective of inquiry is, as in our approaching car case, How much? How much faster? How much sooner? How much nearer? How much easier? The comparative degree of the "adverb" is primary in reflective experience, in its participation in the mutual involvement of "verbs" in the universe of action. Inquiry seeks how "verbs" are operating, how they are interacting and cooperating. It goes on to seek how their ways of operating are related to each other—the correlations between "adverbs" that are scientific "laws" or formulations. It distinguishes the "more or less" of the "hows" or "adverbs," and the precise "more" and "less": "how much more," "how much less." In developed inquiry and knowing—in "exact science"—in the measure that the knowledge of how something can be done is to be achieved, we must find how much more, how much less. From this follows the immense importance of the measurement of ways of operating, of "adverbs," and of their mathematical formulation in general—of the whole emphasis on quantitative analysis and on exact mathematical distinctions.

We have been speaking of "adverbs" or Structure as distinguished from "verbs" in reflective, linguistic experience. But the discrimination between operatings and their ways of operating is also encountered in any cooperation with Substance, in prelinguistic behavior as well as in discourse. I have attempted to work out a behavioristic account of the organic discriminations which underlie these formulated distinctions, a behavioristic account of the way in which Structure is discovered in our encounters with the world. This points to a behavioristic theory of signs, which would make "signifying" or "meaning," not a mysterious addition to the Substance we encounter, but rather something present at the lowest level of organic cooperation in the Situation. It is also a way of giving due meed to both "nominalism" and "realism" on the question of the status of "universals." It can be pushed into an account of the functioning of linguistic signs, or language; and that in turn leads to the exploration of non-representative symbols, and Connectives or "conjunctions" in general. In Chapter 9, "An Empirical and Naturalistic Theory of Signs, Signification, Universals, and Symbols," three of these four levels of human dealing with Structure, made possible by the encountered discrimination between operations and their ways, are elaborated a little further. The analysis of language and communication, which involves a combination of signs and symbols, of representative and non-representative factors, is not there included.

VII

So far we have distinguished "verbs" and "adverbs," "operations" and their "ways"—activities and structures, functioning as a particular and functioning universally. But in the universe of action we encounter a further discrimination: that between the activity or operation, and the factors "responsible for" the activity—*τὰ αἴτια*—the factors that *are* operating as means and mechanisms in the process. In the universe of action we encounter complex means-end structures; we discriminate practically between activity and "its" means, between behaviors and "their" mechanisms. Further reflective analysis reveals that these directly discriminated factors are not the only "factors responsible," and human manipulation, control, and art may well have to work with many others as well. That is, we encounter "agents," "things acting," in the ordinary sense. There is here no attempt to deny this obvious fact of ordinary experience, the presence of things acting. But I want to put them into the context from which they are selected by our practical interests of responding and acting ourselves, and selected also by ordinary language, which is so heavily molded on practical interests. Such agents are expressed in ordinary language by "nouns," with all their powers and attributes. In all non-cognitive experience, we encounter "things" or "agents," acting, functioning, behaving in various ways; and it is to such "things" that we respond, practically and emotionally. We do not get from "actings encountered" to "agents acting," or things, by any process of "inference," as is maintained in the construing of experience in dualistic or Lockean empiricism. The position of Bertrand Russell, that we proceed from encountered "sensa" to "objects in the external world" by a process of inference, and the position of Santayana, that we pass from "intuited essences" to common sense objects only by an act of "animal faith," spring from the dialectical elaboration of the Lockean assumptions, not from an analysis of encountered situations. Agents or objects are immediately encountered: they are "data"—or better, "prehensa"—discriminated and selected in the universe of action by our organic responses. Of course, just what they are—their precise powers—needs further inquiry and discovery through reflective and linguistic experience.

We encounter factors functioning in operations as "actings," and factors functioning as "active means," as "agents"—as "verbs" in the present tense, and as subjects of "verbs"—as "nouns." We encounter factors functioning "verbally," and other factors functioning "nominally." With some "verbs" or actings, like "it's raining," "it's snowing," etc., we do not usually distinguish the "nouns" or agents, the means or mechanisms of the process, just because we cannot do anything about the weather: it is not practically manipulable. When we think we can, by prayer, sacrifice, or ritual dance, we pray to Jupiter Pluvius. When it is not yet raining, when we *can* take precautions, we distinguish the "active powers" of the clouds, the wind, the temperature, etc.

This discrimination is reflected, formulated as a distinction, and sharpened by language. But it is not created by language. The discrimination between "nouns" and "verbs" is a practical discrimination encountered in the universe of action. It is of immense importance. It focuses attention on "nouns" as means to action, as "active powers" of operating, in cooperation with other means, "conditioning" means, that is, other "nouns" distinguished in the operation by their functioning as "passive powers," powers of "being acted upon." The distinction between "active" and "passive" powers is itself a discrimination made in the universe of action, in practice. In discourse, and especially in the formalized discourse of scientific formulation, it appears as "conventional": there is no reason for adopting "this" factor as functionally correlated with "that" one, and hence as the "agent" or "efficient cause," rather than the other way round. In the language of science it is the same correlation. The notion of "efficient causation" hence tends to disappear from formalized and exact science. In mathematics, there are obviously no efficient causes, only formal causes. In mechanics and dynamics, events are not said to be "caused," but rather to be instances of, illustrations of, the laws of the sciences—more precisely still, to be values derivable from the equations.

But for action and practice, for art and manipulation, the distinction is far from "arbitrary." As Aristotle puts it, the case of "acting" and "being acted upon" is like the road from Athens to Thebes, which is the same road as that from Thebes to Athens; the "two" roads, as distinguished in λόγος, are two alternative expressions. Similarly, "acting" and "being acted upon" are the same process, viewed from two different poles. In language the distinction is "conventional." But for action, for art, it is anything but "arbitrary." It makes a great difference whether you are in Athens or in Thebes. And likewise it makes a great difference which factor you manipulate in the situation.[26] For action, the agent, the active power, the "cause" in the ordinary sense of "efficient cause," is the manipulable, the handle or leverage for producing, stopping, or altering the operation, or for predicting how it will take place. "Cause" and "effect" is thus a practical rather than a theoretical distinction: the "cause" is the means to some activity.[27]

This suggests that Hume's analysis of causation proceeds from a pure "spectator theory" of experience and knowing. Our only relation to "impressions" or events, it assumes, is that we can "observe" them as spectators. We then find, of course, no "necessary connection," but only "constant conjunction"—indeed, only "frequent conjunction."[28] This spectator analysis of causation culminates in John Stuart Mill, for whom ultimately the entire state of the universe at one instant is the "cause" of the entire state of the universe at the "next" instant—a wholly unintelligible and futile outcome. It has not even the clear meaning and utility of taking "causation" as mathematical correlation —a notion in which there is no trace, incidentally, of the empiricist's notion that causation is essentially "succession," which is naturally all a spectator can observe. As spectators, of course, we can never see or observe the relation of means and ends, or functional structure, of "effi-

[26] *Physica* 202b.

[27] Compare Dewey: "A 'cause' is not merely an antecedent; it is that antecedent which if manipulated regulates the occurrence of the consequent. That is why the sun rather than night is the causal condition of day." *Experience and Nature* (New York, 1929), p. 109. As in this case, the manipulation can take place in imagination.

[28] See the author's "David Hume: Radical Empiricist and Pragmatist," in Hook and Konvitz, eds., *Freedom and Experience*, pp. 308–11.

cient causation." The attempts to do so are always futile, like Whitehead's, who comes out with the curious notion that we are "aware" of our eyes in seeing, and that this is an "answer" to Hume.

We encounter means and ends, efficient causation, not as spectators, but in action, whenever we try to do something to or with something else, and we refine it with further conscious manipulation. We find we must do it in certain ways, and cannot do it in other ways. The shift from the observational and descriptive science with which Hume was familiar, which lent itself to the assumptions of the spectator conception of experience and knowledge, to a genuinely experimental and manipulative science, has made Hume's analysis irrelevant. Causation for such an experimental science becomes a matter, not of necessary *connections* —the theory of the rationalistic, Spinozistic kind of science Hume was rightly criticising—but of necessary *conditions.* Hume was right to read "simple necessity"—the mechanical, inexorable necessity of Newtonian science—out of all matters of fact. He was wrong in failing to recognize that in such matters of fact, the necessity is not "simple" but "hypothetical"—it is conditions, means, mechanisms that are necessary, not the "effects" of antecedent "causes."

What a means *is,* as a mechanism or cause in an operation, is how it acts in cooperation with other conditions or passive powers. The means *is* its specific and determinate powers to act in a certain way. The powers of means and causes are encountered only in their functioning: all knowledge of those powers is derived from operatings. Hence "for us," "in experience," operations, "verbs," are primary. A "noun" is a power, or a set of powers. The content of "nouns" is derived from "verbs": the "nature" of what functions as a means is "to act" in a certain way. The "nature" of a "noun" is always a "verb": a "noun" is a power to act.

"Ways" of operating are likewise translatable into "kinds" of powers or means: "adverbs" modifying "verbs" are convertible into "adjectives" characterizing "nouns." The "nature" of a means is expressed as what is "essential" to its functioning as that kind of means, and is expressed equally as what is essential to its functioning in that way. The way of growing of the seed, for instance, is translatable into a certain kind of power. The way of acting of masses is translatable into the "proper powers" or "properties" of masses. Thus the functional structure of operations and behaviors can be formulated equally as the "properties" of powers.

In a sense, it is the same structure of behaving discriminated in processes than can be expressed equally as "ways" of operating, or as "properties" of "kinds" of powers: that is why the linguistic translation is possible. But, though it is the same structure, it is that structure functioning in two quite different ways: in the one case, as the structure of encountered and empirically observed operations, in the other, as the structure of powers. This structure is encountered directly in action as the structure of an operation; through the translation made possible by language, it can be encountered in reflective experience as the structure of a power.

In putting it this way, I do not mean that language "creates" the distinction between an operation and a power, or that the difference between the two ways of talking about the same structure is in any sense "arbitrary." The discrimination between operations and powers is encountered in the universe of action: it is encountered as two different ways of functioning in Substance. The discrimination is for action perfectly "objective," and the formulated distinction is for reflective experience also perfectly "objective." It can be refined and made more precise by inquiry, which can discover the various powers involved in any cooperation.

What language does do, is not to "create" an additional way in which the encountered structure of an operation can function: namely, the way of functioning as the structure of a "power." It is rather to manipulate that structure and to reformulate it, so that we can *treat* things *as powers* that can exhibit that structure in their operating, and thus anticipate their way of operating, with all that such anticipation or prediction holds for both knowledge and action. Language does not create powers, it enables us to make use of them *as means,* to treat them as means and causes, both intellectually and practically—through the grasp that reformulation or translation gives us upon their structures.[29]

[29] Compare Dewey's insistence on our "direct experience" of "possibilities": "Genuinely complete empirical philosophy requires that there be a determination *in terms of experience* of the relation that exists between physical subject-matter and the things of direct perception, use, and enjoyment [this is the central problem for Whitehead also]. It would seem clear that historic empiricism, because of its commitment to sensationalism, failed to meet this need. The

In the universe of action, both the practical discrimination of agents and their reformulation in reflective experience and discourse as means, mechanisms, and causes are vital. To seize an operation discriminated in the situation, and to treat it as a means or power, is to get a leverage for manipulation. It is to treat it as "signifying" what it can do, and as "suggesting" what can be done with it—as signifying both expectations, and the possibilities of our further cooperation with it.[30]

Ordinary language is, in fact, so practical in its genesis and character, so orientated toward the functional structure of means and ends, of things and their powers to act, of agents and activities, that it can hardly "describe" encountered operations at all. It takes a sophisticated "verb language" artificially invented for the critical purpose of calling us back to the directly experienced world, to get anywhere near the discriminations encountered in the universe of action, the actual operations of Substance. Science likewise, in its concern with structures as means, pushes the "noun language" of common sense into a generalized formulation of the "powers" exhibited in particular cooperations, as "properties" proper to that kind of means in diversified contexts.

The verb language and the noun language are thus two different

---

obvious way of meeting the requirement is through explicit acknowledgment that direct experience contains, as a highly important direct ingredient of itself, a wealth of *possible* objects. There is no inconsistency between the idea of direct experience and the idea of objects of that experience that are as yet unrealized. For these latter objects are directly experienced *as* possibilities. Every plan, every prediction, yes, every forecast and anticipation, is an experience in which some non-directly experienced object is directly experienced *as a possibility*. And, as previously suggested, modern experience is marked by the extent to which directly perceived, enjoyed, and suffered objects are treated as signs, indications, of what has *not* been experienced in and of itself, or/and are treated as means for the realization of these things of possible experience. Because historic empirical philosophy failed to take cognizance of this fact, it was not able to take account of one of the most striking features of scientific method and scientific conclusions—preoccupation with generality as such." John Dewey, "The Objectivism-Subjectivism of Modern Philosophy," in *Problems of Men,* pp. 317–18. Quotation used by permission of the Philosophical Library, Inc.

This suggests how Dewey deals with Whitehead's central problem in his philosophy of nature (*The Concept of Nature* [Cambridge, 1920], which remains Whitehead's most suggestive and most constructive book) in terms of his own conception of "direct experience."

30 For a further development of this analysis of signification, see Chapter 9, "An Empirical and Naturalistic Theory of Signs, Signification, Universals, and Symbols."

ways of formulating the same functional structure of processes, of manipulating the same material. In contemporary philosophical inquiry, this distinction has been emphasized by many thinkers, of whom perhaps Cassirer and Dewey are the most suggestive. Cassirer has made much of the distinction between "concepts of function" and "concepts of substance."[31] Dewey distinguishes between "categories" and "classes," the outcome respectively of "universal" and "generic" propositions. The distinction seems close to the one we have been making between "ways" of acting and "kinds" of power. The relation we have called "translatability" between operations and powers, "verbs" and "nouns," Dewey calls "conjugate." The basic point, that "kinds" or "classes" are derived from "ways" or "categories" (Dewey's term), he puts: "No grounded generic propositions can be formed save as they are the products of the performance of operations indicated as possible by universal propositions."[32] This distinction has even been pushed recently to the contrast between two different kinds of "logic." Be that as it may, there are certainly two different kinds of linguistic instrument. And we might well follow Dewey in saying, there are two different ways of functioning "logically" in inquiry, or, more broadly, in the communicative or language situation: "universal" and "generic" propositions, "ways" and "kinds," taken as two different ways of functioning universally.

The different functions of these two languages would require detailed analysis; only an approach can be suggested here. The noun language seizes on operations encountered in the universe of action, and treats them as means, as powers, in order to get a leverage for manipulation. The danger always is that it may single out in the operation to express as a "noun" what is not in fact a means—it may fail in practice. Or it may treat an operation as its own mechanism, and take such operations as "life," "consciousness," "mind," or "soul" as "nouns" or agents, causes. The fact that we can talk about any factor, and treat any one as a subject, a means or agent, by translating it into a "noun,"[33] often leads to what we call an "hypostatizing" or "substantializing" of what

[31] See Ernst Cassirer, *Substance and Function* (Eng. tr., Chicago, 1923; reprinted, New York, 1953).

[32] Dewey, *Logic,* p. 275.

[33] Just as we have here been converting "adverbs" into nouns, and speaking of them as "ways." In similar fashion, treating any of the factors in Substance as an object of inquiry converts it into a "how," an adverb.

are in fact processes. To treat operations as "things," "means," "mechanisms," is valid only when it isolates from a cooperation a genuine mechanism. Hence the noun language is in constant need of clarifying through an "operational" analysis. The rule is *Cherchez le verbe,* translate "nouns" back into the factor or the trait of a factor in the operation which it originally selected and converted into a "noun" or power. Translate the structure expressed in the noun language as the power of of a "noun" into that structure expressed as a way of operating.

In contrast, the verb language remains closer to the discriminations encountered in action, to the subject-matter directly "taken" from the universe of action. It involves much less manipulation of its selected materials. It can hence serve the function of criticising the noun language, of calling it back to the directly experienced world. It is therefore beloved of "empiricists" and "positivists"—unless indeed they have converted experience itself from a process into a noun, a subject-matter, and broken it up into atomic nouns, "sense data," in which case they remain content with the noun language and its hypostatization of experience and its elements. The verb language is closer to the ultimate "denotata" of language and knowing. The verb language also serves a purely "aesthetic," "descriptive," "phenomenological," or "theoretical" interest. It can be "emotive," as expressing immediately encountered qualities, as contrasted with the practical, artistic, manipulative interest, which seizes on means rather than such consummations. A pure verb language would be a mere pointing, mere denotation—what Whitehead perversely calls "speculative demonstration"—that is, it would cease to be a language at all, and would become a mere "notation" of factors.

The noun language involves much more manipulation and reconstruction of its selected materials discriminated in action. In selecting means, and treating them as powers, both active and passive, it takes them, not as complete in themselves, like operations or processes encountered, but as suggesting what they can do, and what can be done with them, as suggesting expectations of future behavior, and possibilities of future manipulation. It serves the practical functions, and is closer to common sense. It converts the practical discriminations of action into formulated signs and "meanings," it makes them available for the practical functions of language. It refines its material, "formulates the meaning of events," as Dewey puts it, and extends that meaning: for by seizing on means and active powers, it gets a handle and leverage for grasping other powers of the means there involved. It finds the "properties" of those means, their powers as revealed in a variety of situations and contexts. It enlarges the range of the powers available, by pushing them far beyond the particular operation encountered.

Science extends the noun language into a generalized formulation of powers as properties "invariant" or "proper to" that kind of means through a wide range of contexts. It isolates powers, and gives them and their relations to other powers a mathematical formulation. It aims at the perfect noun language, which would state the proper operations of things as they have so far been discovered—the objective of formalized and systematized science. It needs the constant recall to the verb language, to encountered operations, in order to extend our knowledge by discovering further powers in things, and thus enlarge our formulations of their proper operations.

Properties are generalized powers, relatively invariant, relatively isolated from any specific functional context. Properties never succeed in becoming wholly generalized. They remain powers, and they point to and are warranted by specific operations. They are "properties" only through a certain range, specified or implicit, of conditions. Thus the chemical properties of the seed remain the generalized powers it exhibits in the context of chemical operations. Properties are the functional structure of the powers a thing exhibits through a range of contexts. This structure of properties is thus not a particular but a universal: it is a structure functioning universally. Science aims to generalize the powers encountered in specific situations—in the experimental situation—into properties that will hold for an entire range—though they always remain powers of cooperating *for* that specified range of situations, and the final reference is to the operation of the scientific enterprise as a social institution. The procedure of scientific criticism of formulated properties is to delimit them as "powers *for*" a determinate range—to find the context, the limits of the range of situations within which they *are* powers, within which a "noun" will exhibit such properties. What, e.g., are the limits of "capitalism," within which its formulated economic laws hold, and beyond which they do not apply? What are the limits of molar mechanics, beyond which, at the extra-galactic and at the sub-atomic levels, they no longer obtain?

It should be obvious at this point that the function of metaphysical inquiry, as stated by most of the philosophies of experience since the time of Hegel's *Phenomenology,* to serve as the *criticism of abstractions,* can be stated as the criticism of the noun language, both that of practical common sense and that of formalized and systematized science, by recalling it to the world as directly experienced. In this way we can bring together both the appeal to "immediate experience" of American philosophies of experience like those of James, Dewey, and Whitehead, and the "phenomenological method" of criticism of the Continental philosophies of experience stemming from Husserl and Heidegger. And to them we can join also the British critiques of language and the similar critiques of the logical positivists. For the method suggested is to work out what has already been here called "an artificial and sophisticated verb language" that can express more clearly and adequately the generic traits of, and the distinctions forced in, Substance, or the world as directly encountered: in the world "immediately experienced," say the Americans; in the experienced world "phenomenologically described," say the Continentals; in the world adequately described "in protocol sentences," say the logical empiricists; in the world set forth and implied in the manifold ways we use ordinary language, say the elucidators of the uses of language. In pursuing this task and this method myself, I have been following the attempts of philosophers as diverse as Aristotle, Woodbridge, Dewey, Whitehead, and Heidegger, to elaborate a verb language—sometimes called today a "process philosophy"—in which to state a functional realism in such a way as to serve this critical end.

VIII

We have distinguished, as ways of functioning in Substance, operations and their ways, powers and their kinds. I have emphasized that these distinctions in discourse, or "categories," taken as what the factors functioning in Substance can be said to be, are formulations in language of discriminations encountered in action. They are "types of factor" in our experienced world which our transactions with it discriminate in nonreflective experience before reflective experience, taken as that transaction with the experienced world that is discourse and language, expresses, formulates, and communicates them.

But it must also be emphasized, these discriminations are not "absolute"—they are not rigid and fixed for every situation and context. They are always relative to a determinate universe of action or situation, just as what constitutes that situation is itself relative to its "action" or "objective," that is, is selected by that "action" from the immense complex of cooperating processes that is Nature. These discriminations are relative to or functional in that determinate situation. Hence they are "objective" *for* the objective of that situation. They are not "arbitrary"; they can always be discovered by inquiry. They are not subjectively relative, "just relative," in the sense that brings any further inquiry up short. They are "relative *to*," objectively and determinately relative. This position is not only a *functional realism;* it is also, ontologically speaking, an *objective relativism.*

Activities, "verbs," are what they are: they are what they are encountered as, in every way. But in any determinate situation, they may *function* as instances or signs of a characteristic way—"adverbially"—or as themselves powers to further cooperations—"nominally"—or as instances of properties of kinds of power—"adjectivally." Depending on the specific situation, the same thing or factor, the same activity or process, may on occasion function as, and hence *be,* an operation or a power, an instance of a way or a kind. It may function as a means or as an end, as a cause or as an eventuation. There is no "ultimate context" in which that activity or process is rigidly one of these functionings alone. What we have distinguished as "verbs," "adverbs," "nouns," "adjectives," are thus all different ways of functioning, ways of cooperating in Substance, of entering into processes—ways of "being experienced." As known reflectively, in metaphysical inquiry, they all function as "hows," as "adverbs"; just as when stated in discourse they all become "nouns." There is no factor discriminated in encountered processes that is "inherently" one type of functioning and no other. It assumes its particular functional character only in a specific situation. We have not been distinguishing "kinds" of existence, but ways of functioning *in* existence—or rather, the kinds or types here distinguished are a way of formulating "ways of functioning." In other words, these metaphysical "categories" are *functional* categories, not logical categories. In this sense—and I hope in this innocuous sense alone—this is an ontology without logic.

IX

There remain "conjunctions," factors functioning in Substance as Connectives of all sorts. They are very important, for they include not only the great constellations of linguistic signs and symbols that are language, and the complex elaborations of non-representative symbols like mathematics, logic, and theology, but also all the hypotheses and theories of science, all its systems of temporal and spatial measurement, all moral and legal codes, all human and social ideals, and all myths, both historical and metaphysical. Such Connectives are found functioning, not to be sure in those areas of existence that are never encountered directly but only inferred—those inaccessible to human encountering—but in every humanly encountered situation, whether that encountering be on the level of purely habitual behavior or on that of reflective and linguistic behavior. They pervade the experienced world. They will not be analysed here; the analysis of Connectives and the elaboration of certain types will be found in Chapter 9, "An Empirical and Naturalistic Theory of Signs, Signification, Universals, and Symbols," Section IV.

Just as metaphysical inquiry has no particular starting-point, so there is no point at which it may not for the time break off. Being analytic of existence, it never deserts its inexhaustible subject-matter of existence. It need never worry whether it has omitted anything, for it does not have to create the world out of the factors it discloses. Of how much richer a palette would be needed to paint the portrait of existence, I am fully aware. I am sorely tempted to bring in the nature and status of "mind" at this point,[34] and "time," the temporal aspect of existence.[35] But time invoked proves an imperious master: it has already brought me to a close.

[34] See Chapter 8, "Ways of Construing Mind and Intelligibility."

[35] See Chapters 2 and 3, "On the Understanding of Histories," and "History as an Instrument of Understanding."

CHAPTER 7

Empirical Pluralism and Unifications of Nature

I AM HERE PROPOSING to approach Nature directly, and with none of that preliminary methodological discussion which is so much in the current mode. For I share the distaste of many for those desert sands that stretch on endlessly toward the mirage of confirmability; though I also believe that sand is an important ingredient in the hard roads that can take us places. But I am here inviting neither to excursions, nor to tours to distant scenes. I am proposing rather to explore the old homestead, the familiar Nature with whose accustomed features we have long lived in harmony and compatibility.

The Nature we encounter exhibits a thoroughgoing diversity or plurality. It is a fundamental metaphysical fact that Nature is radically and ineradicably manifold. Since William James's insistence on the "pluriverse" we live in, metaphysical inquiry has rejected all idealistic monism. Some form of ontological pluralism has come to be accepted again by most responsible metaphysicians, just as they have once more come to take time "seriously."

But it is likewise a fundamental metaphysical fact that Nature can *become* unified in human vision. Again and again the world has provoked man to many a different scheme of unification. From the beginning men have seen the world whole, through the vision that is myth and symbol, through the great creation myths of primitive cultures. More recently, some have tried to see it entire through the vision that is knowledge and science, through the working out of progressively more unified general ideas and theories, that seem to point to an eventual unification in a single unified formula—a unified field theory, perhaps.

Whether in the end "knowledge" and "science" operate to unify Nature in a way that is fundamentally different from the way of myth and symbol—whether science is, as we say, less "symbolic" and more "literal"—has been a vexed philosophical issue, especially in modern times. I have tried to frame the question—and I might indeed claim that this is one fruit of the metaphysical leading principles here set forth—in such a way as to transform what has been an "issue" to be interminably debated, into a problem that can be inquired into, with some hope that inquiry can bring to light pertinent facts. Knowledge and science are certainly no less—and no more—"human" than are myths and symbols; and no less—and no more—"natural." Both ways of seeing the world whole employ characteristic instruments of unification. In their unifying function, scientific hypotheses, theories, and systems, together with myths and symbols, "regulative ideas" and human ideals, and such complex elaborations of symbols as mathematics, logic, and theology, and the greatest of all, discourse and language itself—all these varied instruments of unification seem to possess much in common. They all seem to enjoy the same happy ontological status: they all fall, in my metaphysical classification of "predicables," or ways of functioning,[1] into the group called "Connectives" or "Conjunctions." They are all "functionally real," they are all "real" as functioning to institute objective relations. They are all human ways of cooperating with other natural processes. Their distinctive ways of functioning, their characteristic behavior, at times their misbehavior, is a matter for detailed inquiry into facts.

The position here being developed may hence be called a "functional realism." So important are Connectives in any unification of Nature that their status demands an initial clarification. In general, the structures and characters grasped and formulated in knowledge and "warranted discourse" have a determinate status in the world encountered. They are "there," in Substance—in the language of medieval realism, they are "in re." They are discoverable "there" in Substance experienced, in its complex cooperation of powers—they are there in the universe of action or the situation. Now, certain structures and factors can be said to be "there," and to be discoverable, even when the factor of which they are the structure is not functioning in a process. Examples of such structures would be the physico-chemical structure of the seed, the me-

[1] See Chapter 6, "Substance as a Cooperation of Processes," pp. 176, 194.

chanical structure of the sewing machine, the psychological structure of human nature, or the musical structure of the symphony. Such structures we have called "formal" or "constitutive" structures, and have found them as the frames of mechanisms and materials that can, on occasion, function as means or powers in processes. Other structures and characters are not "there," are not discoverable, unless these factors are functioning as means in a process—unless the seed is growing, the sewing machine sewing, the men acting, the symphony being performed and heard. Such characters and structures we have called "functional structures."

But such functional structures enjoy an equally determinate status in the world encountered, in Substance. They are equally discoverable in its processes, they are equally "real," equally "in re." Their locus is *not* in things apart from their functioning, but in that functioning of powers; they are "there," they are "real," in their functioning in a specific cooperation of powers. They are "real" as belonging to and as discoverable in that cooperation. Their "reality" can be said to be precisely their functioning. They can be said to be "functionally real," and to enjoy a "functional" status. In general, that is "real" which functions determinately and discoverably in the complex of processes that is Substance.

Now, much that is in this sense "functionally real," that has its locus and status and is discoverable in a cooperation of powers, is not operative or "actual" if because of the absence of certain necessary conditions the cooperation does not take place—if the seed does not grow, but remains a mere set of powers, or if the symphony remains a mere score. And likewise, there is much that is "functionally real" and discoverable in Substance encountered that is not operative or "actual" in the absence of the participation of *human* activities in Substance. It is here that Connectives belong. Thus the so-called "values" that function in human experience of the world, in action, art, and science, are not operative in the absence of that human participation—when they are not functioning as means to human ends. But when, with man as one factor in the situation, they are so operative, they are then "functionally real" and "objective": they are not "subjective," but are objectively determinable—they are "good for" in the perfectly objective sense of being "good for men." The same holds true for all Connectives. Thus, in the chief Connective, language, the structures of discourse are not functioning factors unless men are talking and communicating. But they have their locus and status, they are "functionally real," in the process of communication—in Substance expressed and communicated, in Substance reflectively experienced, in Substance participated in through discourse. Just how these various factors function in Substance—i.e., how they act —how precisely they are "real"—is in each case an objective for inquiry. And the answer is always relative to the process or situation in which they are functioning as cooperating factors.

It is in this sense that the Connectives that operate in unifications of Nature can be said to be "functionally real."

II

I want to push a little further what is implied in each of the two aspects of Nature emphasized: the fact that the world is encountered as *plural,* and the fact that it lends itself to *unifications* through the functioning of Connectives.

I start with the fact that Substance is radically plural. Substance, it will be recalled, is defined as "the encountered context, or situation," within which reflective experience can distinguish a variety of processes and structures. Substance is always encountered as specific and determinable, and this means as "relative"—relative to the direction or end the encountering itself generates. The field or situation can be extended indefinitely, as that end makes more and more of Nature relevant to itself. But we never reach or encounter "the ultimate field, context, or situation." We encounter only the field, situation, or context that is "ultimate for" that particular substance or situation.

This suggests certain further implications of the metaphysical pluralism here being explored—the Aristotelian pluralism of "determinate substances," expressed in the language of the philosophies of being, and the Deweyan pluralism of "specific situations," expressed in the language of the philosophies of experience. Every substance, every situation, every universe of action and experience—whatever name we choose to give the complex of cooperating processes that is encountered —is always encountered as something specific and determinable—as *a* substance, *a* situation, *a* universe of interaction. We never encounter *"the* Universe": we never act toward, experience, or feel being or existence as "a whole." Despite Santayana and others of like habit of speech, "pure being" seems to be pure bunk. Our encountered and experienced world is always selective and determinate. We can indeed *talk* significantly about "the Universe." But when we do, we are talking distributively, about *every* universe of action and experience, about *every* situation, substance, or field. We are not talking about some unified, all-embracing Substance or Field.

There is hence no discoverable "ultimate context," no "ultimate substance." There is only the widest context that is relevant to any particular activity, process, or specific cooperation of processes, and is hence "ultimate for" that cooperation. "Ultimate," that is, is always relative, never "absolute"; it is always "ultimate for." Talking, discourse, has the widest context of all: we can talk significantly of any or all universes of discourse, and these universes of discourse tend to become more and more unified in the talking. The only sense in which we can speak meaningfully of "the Universe" is as the widest "universe of discourse." But there is no discoverable "ultimate context" of discourse, save all the *other* contexts: there is no discoverable "context of contexts." In other words, Spinoza was wrong, and Kant was right: we can say nothing valid about "the Universe as a whole," or as a "totality," because we can never encounter or experience it as a whole or a totality, even in reflective experience. We possess no "adequate knowledge of the infinite and eternal essence of Nature." This may be called the "empirical principle": its fundamental character justifies calling this metaphysical pluralism an "empirical pluralism."

Hence "the Universe," or "Nature," is not "a process"—a single process—though any "universe of action and experience" is a complex of processes. Nor has "the Universe," or "Nature," any "meaning"—any single meaning—as a whole, save as the sheer *locus* of all processes, contexts, and meanings. Every process has a context or field of other cooperating processes, in terms of which it has a discoverable meaning—a "meaning *for*" that context. The "meaning" of any process is the way it functions in its context. What has no context can have no function, and hence no "meaning."

Now of course it is quite possible to take "the Universe" as a single process, with a single "meaning." Most of the greatest philosophies have done just this, to say nothing of a multitude of religious schemes. But when this is done, we find that we must then invent a further "context" for "the Universe," or Nature. We must go beyond metaphysics to *philosophical theology*. We can indeed thus generalize and unify our analysis of determinate processes, as many a philosopher and philosophic theologian has done. Finding, for instance, that every particular process is always directed toward a correlative objective or "stimulus" *external* to that process—*χωριστός*—in the context of other cooperating processes, we may then, with Aristotle, generalize that external objective or stimulus to be found in every determinate process, into an objective or stimulus—a unified "Unmoved Mover"—external to all determinate processes. Or, finding that every process is always conditioned by its context, we may then, with Spinoza, generalize that conditioning context of every determinate process into an "Unconditioned Conditioner" of all processes. Again, finding that every process has a "source" or "origin" in antecedent processes, we may then generalize that circumstance into a Source or Origin of all processes—into a "First Cause" antecedent to all "secondary causes."

But in terms of the empirical principle, apart from their function as unifying devices, there *is* no discoverable or implied Unmoved Mover, there *is* no Unconditioned Conditioner, there *is* no Source or Origin of "the Universe." Such generalizations of factors revealed by analysis in particular processes are "metaphysical myths." [2] They are logical constructions or extrapolations, like physical theories, and they possess similar functions. In their ontological status, they are what I have called unifying Connectives or "Conjunctions." Metaphysics can say nothing about "the Universe"; it can speak only of *any* "universe of interaction." It can say nothing about "the ultimate context" or "the ultimate field"; it can speak only of *any* context or field. This our philosophies of experience, from Kant down, have taught us. The attempt so to speak leads to the invention and employment of myths or Connectives.

Now, such myths are very far from being "meaningless." Like all Connectives, they have a perfectly definite function which can be objectively inquired into. They may well be basic in the living of human life, which often enough gets *its* "meaning" from their use—or rather, which uses them to find and express its "meaning." It may even be true that though "the Universe" has no meaning in terms of a context ex-

[2] See the classification of myths on p. 262.

ternal to itself, human life derives its meaning by making use of just such a "mythical" context—just such a metaphysical myth, or Connective. It may be true, as Woodbridge puts it, that though Nature has no "justification," man is "justified" by "the Supernatural"—that is, by the Ideal. The pursuit of knowledge, he maintains, does not and cannot take us beyond Nature; but the pursuit of happiness does. This may indeed be true: as Woodbridge puts it, the "judgment of the race" has maintained it. But nevertheless, Woodbridge insists, "it is faith, and not knowledge, that 'justifies.'" And no very intelligible meaning seems to be involved in saying that "the Supernatural" or "the Ideal" lies "outside Nature," or "outside history," as is often said by theologians nowadays. To be sure, "the Supernatural" certainly can be said to lie "outside" this or that particular human life, until it "comes into" it—in theological terms, until it "breaks through"—and it may well "extend beyond" all human life, and thus be "transcendent." All these ways of speaking seem to refer to facts that are familiar to those who have some sense of the religious dimension of experience.

But if this be indeed so, then "Nature" must find some secure place in her domain for "the Ideal," "the Transcendent," and even for "the Supernatural." Indeed, it is clear that any adequate philosophical "naturalism" must have room for all the genuine and obvious facts that such Connectives as "the Supernatural" have referred to; and in that sense, must find some place for "the Supernatural" itself.

Such myths or Connectives—of "the meaning" of "the Universe" in the mythical context of the Unmoved Mover, of the Unconditioned, of the Supernatural, of the Ideal, of God—are not, so long as metaphysics maintains the empirical principle, parts of metaphysical knowledge. Metaphysics can only inquire, What is implied in the fact that human life can employ them to give "meaning" to itself? How do they function to organize the values of existence? How is the actual unified in the light of the Ideal?

I am by no means suggesting that a wise philosophy will of necessity confine itself to what metaphysics can exhibit and denote, and will refuse to go on to "philosophical theology" and its myths. I have myself a great respect for philosophical theology—far more than most theologians today, who seem to have rejected it for an exclusive emphasis on kerygmatic theology. I find men today do not *know* nearly enough about God—not even those who talk of Him with the greatest familiarity. But philosophical theology is a different discipline from metaphysics. Metaphysics has nothing to say about "God" or "the Universe" as the "ultimate context" of existence. But it has much to say about the way such myths or Connectives function in the particular contexts of human living—about any "God," or any "universe as a whole." For such metaphysical myths or Connectives are factors encountered in Substance. They are "objective facts"; and what they do, how they work, what values they achieve, are likewise objective "facts." Myths and Connectives have a natural and objective function to perform in Nature's complex cooperation of processes. To function as a Connective, or a myth, is one of the fundamental ways in which natural processes can function.

III

This empirical pluralism, implied in the fact that what is encountered as Substance, as a situation or universe of action, is always encountered or experienced as specific and determinate—or determinable—even in reflective experience or discourse, does not deny the possibility or the value of the search for unification, so intimately bound up with the search for control, for the power of manipulation. I now wish to turn to the other aspect of Nature, to examine those unifications she brings about, and some of the ways in which they are achieved.

The demand for unification is impressive. It is persistent, and doubtless ineradicable. We have only to reflect on the tremendous kick the most unlikely men manage to get out of "Oneness" and "Unity." What do our hard-boiled and sceptical positivists today cherish above all other concerns? Nothing other than "Unity"—the unity of science. I am sure any good *Existenzphilosoph* could find this craving for "unity" and "integrity" rooted in "the human situation," springing from the disunities and "dialectical tensions" to which the contemporary German "soul" at least has fallen prey. Gilbert Murray has sought to explain it by another myth: he calls it "the groping of a lonely-souled gregarious animal to find its herd or its herd-leader." But however we attempt to account for the craving for unity, it seems to be a deeply-rooted human demand. Like James's "sentiment of rationality," which is indeed but a particular variant of it, it is a sentiment and a demand long before it is justified by any discovered facts.

Logically, of course, the demand for unification and unity is a colossal assumption. Consider the insistence that existence, what is encountered, be found somehow to be a system and order, despite the inexhaustible and ineradicable variety and individuality it exhibits. Man requires that existence exhibit a common set of principles and laws, as the very condition of being found "intelligible" to the human mind. When imposing philosophies, like those of Thomas or Kant, in the process of working out an adjustment between two different sets of beliefs which for historical reasons have come into conflict, arrive at a division between different sets of principles for different "realms" of experience, this neat partition always seems unsatisfactory, and inevitably proves unstable. In the next generation these two sets of principles are unified in a common system, in the thought of a Duns Scotus or a Hegel. When a Descartes—or a Kant—divides the world between the two realms of what his intellectual method can deal with, and what it cannot, that soon appears as a methodological inadequacy, and men like Spinoza and Leibniz—or the whole generation of post-Kantians—set to work to develop a more adequate method that will not clash with the required unity of knowledge. The great historic dualisms, based on the distinction between what a given method can handle and what it cannot—Platonic, Cartesian, or Kantian—always tend toward unification—even if only by making the latter the "appearance" or the "expression" of the former.

Or consider those unifications accomplished not through a logical system of principles, but through a temporal scheme of history. There are the great creation myths, which achieve unification through deriving existence from a common source and origin. There is that most imaginative of all temporal myths, the idea of "evolution." When we ask why it is that men have so often turned to history in their craving for unification, the answer seems clear. Time itself is indeed the great unifier. For historical understanding is always unified in the focus of the present or the future. Consider the power of the "Christian epic" and its unification of the world in the eschatological myth of the Last Judgment—or of its Marxian variant, the revolution that will produce the "classless society."

Then too there is the practical motive for unification, embodied in the demand for a unity of Nature that will sustain a continuity of method: the conviction so strong in our own Augustinian and Baconian tradition, that power and control will come from the universal application of the method that has proved successful within some particular field. There must be a universal method—the Platonic dialectic, the Cartesian mathematical interpretation of Nature, the Baconian induction—that will render men the masters and possessors of Nature. And so men pass lightly over the specific conditions of different subject-matters. Consider the many earnest attempts to carry over into human affairs the different methods developed in the successive stages of the enterprise of natural science, from the "geometrical method" of Spinoza in the seventeenth century to the statistical methods of our sociologists today, or the hypothetico-experimental method of Dewey. Or take the drive to make politics into a human engineering, to be treated by technological methods—despite the inadequacy of what has so far been achieved, in comparison with the continued power of the age-old political and religious methods for enlisting for what has to be done the cooperative support and action of men.

But though these various demands for unification rest upon faith rather than proof, it is a faith that has flowered in good works. That both understanding and power do come with increasing unification, is scarcely to be denied. To be sure, it never turns out to be quite so simple a matter as we assume, whether in our logical schemes of laws and principles, in our historical unifications through myths, or in our universalized methods. In the variety of Nature's riches, all these schemes inevitably leave out of account those traits and characters they are unable to handle. That is why they require constant and unremitting criticism, an ever-renewed confrontation with Substance encountered, with Nature in the raw, before she has been washed and brushed and tidied up, her hair done in the latest fashion and her nose carefully powdered. Ceaseless vigilance is the price of metaphysical adequacy.

And inevitably these schemes of unification demand the use of unifying Connectives of one sort or another—of myths and symbols, of logical constructions like physical theories, of philosophies of history, of social and political ideals. All these varied types of Connectives function to unify different substances and situations that are in fact encountered as plural and disparate. The "unity" of experience, or of the world, is not a simple discovery. It is rather a process—a *process of unification,* whose achievement demands a heavy reliance on Connectives—on myths, symbols, hypotheses, theories, ideals.

These unifications that Nature achieves in cooperation with man are clearly not "merely human"; above all, they are not "subjective," in that sense that divorces man from Nature and leaves him in splendid isolation in an alien world. To be sure, those unifications attained in vision and in knowledge all involve human cooperations with other natural operations. But it is not man alone—above all, it is not man descending from another realm and trailing clouds of glory—who connects and unifies and brings Nature to a focus in his transcendent lens. It is Nature herself, existence cooperating with men. These unifying Connectives, like the greatest of all, Discourse herself, and her noble daughter Mathematics, are factors in Substance, and function in interaction with other factors in its complex transactions. They are, as we have insisted, functionally real and objective. They may be conventional, but they are not arbitrary.

IV

In preliminary summary, then:

1) Nature is not a "unity"—of substances.

2) Nature is a *continuity*—of natural processes, making possible a continuity of analysis, of knowledge, and of scientific methods.

3) But Nature is not a continuity of ends or outcomes, in any sense that would obliterate encountered distinctions of value. Uniqueness and individuality are characteristic of Nature's productions. Nature exhibits a variety of "dimensions" in her achievements: she is not "one-dimensional"—though this is often said by those whose primary interest lies in realms of being that lie "beyond" Nature, and are thus in the literal sense "supernatural." Nature is rather "multi-dimensional": she possesses, and exhibits in her products and outcomes all those varied "dimensions" she is found to display.

This fact is sometimes expressed: Nature exhibits many different "levels." But this doctrine of "levels" has for the most part been captured by the supernaturalists, alas! who are concerned to deny the continuity of the mechanisms by means of which Nature effects her ends, and the consequent continuity of analysis, which has led to the triumphs of scientific inquiry. Here it is insisted that Nature exhibits different "levels" of ends and outcomes, and at the same time a continuity of means and mechanisms: the former is in no wise incompatible with the latter circumstance. The greatest conceivable difference in value between the ends of Nature's productivity sets no limits to the discovery of as much continuity as we can find between the mechanisms on which that production depends. There are no antecedent limits set to the experimental exploration of the structure of means.

This would seem not to be controversial. Yet in the same mail there were received two papers, controverting it from opposed positions. One was a defense, naive and revealing, of "materialism," by a college instructor. It ran, "Only matter exists"—that is, only means and mechanisms exist. "Love" and "beauty" do not "exist": they are "words only, for material states and situations." What is effected by mechanisms—activities, processes, outcomes, eventuations—these do not "exist." In the rendition of a violin sonata, all that can be said to "exist" is "the dragging of the tail of a dead horse across the entrails of a dead cat." Of course, the music is "delightful," it is "important," it may even be called "real"; and the author goes on to distinguish between "what exists in a simple location"—his criterion of "existence" —and "what is merely 'real.' "

In so far as this is not a mere quibble about the meaning of the term "exist," and an undue restriction of that meaning, this illustrates where one gets when one does not take activities and processes as primary and irreducible subject-matter. A sound metaphysics would say, activities, operations, and processes "exist," and are effected by means of mechanisms distinguished as factors involved in those processes. "Materialism" locates the means and mechanisms involved; then by reductive analysis, holds that *only* these mechanisms can be said to "exist"—what they *do* does not "exist," but is merely something else.

The other paper was a defense, likewise naive and revealing, of "dualism." It happened to be by another instructor at the same college: there has never been any unity of knowledge at this seat of learning. This paper ran: Because man acts in certain distinctive ways, not encountered as the ways of acting of any other being, and therefore distinctively human ways (the paper was defending the "Humanism" of Irving Babbitt) he must perform these acts by means of a mechanism specifically different from the continuity of mechanisms by which all other natural processes are effected. The argument runs: Man perceives universals, therefore man must "have" a "simple unextended immaterial spiritual principle" by means of which to do it. This argument starts with an activity, which *is* distinctive and of "unique" value, and then assumes a mechanism not only distinctive, like all specific mechanisms, but also unanalysable ("simple") and discontinuous with all other natural mechanisms. Where can such an argument stop? with a unique and discontinuous mechanism for each distinctive way of acting encountered in the world? The author, being a Catholic, goes on from what he calls "Dualistic Integral Humanism" to "Trialistic Supernaturalized Humanism": certain human activities demand a third unique mechanism, the "grace of God." And so on, *ad infinitum*.

Does Nature, in addition to this continuity of mechanisms, display also a continuity of genesis, as the early evolutionists believed? The last generation were much concerned to set forth how human experience, in all its manifold variety and complexity, might have "arisen" out of a pre-human and sub-human "experience," in the evolutionary process. Much indeed of the evolutionary emphasis is left over in the thought of those who, like Dewey, in their own lifetime fought through these intellectual battles of the Darwinian age.

Today, the question of the "genesis" of human experience out of lower forms has pretty much ceased to be a debatable issue. It is accepted on every hand as an undoubted fact; the details have become a problem for factual inquiry. But at the same time we have come to have grave doubts about the validity of the speculative anthropology in which our fathers so easily engaged—Dewey among the best of them! We realize we were not there when it all happened, and have doubts as to whether that prehistory can be recovered. And we have come to have even graver doubts of the explanatory value of such an account of the way in which our familiar experience "arose," even if we had accurate details. Our human problem, we have come to feel, is to understand things in terms of the way they function and operate now; that is at least something that is experimentally observable. The genetic problem of how things came to be as they are, is, after all, Nature's problem of Creation—or God's. Man's primary problem, our generation holds, is rather to understand the ways in which what is, however it may have been created, continues to operate and function.

When we approach this human problem, in sober truth, the structures distinguished in Substance by reflective experience, and formulated in discourse and knowledge, are found to be bound up with and involved in structures of other substances and situations. These relatednesses, this continuity of structure, can be explored and followed on indefinitely; and in such inquiry and discourse they tend to become more and more unified. In this process of exploration, we find structures that are not functions of any particular universe of action or any particular encountered complex of processes, but seem to be involved in all processes, in all actions and cooperations. These structures are found to be "invariant" throughout a great variety of contexts. They can hence be "isolated" from any particular context: they "transcend" the limitations of any determinate situation or substance. This fact makes them of fundamental importance for human knowledge and action. A knowledge of such structures proves to be of the widest instrumental value in all contexts. These "invariant" structures can be used, and must be conformed to, in *any* "universe of interaction," in *any* situation.

Expressing this fact as an experimental discovery, we may say, the exploration of the continuity of mechanisms by which Nature operates has led us to formulate those ways of operating in terms of physical and chemical laws. It would perhaps be more accurate to say, that those structures that are invariant through the widest diversity of contexts constitute a delimitation of the subject-matter of physico-chemical inquiry. We find also, of course, structures that obtain in more limited types of context, that possess a more limited range of invariance. And these structures are formulated as the "laws" of more restricted "fields," more limited ways of acting, in other sciences.

This encountered unification of structures of a certain type has suggested to many not only a factually verifiable continuity of processes in Nature, but also an eventual "unity" of discovered structure. Such a thoroughgoing unity of the objective of knowledge, making possible the eventual unification of knowledge into a single system, possesses great value as an ideal of knowledge and of formulated discourse—as what Kant calls a "regulative idea." It also unquestionably possesses great dangers, and conceals many pitfalls. Witness the "Unity" of the Neoplatonic dialectic, which came to be elevated above the subject-matter of which it was originally taken to be the "unity," and set over against it, making of what it was at first intended to organize a "mere appearance." Witness also the "Absolute" of the post-Kantians, like F. H. Bradley, and the many purely dialectical and hence completely unreal problems in which it involved its adherents.

We may, then, with due caution, envisage an eventual unification of structure. But the process of the encountered continual unification of structure does not suggest any "unity of substance"—even "eventually." This is not even a "regulative idea." Spinoza's use of the term "Substance" to designate the unified structure of the universe—the "Order of Nature"—is perverse and misleading—even when repeated in so good a pluralistic Aristotelian as Woodbridge.[3] To avoid obliterating a fundamental distinction, it is well to follow Aristotle on this basic point. "Substance," the subject-matter encountered in any universe of action, is *never* a comprehensive, all-embracing Unity, Whole, or Totality. It remains particular and τόδε τι.[4]

V

In conclusion, I should like to raise certain questions about one of the most characteristic ways in which Nature achieves unification—through cumulative temporal development, in the many *histories* she brings to pass. These unifications I find of peculiar interest. For when man cooperates with other natural processes to push further Nature's temporal unifications in the unifying focus of his own history, he and Nature find themselves compelled to employ that particular variety of Connective we call in the more precise sense "myths." The way in which Nature achieves unification through the operation of "myths" has been far less explored than the way she gains it through logical constructions and mathematical theories.

[3] See F. J. E. Woodbridge, *Nature and Mind* (New York, 1937), "Structure," pp. 148–59.

[4] For a fuller treatment of unities in knowledge, see Epilogue, "Unifications of Knowledge."

Now the "history" of anything—the history that thing possesses as the outcome of its fortunes among the other impinging processes of Nature, the "history" that historical knowledge attempts to understand, not the "history" that is that understanding itself—is the significant or relevant past of that thing, the past that is relevant for what it now is. A thing's history is those processes and events that have contributed to its being, gathered into a focus in the present.[5]

Nature is full of such temporal "gatherings into a focus," such "historical unifications," such cumulative outcomes and achievements. Galaxies and stars, mountain-ranges and forests, as well as human societies, institutions, and ideas, are all what they are because of their respective pasts. They are "concretions" and "cumulative conservations" of the cooperations of processes into which they have previously entered. If Nature were in truth mere "flux," if she did not exhibit countless patterns of historical unification, and hosts of teleological structures of means and eventuations with a temporal spread, then human histories would indeed be wholly anomalous. Men's unification of their own history, their discovery of the significance of their own past, through knowledge or vision, would be quite impossible. So likewise would be any discovery of "the meaning" of the world, or of human life.

But Nature being what she inescapably is, such human unifications in knowledge or vision are but a pushing further of Nature's own unifying powers. So important is this ability of men to extend further the cumulative unifications of Nature that, in order to be emphatic about it, some have said that this power of man to understand his own history "transcends Nature"—forgetting that it is a fundamental character of Nature to be forever "transcending" herself, to be productive, and creative of new outcomes—nowhere more clearly than in her human parts.

When men bring Nature to a focus in the discovered "meaning" of human history, the past becomes unified in the perspective of the present, and is understood as leading up to our own goings on, to our own ideas and problems. Such a temporal unification of the life of man in Nature we usually call a "philosophy of history." These attempts to find an interpretation of "history as a whole" involve an

[5] See pp. 35–36.

appraisal of the present in the light of the future it suggests. They interpret the past, whose deposit constitutes our resources, in terms of the envisaged future. The nature of the world and of human societies is such as to generate philosophies of history.

A philosophy of history attempting to construe history "as a whole" thus involves two kinds of unification. History can be unified in terms of its materials and resources, of the significant past; and it can also be unified in terms of its envisaged future. Thus philosophies of history normally employ two somewhat different kinds of unifying Connectives or myths: myths of origin and myths of outcome, creation myths and eschatological myths. The origin myths serve primarily to reveal the character of the materials of history: the nature of men and their behavior, or the nature of those groups that play the role of dramatic protagonists in history—races, nations, or classes. Thus we are led to see history whole in terms of the fall of man, or of the state of nature, or of primitive communism. For centuries we could not understand our history except as beginning in a "state of nature." Today we are more apt to call it "primitive society," and to go to anthropology to find the significance of the history of our own institutions. When the Germans used to do it, and discoursed passionately of blonde beasts, we smiled—or swore—according to the degree of our philosophical resignation. When we do it ourselves, and dwell upon the Kwakiutls, the Bushmen, the Andaman Islanders, and coming of age in Samoa, we are sometimes convinced that in drawing upon the anthropologists for an understanding of our own history, we are being very "scientific" indeed.

In their purest form these origin myths describe the emergence of human nature from non-human nature. When we used to consider man a fallen angel, the meaning of human history depended on the history and fall of the angels. Now that we are inclined to look on him rather as a great ape that has almost made good, the meaning of human history clearly depends on the history of the success-story of the great apes—on the history of the "evolution of mankind." These pre-human histories are wonderfully illuminating—in both cases, that of the angels and that of the apes. The only problem is how this "pre-history" can be so illuminating, since we know hardly anything about it: our actual knowledge of the history of the apes is about as sketchy as that of the angels. Human history as a whole, clearly, seems to take on a meaning only when we view it as springing full-blown out of an antecedent myth.

On the other hand, a philosophy of history can also achieve its unification by considering the present in terms of the possible future, of the ends implicit in it, and the means to their attainment. It is selective in its focus: it involves a choice among the determinate possibilities of the present of that "tendency," or predicted future, which we judge to be "dynamic" or "controlling." This choice of focus involves a choice of allegiance, a faith—the faith that the future will display a certain character. Normally again this faith in one kind of outcome is expressed in terms of a myth—the millennium, the kingdom of God, the classless society, or the triumph of social intelligence.

Both origin myths and outcome myths are instruments for unifying our history, for bringing it to a focus from which it can be understood as a whole, and can reveal its significance and meaning. The actual way these myths function is very complex, and demands careful exploration. The two kinds seem to operate rather differently, yet both are clearly involved in historical unifications. There seems to be no discoverable "meaning of history as a whole" without some outcome myth—without some "ideal," which is another name we give to such Connectives. We can no more find the significance of "history as a whole" without an ideal than we can find the significance of life—or of the world—without one. History would then indeed be as meaningless and futile as would life, a meaningless "flux."

But history, life, or Nature herself is a "flux" only to ignorance. Each is full of implicit ends or ideals, full of values, because each alike is an affair of processes, of mechanisms producing outcomes, of causes and necessary conditions of results, of means and ends. They are all alike full, that is, of things that are "better" and "worse" for other things. Nature is in truth teeming with "entelechies"; and it takes but a single flower to refute the absurd contention that there are no "values" in Nature, no achievement of ends through valuable means. We can even say that it is obviously "good for" the planet to go round and round.

Of course, neither the flower nor the planet can be said to "find" it good: in our experience, only men "find" anything. But surely it does not follow that because only men find anything, what they find is not found. The finding is a genuine cooperation of men with Nature. Ideal Connectives are not "fictions," not "imaginary" or "arbitrary." They are as "natural," as "objective," as any other way in which existence functions in Substance. They all, to be sure, involve human cooperations with other natural operations. Without man's activities, they would remain as powers of Substance. But it is not man alone who connects and unifies: it is existence cooperating with men. And the powers of existence to connect and be connected, to unify and become unified in vision, are essential to the character of existence.

Of course, it is the significance of *our* history *for us* that we discover through the unifying foci of myths or ideals—just as it is the meaning of the world for us that any Connective can generate. A star might well find a different meaning—or a being from Mars. However, there is no evidence that stars find anything significant; and if there be Martians, their philosophies remain unknown. But the fact that we must understand Nature from a human focus is not only a fact about human understanding—and, since human understanding is the only one we know of, a fact about all understanding; it is also a fact about Nature. Nature is brought to a selective unification only in a focus, an ideal, that Nature has herself generated in revealing her possibilities to men. Likewise, the fact that we must understand our history in the light of a selective unification, an outcome myth, that history has itself generated, does not mean that we cannot understand it.

We can understand it best, in the degree to which the suggested focus or outcome is based on knowledge—in which it unifies what we are, what we are doing, and what we still can and must do. It is sometimes said that the ideal which reveals the significance of our history must itself stand "outside history." What this means seems clear: it must be a genuine ideal. But unless that ideal stands at the same time "inside history"—unless it is *our* ideal, rooted in what we are and in what we can become, and relevant to our problems—it will not give us a genuine understanding, or reveal the significance and pattern of our history. Nature, and history, can achieve genuine unification only through Connectives and myths which, though they be conventional, are nevertheless not arbitrary, but are rooted in the very nature of things.

If we start with the world as a *unity,* it is impossible to get from that unity to the encountered plurality of things, which remains therefore a mystery. Only God has been able to turn that trick, and he has not revealed how he has done it: human theologians have never been able to explain the process, not even the evolutionists. But if we start with the encountered plurality, there is nothing to prevent us from tracing as much of *unification* as we may. Such unity as has been achieved, in our vision or in our knowledge, is the outcome of our processes of unification.

CHAPTER 8

Ways of Construing Mind and Intelligibility

IT HAS BECOME THE FASHION in metaphysical analysis to treat man's reflective experience in terms of "Mind." I am not myself at all sure that as a metaphysical term "Mind" is very satisfactory. It has acquired through hard usage and gross abuse a whole cluster of connotations which are almost impossible to put aside. It has become pretty inextricably bound up with the ontological dualism and supernaturalism —what Dewey calls the "extra-naturalism"—of modern philosophy, so that the very term awakens memories of the old saw, "What is Matter? Never Mind! What is Mind? No Matter!" I should myself be most happy to join iconoclasts like the Positivists, if they would only propose that we all forthwith resolve to lose our "minds." We were all doubtless better off were "Mind" abolished, as James destroyed "consciousness"—we could then get on with really important problems. Those of us who would thus lose the major portion of our stock in trade, would really be in an improved position, were we forced to establish our philosophic credit anew in order to secure further intellectual capital. The alternative to continuing business at the old stand with the very shopworn concept of "Mind" is, *Cherchez le verbe!*—find the activity or operation which "Mind" has been traditionally used to account for.

Moreover, "Mind" is bound up also with the provincialism of a single philosophical tradition—or, as I like to put it, a single philosophical "language"—the very insular thought of the British, whose philosophical journal is most appropriately entitled *Mind.* I remember the amazement I once created quite unintentionally, when I remarked casually that Brand Blanshard is the American representative of *Mind*—a state-

---

This chapter draws on material appearing in "A Note on Mr. Sheldon's Mind," *Journal of Philosophy,* XLIII (1946), 209–14.

ment I am sure Mr. Blanshard would himself endorse, in every sense of the term. The words which express the ultimate conceptions of the intellectual life in any language are literally untranslatable into any other—they concentrate in themselves the essence of an entire culture. There is the "Mind" of the British, the *Geist* of the Germans, the *Nous* of the Greeks, the *Intellectus* of the Latin schoolmen, the *Raison* of the French—they defy mutual translatability. The analogous American term is obviously "Intelligence," whose meaning is certainly complex, but at the same time is clearly the most functional of all, the hardest to hypostatize, or to convert into a "thing," a "substance." To be sure, the early intelligence testers did a pretty good job of hypostatizing. They made their "intelligence" a fixed thing, a "simple substance" with inherent properties, the same in every context—that is, something quite non-relational. And it took some little time to get over their aberrations.

Like most things Greek, *Nous* is far preferable to "Mind," especially in its Aristotelian interpretation as the "rational psyche" or "life," the "Life of Reason," or "life lived on the reflective level." In Aristotle, Νοῦς is a δύναμις or "power;" that is, like all "powers," it is construed completely in terms of what it does, of how it operates—it is defined wholly in functional terms.

Formally considered, all these ultimate terms for dealing with the intellectual life are "nouns"—that is, metaphysically speaking, they are all "powers," powers to act in certain specific and determinable ways. Thus, when pushed to their source in our experience of the world, they all become ultimately "adverbs"—that is, they designate "ways of acting." This functional conception is probably best expressed in the American term "Intelligence," which means the power of "operating intelligently," or even, if you prefer, "operating intellectually," functioning "as Mind," or functioning "cognitively."

But, as in the case of all these ways of operating, that adverb is translatable into all the other ontological types of functioning. Traditionally, "Mind" has been taken as 1) inherently a noun, a "thing" or "substance"—an "immaterial substance." Thus has it long been construed in the traditions of the Neoplatonists, the Thomists, and the Cartesians. Again, "Mind" has been taken as 2) inherently an adjective, as a certain kind of power, as a distinctive quality. This view has been characteristic of the British tradition, in which Mind has been interpreted as "being conscious," which becomes, when translated into a noun, "consciousness." This view appears in Russell, and on a large scale in Alexander. There is likewise a notorious British flavor in Santayana. For him, "consciousness" is "the rainbow on the fountain," a characteristic "quality." "Spirit," Santayana's most recent term for this intellectual "quality," is "the inner light of actuality or attention," a "spiritual quality," the "product of combustion," a "leaping flame," a "mirror reflecting the perspectives of nature," a "character" which "psyches" take on. For Santayana the "psyche" is a thoroughly functional conception: it is a power, a tendency of the organism to act. And formally considered "spirit" must also be for him in the last analysis a functional conception. As always in the later "Realms of Being," the difficulties lie in Santayana's sharp separation of functions—in his "realminess." Finally, "Mind" has also long been taken as 3) inherently a conjunction, or a relatedness—as in the Averroists, in Spinoza, in T. H. Green, and recently in Whitehead.

Now, I submit, each of these ways of construing the fact of "Mind"—like the nine and forty ways of writing tribal lays—is "right." There is a sense in which Mind can be construed as each of these ontological functions—especially if the others be not denied, and if the possibility of alternative construings be not forgotten. Each of these several ways has its own advantages: it was devised to deal with particular facts and problems of man's reflective experience, and it is naturally best fitted for treating the particular problems it originally undertook to treat. Each, likewise, has its own disadvantages—it confronts its own particular dilemmas and difficulties. If each of these various ways of construing Mind were worked out to take account of all the facts of man's reflective experience, honestly and without bias, the various ways would be mutually translatable. Historically, I think, it can be established that this goal of intertranslatability has been at least approached. A candid thinker must therefore admit that they all have explanatory possibilities, especially if each does not neglect or minimize the facts which the others were elaborated to illuminate—a neglect which in practice, to be sure, each way of construing tends to do.

I

Of these five ways of construing Mind, to take it as an "immaterial substance" seems, on the basis of an experience extending in the Western tradition over several millennia, to have now become the least fruitful. That is, it has already had full opportunity to bring to bear all the illumination it can throw on the familiar facts. On the other hand, to take Mind as "acting intelligently" seems to possess the greatest suggestiveness, and to point to the greatest possibility of discovering fresh facts about the intellectual life. To be sure, to construe Mind as an "immaterial substance" is no less fruitful than the corresponding construing of the mechanisms by which processes are effected as "material substances." But both construings seem at this late date to have largely exhausted their explanatory possibilities; and hence metaphysical inquiry today has preferred to abandon both of these traditional conceptions.

Just why does it not seem to present-day metaphysicians very fruitful to continue these traditional construings of Mind as an "immaterial substance"? I would emphasize three major reasons. In the first place, to take "Mind" as an immaterial substance, or even, as many metaphysicians preferred in the last century, to take it as "mental processes," meaning thereby processes so unique and so discontinuous and cut off from other natural processes that they demand a wholly unique mechanism for their performance, is to introduce a principle of explanation which, if followed out consistently and carried to its logical conclusion, would destroy all possibility of explanation at all, would destroy all intelligibility.

Ontological "dualism" illustrates this logical shortcoming beautifully. Because man acts in certain distinctive ways, it holds, not encountered as the ways of acting of any other being—because he acts in certain distinctively "human" ways—he must necessarily act *by means of* a mechanism specifically different from the continuity of mechanisms by which all other natural processes are effected. The classic argument runs: man perceives universals; therefore man must "have" or "possess" a "simple unextended immaterial spiritual principle" *with which* to do it! [1]

[1] See Chapter 9, Section II, on Universals.

The argument starts with an activity, which *is* distinctive of man, and certainly of unique value. It goes on to assume a "mechanism" for accomplishing this activity which is not only "distinctive," like all mechanisms, but also "unanalysable" (or "simple"), and discontinuous with all the other mechanisms found to be involved as the necessary conditions of natural processes. If this principle of explanation be adopted, where are we to stop? With a unique mechanism for every distinctive way of acting? What would be left of our science should we really follow out this principle consistently? Every distinguishable process of Nature would then have to be accomplished by a principle unique and proper to itself. Imagine the task and the countenance of physics, had Nature been really so constituted that each of her distinguishable productions required a specifically different mechanism as its necessary condition!

In the second place, to construe "Mind" as an immaterial substance seems to convert the operation of a "power" into its own mechanism and conditions. In setting up a unique mechanism for the operations of "Mind," we seem to be closing all further inquiry into the complex conditions under which these operations are actually found to occur. To attribute the facts of "Mind" to a unique mechanism obscures the search for the various complicated means and conditions involved in "functioning intelligently," or "cognitively." Of an "immaterial substance," even if conceived as "mental processes," we can examine only what it does, its specific mode of behavior. We are cut off by the dirty adjective from the possibility of exploring the complex *means,* both material and non-material, *by which* such a "mind" performs these functions. We are tempted to locate all the means involved somehow within that "immaterial substance" or "mental realm." Such a construing is strictly analogous to Molière's satirical example of trying to "explain" the observed action of opium upon the human organism as due to its "dormitive powers." To explain the operations of "acting intelligently" in terms of a "mind" construed merely as the "power" so to act, is to remain with a mere statement of the observed facts, without attempting any further analysis of the complex mechanisms involved. It is a resting content with the "fact that," without attempting to go on to investigate the "reason why."

In consequence, and thirdly, to construe "Mind" as a unique kind of substance, as a "noun," is to make these conditioning factors wholly private and inaccessible, and to remove them from the possibility of any scientific investigation and analysis. It obscures all the cultural and environmental factors which are in reality necessary conditions of any "functioning mentally." The explanatory possibilities of an alternative approach to the facts of "Mind," which would take "functioning intelligently" as a publicly observable form of human behavior, will emerge in our subsequent analysis. We are at this point anxious primarily to set forth the limitations of the essentially "private" and "subjective" construing of the facts of intellectual experience.

II

Metaphysically speaking, then, Mind can be construed in five major ways, in terms of each of the five types of ontological functioning it has here been attempted to distinguish.[2] Mind can be taken as a "power" or as an "operation," as a specific "kind" of power or as a specific "way" of operating, or as a "Connective." That is, it can be designated fundamentally by a "noun" or a "verb," by an "adjective" or an "adverb," or by a "conjunction."

Whichever of these five ways of construing Mind we choose to adopt, there are two major reminders it would be well to emphasize—reminders not to forget the outcome of the general metaphysical analysis of these ways of functioning in Substance when we come to analyse this particular instance, "Substance functioning mentally"—or, in the alternative terminology of the philosophies of experience, "the mental situation," the situation in which "Mind" is involved as a factor.

In the first place, if we take Mind as a "power" to act in certain ways, we must not forget that, like all powers, Mind is a power exhibited not by a single factor in Substance taken by itself, but by Substance or the Situation as a whole. It is a power exhibited by the complex cooperation of processes to be found in some determinate situations. Mind is thus not a power possessed and displayed by a particular physical organism taken alone and in isolation. It is not a power that belongs to one distinctive instrument or mechanism involved in "functioning mentally," the particular human organism that is said "to think." Mind as we encounter it in "the mental situation" is rather

[2] See Chapter 6, Section VI.

a complex set of powers of cooperating in that mental functioning. It involves a variety of factors, mechanisms, or necessary conditions in the "mental situation" in which it occurs. To concentrate solely on the "agent" or active mechanism involved in thinking, on the human thinker, leads to the neglect of the other necessary conditions present in the thinking situation, and obscures the continuity between the process of thinking and other natural processes.

Mind can be said, in Santayana's phrase, "to inhabit particular animal bodies" only as one specific power, or, more precisely, as one set of powers, distinguished in terms of a specific mechanism, the "animal body," from other specific powers of the environment and of the materials of thinking. To function itself as a power, Mind demands the presence of these other powers. Strictly speaking, Mind in this personal sense is a power, not of operating, but of *co*operating with other powers. Mind is thus, like all powers, a relational power. How it will operate depends on the operation of the other powers in the Situation, and on the way in which this power of the organism cooperates with them.

Hence, if we take Mind as a power to act in certain ways, we must not forget that this power belongs to what is encountered as well as to the encounterer, the so-called human "agent" in thinking. Strictly speaking, and in the full sense, Mind as a power belongs to the *process* of encountering, to the process which includes the cooperation of all the various factors involved as necessary conditions in the mental situation. We can indeed *encounter* Mind as a power exhibited by the agent, the "animal body" or human organism, taken as the locus of the "active powers" involved. But we cannot hope to *understand* Mind if we take it in isolation from all the other manifold powers and conditions involved in the thinking situation.

Consequently, the question, "What is it that thinks?" becomes the question, "What are the different powers that cooperate in the process of thinking?" And this latter question in turn becomes, in terms of our analysis, a practical question relevant to the particular problem under investigation. Is it the brain that thinks, the nervous system, or the organism as a whole? All are powers necessary for the cooperation that is thinking: all are necessary instruments or mechanisms involved in any case of actual thinking, in that no thinking can take place without them. But they are far from being the only necessary factors or powers. There are also required all those cultural and environmental factors which are equally necessary conditions of any "mental situation," of any case of "functioning mentally." Brains, nervous systems, the body as a whole, and all such "material" mechanisms located *within* the organism are far from being the only instruments necessary for the occurrence of thinking. Equally necessary are such public, extra-personal, and "immaterial" instruments as language, previous experience with a world, and the intelligible structure of some subject-matter. Here belong all those impersonal cultural factors which Hegel treats as *Objektiver Geist,* and which the anthropologists call "institutionalized behavior" and "culture patterns."

Metaphysically considered, it is really just as accurate to say, for example, that "discourse thinks," or that "language thinks," *in* individual men, as it is to say that a particular brain thinks, as the materialist would have it. Both ways of putting the matter are inadequate and incomplete, because each singles out but one necessary condition or power involved in the thinking situation. There is indeed more justification for the former locution, for language or discourse is clearly the "active power" in thinking. To be consistent with his own analysis, to say nothing of coming to terms with our present-day knowledge, Aristotle should have identified his "active intellect" with "logos," discourse or language—not with the Divine Logos, like the Augustinians, but with human logos, or communication—though the Augustinians were right in making logos extra-personal. Discourse is certainly far more manipulable than any of the other factors involved in thinking, which is the conclusive test for the locus of an "active power." More precisely, thinking is a process that occurs *by means of* brains, language, subject-matters, and a host of other varied factors to which the harsh distinction between "physical" and "mental" seems rather irrelevant. To conceive Mind functionally, as a certain way of behaving which Substance exhibits under determinate conditions, when it is functioning in a "mental situation," has the advantage of directing attention to *all* these necessary conditions and Powers.

In this connection it is interesting to quote one of those yellow-paper notes Woodbridge was always making: this one is evidently upon a contention advanced by William R. Dennes.

It is well to describe the mental as activity, and as an activity not describable in terms of its field. The agent of the activity should now be identified, and some attention given to the discrimination of his activities. What difference is there then between attention, discrimination with its consequences, and "the activity of interpreting"? Why not say "thinking" at once and be done with it? But thinking is barren without something to think about, and with something to think about it is wayward. What controls or constrains its waywardness? Things thought about, seems to be the answer. If we now ask, how do they do it? what is the answer? Is the answer a discovery about thinking, or about them?

Woodbridge's own reply is clearly, the latter. But in terms of the present analysis the reply is obviously, it is a discovery about both.

Ultimately, we can say that it is "the Situation" that thinks, the determinate "Substance" that thinks. As Dewey puts it, what is primary is the fact that "It thinks," "It experiences"—i.e., there *is* thinking, there *is* experiencing. This is the basis of his attack on the absolutizing of the "subject-object distinction," of his contention that this distinction is not primary but derivative, and is a practical distinction that arises *in* process, *in* the thinking situation. Such a view, of course, is also wholly traditional, though it has not always been embraced by orthodoxy. Thus Aristotle always says that an "art" acts by means of the artist; and Spinoza puts it, that the universe itself thinks *in* men, and *by means of* men—a position that is clearly metaphysically sound. The Averroism of my position—and Spinoza's—will not escape the medievalist.

Of course, the thinking of the Situation—or more broadly, of the world—can *become individualized*—though this hardly occurs as frequently as we usually flatter ourselves it does. It is then in a genuine sense "we" who think. But this "we"—like any case of individualization, or of personalization in general—becomes itself a process, an operation. "We," "I," or "the Self," is thus ultimately a "verb": individuality and personality are really past participles, achievements that *have been brought about.* "The Self" appears as "Substance *individualized";* a "person" as "Substance *personalized.*" This view can be pushed into an analysis of "the moral situation," or "functioning morally." The implications are suggestive.

So far it has been emphasized that Mind taken as a power must be a power exhibited by the Situation or Substance as a whole. The *second* reminder is that this holds also of Mind taken rather as an activity, an operation—as a "verb." Mind considered as an operation must likewise be the operation of "Substance" or "the Situation as a whole," not solely an activity of the agent of thinking taken alone. And whatever the agent of thinking, the particular human organism, actually does in the transaction that is thinking, all his activities and procedures have a definite locus in Substance and its cooperation of processes. His intellectual activities, therefore, are all as "real" and as "objective" as any of the other processes involved in the cooperation of thinking.

In considering Mind as a power, we usually tend to overlook all those powers whose locus is not clearly in the agent of thinking, the organism itself. In considering Mind as an operation, as "functioning intelligently" or "cognitively," we tend rather to minimize the activities of the agent, and to regard them as "subjective," with no real place in the cognitive situation. But the activities of the so-called "subject" are clearly as "real," as "objective," as any of the other processes involved in the total cooperation. They have just as valid a claim to a legitimate ontological status in Substance. This holds for all the operations of inquiry and investigation, with their structures or "forms"—as it holds for all the operations of language, and for those of measurement—as it holds, in fact, for all the operations and functionings of Connectives in general. Connectives all have a status in Substance that is "functionally real," "real" as functioning.

Those activities of the agent of thinking, the "knower," that are involved in all his cognitive functionings, are taken by non-functional or purely "structural" epistemological "realists," like G. E. Moore, Samuel Alexander, Whitehead, and William Pepperell Montague, as "psychic additions," in Whitehead's phrase, and as somehow epistemologically illegitimate. They really ought not to be there. At best they are a kind of scaffolding, to be discreetly cleared away when the inquiry or the knowing is completed. On such a view, "knowing" is not really an activity or an operation at all; far less can it be construed as an *art* of interpretation, in which something novel is *made* out of some material, as on Dewey's view. I remember Moore's once expressing surprise that correct English usage should speak of an "act" of perception, when there is so obviously nothing "active" about that "relation" at all! Being quite innocent historically, Moore did not realize that an *actus perceptionis* is a specific actualization of the "power *to be acted upon*" by sensible forms.

Such non-functional realists hence try to minimize any "activity" of Mind in the process of knowing. They endeavor to reduce Mind to the pure *relation* of "cognition," somehow obtaining between a passive "knower" and the world. They must hence necessarily plaster upon the world's countenance itself all those structures, like simultaneously alternative time-series, which theories of Mind as an activity and operation are able to locate within the processes of thinking itself. The classic recent illustration is Whitehead. For him thinking becomes a kind of spatio-temporal "perspective" upon the complex structures and "propositions" inhabiting a realm of Eternal Objects.

In sober truth, there seems no compelling reason to take these activities of the agent of thinking, or of functioning intelligently—all the manifold employment of Connectives, like mathematics, scientific theories, hypotheses, or language itself—as in any sense illicit. They seem rather to be integral functions encountered in the "thinking" or "mental situation." They are all, to be sure, "additions" to that Situation, in the sense that the operation of any power of Substance is an "addition" to its non-operation. They can be said to "emerge" in the cooperation of Powers—to "accrue" to the situation with the occurrence of "new interactions," as Dewey puts it. But they are not "psychic" additions, in the sense that they are located *in* some "psyche" which is itself shut up *within* an organism—or *within* a brain, as I believe Hobbes, Russell, and Montague rather curiously hold. Such Connectives are not "subjective"—in the sense that they have a different and unique ontological status. Though their functioning involves men as its mechanism, they are not "merely" human. They are certainly not "psychic" in the sense of being inaccessible and inherently "private," wholly closed to public inquiry. There is, for instance, obviously nothing "private" about such Connectives as mathematics, language, or physical theory.

This holds likewise for *all* the operations of Mind in reflective experience, for the functioning of non-cognitive as well as of cognitive Connectives. These non-cognitive intellectual operations also have a perfectly "objective" status in the mental situation. They are, to be sure, often taken as "expressing feelings," conceived as something "private" and "subjective," with all that conventionally entails. Thus the operations of the process of "evaluation" in "mental situations" are often treated as the "expression of subjective feelings," to the subversion of all sound metaphysics! And the various arts are often said to use their non-cognitive "systems of symbols" or "languages" to "express human experience," taken as something "subjectively" conceived, in contrast with the employment of cognitive symbol-systems to express "statements of fact"—the particular erroneous distinction I find in Susanne Langer. Actually, there is no reason to suspect that scientific Connectives—or languages and symbol-systems—enjoy any different ontological status from poetic and religious Connectives. Both function "objectively" in Substance, and use, for their quite distinctive purposes, objective relations and qualities of Substance. The specific functions of scientific Connectives undoubtedly differ from those of poetic and religious Connectives. Their operations are undoubtedly distinctive, as are the specific factors they select from Substance to "connect" and unify, and the way they manipulate their selected materials. But *for* the situation in which they are functioning, their ontological status is perfectly objective.

For the practical purposes of some particular inquiry, these activities of the agent in the mental situation may be said to have a distinguishable locus *in* the agent. Certainly it is *through* the agent that they are subject to manipulation, which is the test of primary location. And some traits of these activities may be said to be "private" or even "subjective." The distinction between "private" and "public" is undoubtedly far superior to the older one between "subjective" and "objective." The latter is misleading and non-functional, and is so bound up with traditional metaphysical and epistemological confusions that it would probably be highly advisable to abolish it entirely. If we are unable to resort to this saving clarification in our thinking, it is at least important to recognize that "subjective" is always a practical distinction in a specific situation. Ultimately, what is so distinguished as "subjective" has an "objective" locus in Substance. There is nothing that is ultimately "subjective." Or, to put it differently, "subjectivity" is a certain distinctive way of functioning, not a unique kind of material.

With his usual inimitable clarity, Ernest Nagel gives a suggestive statement of the "objective" character of the activities of the agent in the thinking situation. He is writing of Dewey's conception of the status of logical principles and forms—a view its author, to put it mildly, for the Department of Understatement, did not always express with Mr. Nagel's precision.

> This way of looking upon the matter represents a self-conscious attempt to steer a median course between an empiricism for which logical traits are psychological, in the sense of being mental, and a realism for which logic sets a priori limits upon the characters of existence. Dewey's conception of logic thus offers the alternative hypothesis, according to which logical forms are not mentalistic, and yet are traits of things (that is, modes of [their] behavior) only when things are caught up in reflective inquiry and are subjected to the conditions required for inference. . . .
>
> It must, however, be noted that while logical principles are not formulations of relations between things independently of their occurrence in inquiry, they are not arbitrary rules. On Dewey's view, what the conditions are for satisfactory inquiry is a discovery about them, and is as much a discovery as that the human body needs food to survive or that sound requires a material medium for its transmission. In general, therefore, logical principles are just one special class of formulations which state the conditions or means for the attainment of ends or consequences. If the notion of logical principles as instruments or tools is taken seriously, their adequacy must evidently be contingent upon the character of the materials upon which they are employed and upon the objectives they are to attain; and there is no way of discovering whether they are indeed adequate until we have made the attempt to use them. Dewey is thus in agreement with all those who have maintained (sometimes in criticism of what they take to be his position) that in some sense principles of inquiry are grounded in the nature of things. They are, for him, grounded in the requirements of controlled inquiries, which are manifestly matters of existence. But one must add that just as wood-pulp is not paper, and is potentially paper only in relation to determinate chemical transformations, so a segment of existence is not intrinsically evidence or datum, and it possesses such logical functions only in relation to the equally determinate operations of controlled inquiry.[3]

[3] *The Philosopher of the Common Man,* ed. S. Ratner (New York, 1940), "Dewey's Reconstruction of Logical Theory," p. 74. Quotation used by permission of G. P. Putnam's Sons.

III

Mind can be construed most adequately and comprehensively, as an adverb, as a certain way of operating or functioning, as a distinctive kind of process; that is, as a certain way operations exhibit of cooperating with each other, when a Substance or a Situation is functioning "mentally" or "intelligently."

Now, what way of operating is "operating mentally"? Or, if we take Mind as the power to act in certain distinctive ways, what ways are they? I wish now primarily to raise some problems concerning the discrimination and identification of "Mind."

Is "Mind" exhibited in all cases of "awareness," of "attention," of acting "consciously"? Is it present whenever that quality or adjective can be said to be present?—granted, that every case of Mind does exhibit that quality. This latter contention is of course often denied today, in theories which make much use of the conception of an "unconscious mind." Whatever the disadvantages of this notion, it has at least the advantage of taking "Mind" as something other than mere "awareness."

Now, "unconscious mind" seems to be a speculative hypothesis invented to account for what *is* publicly observable, "overt behavior"—including speech. That is, "unconscious mind" is a "myth"—metaphysically, a Connective. I am not much impressed by the arguments that it is a good one. At any rate, though the term may designate a Connective in the procedure of the psychologist trying to understand overt behavior, a factor in the "knowing situation," in "behavior known," it does not seem to designate a factor in behavior occurring without the attempt to understand and explain it—though it may well designate the problem of locating the specific factors involved in the complex mechanism by which such behavior operates. It may, for example, point to previous experience, to the past of that mechanism continuing to operate in the present.

Is "Mind," then, to be identified with all cases of "awareness"? The question can be put in two ways, according as we take "awareness" as a *quality,* or as a *way of behaving*. In the second construing, "awareness" becomes identical with selective response, with having a "concern with," or with "feeling" in Whitehead's sense. But selective response as a way of behaving is far too inclusive to serve as a distinguishing trait of what we would normally call "mental behavior." Every cooperation or interacting of processes is really a case of selective response. It is a reaction to the stimulus of a characteristic way of operating, and is itself a characteristic way of responding, capable of being provoked by a variety of stimuli, all of which are instances of a common way of acting. Thus the sun melts wax. So does fire, electricity, friction, etc. The "melting" is a selective "way" of reacting, when the particular operation—of the sun, fire, electricity, frictional force, etc.—is functioning as an instance of a way, "heating." [4]

"Awareness" as an adverb, as a distinctive *way* of responding, thus seems to be exhibited to some extent in every cooperation of processes. We can arrange processes in a scale of increasing selectivity and specificity of response, as we find them in Whitehead, in objective idealism, in Plotinus—and in every form of naturalism. But though we may arbitrarily assign "awareness" to a certain stage of this scale—with Whitehead, for instance, to the prehension of the negative judgment —we have here really no sure basis of discrimination.

This throws us back on the first way of construing "awareness," as an immediate quality. As such, "awareness" is not publicly observable; it is something I can encounter only in my own personal experience, and hence it is not subject to inquiry. This quality is discovered in other men through language—through their reports; and the difficulty of communicating such immediate qualities of personal experience is enormous and notorious. The poets have done best; and poetic language—at least, the language of lyric poetry—has been devised to attempt this process of communicating and sharing "immediate feeling." But the constant complaint of the poet is that he has not succeeded, that he cannot make himself understood.

Santayana has made much of this quality of what he calls "the leaping flame of spirit." Though in the "psyche" he has a perfectly good functional conception of "Mind" as "acting intelligently," he seems to identify "awareness" or "consciousness" with "spirit" and its "intuition of essences." Such intuition, he insists, is "spontaneous and artless"; and he who does not thus "intuit essences" is "merely blind." Now, whatever Santayana may have been, I fear I am never a "pure

[4] See Chapter 9, Section II.

spirit." So I must conclude that I am "merely blind." I find I never "intuit essences"—though I hope I haven't lost consciousness completely. I am "aware" of encountering a number of things. I can even understand Sterling P. Lamprecht's "art of intuition,"[5] by which, with much cultivation and practice, one may finally succeed in selecting and isolating "essences," "sensa," or "ideas." As Whitehead, who seems to share my difficulties, points out, this requires a pretty high degree of sophistication. But I never seem to encounter such abstractions in isolation, as just "given." I am aware that they are the "essences" *of* something. So when Santayana proclaims, "Nothing given exists," I frankly don't know what kind of experience he is talking about. Doubtless individuals differ in this power of "visual imagination." I know I could never say, as I once heard Montague confess, "I do most of my thinking when I am flat on my back *seeing* things." But interesting as are these secret powers of great minds like Santayana and Montague, they do not seem to throw much light for me on the discrimination of "Mind."

Indeed, just because this quality of "awareness" is private, and revealed only through speech, I see no good reason to claim "awareness" as the exclusive possession of men. An oyster, or, for aught I know, a rock, may enjoy "the flame of spirit" too; though, having very imperfect organs of speech, it cannot tell me about the experience. Dewey has suggested that "consciousness" is merely brute and unconditioned "isness," the being what a thing irreducibly is, a particular case of "immediacy," or "matter" as a principle of individuation. And Whitehead holds that "the energetic activity considered in physics is the emotional intensity entertained in life." These scales of continuity may indeed obtain—though it is rather difficult even to imagine what could constitute evidence for them. If "awareness" be a quality of immediacy belonging to every selective response, then every process would presumably bear the "flame of spirit," even if only a very little flicker. But the point is, then all hope of discriminating "Mind" in terms of "awareness" breaks down. "Awareness" cannot be "Mind," in the sense of a distinguishable way of operating.

[5] See Sterling P. Lamprecht, "Animal Faith and the Art of Intuition," in *The Philosophy of George Santayana,* ed. P. A. Schilpp (Evanston, 1940), pp. 113–34.

Is "Mind," then, to be identified with the power "to know"? Does this mean that Mind is exhibited wherever there is "perception"? This raises the question of the "sensing" of modern empiricists, and also of the "intellectual perception" of the Greek tradition—Νοῦς, *θεωρία*, "intellectual intuition or vision." The arguments of the *Theaetetus* seem to me conclusive, that sensing is not knowing—though they seem to have made little impression on Englishmen. And that the power of "sensing" which men share with all animals is not the distinguishing mark of "Mind" seems equally obvious. I should follow Aristotle in drawing the line, not the Descartes whose quite different delimitation has dominated modern philosophy. Perception, I should agree with T. H. Green and Dewey, is not an instance of "knowing" at all; it is a stimulus to inquiry, or to the enjoyment and use of knowledge already gained.

Intellectual vision, Νοῦς, is likewise not "knowing"—though it can be said to be an operation of "Mind," an instance of "operating mentally." Plato, I judge, was right—such vision is the culmination of knowing, and dependent upon it. In knowing, we think until we "see." But *θεωρία*, or "vision," is an enjoyment of knowledge, "knowing" itself immediately experienced, rather than actual "knowing." Knowing is not an immediate seeing, either visual or intellectual, but mediate and functional—not in the sense of having no immediate value, for, like every art, it notoriously does—but in its nature and character. Knowing is an active process, involving the use of many Connectives—hypotheses, ideas, and procedures. This conclusion is supported by our psychology, by the history of science, and by any analysis of the techniques of scientific procedure. "Vision" is neither "understanding why," nor "knowing how." The vision of God is not the knowledge of God—though it may well be more important.

If, then, as the "power to know," Mind is at once something less and something more than "intellectual vision," just what does this power involve? Formally, Mind can be said to be the power to find "intelligibility," or "rationality"—the way things act, what a thing with a specific constitution or formal structure *can* do. We then know what the thing *is,* its "nature," the way it can act as a means to an operation or end. "Control" is found when we find the constitution or "formal structure" of things, when we know the mechanism *by which* it acts as it does—and hence how to produce that consequence, how to manipulate it. The distinction is between "knowing what" a thing does, the way it operates, the consequences it produces, what it leads to—traditionally, knowing its "end" or "final cause"; and "knowing how" it does it, the means "by which" it operates in that way—traditionally, knowing its "efficient cause," which leads to "knowing how" to manipulate and control it.

"Intelligibility" and "control," so defined, are obviously intimately bound up with each other, in a continuous process of inquiry. "Knowing what" things do, their behavior, we are led to inquire "how" they do it, into the structures of the mechanisms and materials involved. The power of manipulation and control thus gained reveals new powers and new limits in the behavior of things, what they can do in relation to other things. This is the conception of knowledge implicit in our own scientific enterprise. We "understand" when we can formulate in exact —at best, in mathematical—terms, the way in which a thing will interact or cooperate with other things under specified conditions. Our own science, that is, is fundamentally "functional" or "teleological," it is "operational" or "behavioristic" in character. It is concerned with ways of interacting, with how processes take place—with "functional structure."

In the measure that we know *what* things can do, their powers, and how they do it, the structure of their mechanisms, we can be said to *understand* things—we know both τὸ ὅτι and τὸ διότι, the "fact that" and the "reason why." In this sense, we say, "he understands horses," or, "he understands mass-production," or "advertising"; or, "he understands the structure of the atom," or, "he understands politics," or, "human nature." "Knowing what" and "knowing how" are bound up together in "understanding why"—in intelligibility or rationality, the "generalized idea of the means-consequence relationship as such," as Dewey [6] puts it. This is the power, I submit, which is Mind, in the fullest sense.

It is often assumed that knowing what things *do* reveals and is equivalent to knowing what they *can* do. The outcome of this assumption is the "scholastic" science of nature, in which intelligibility is taken, not

[6] John Dewey, *Logic* (New York, 1938), p. 10. Cf. F. J. E. Woodbridge, *Nature and Mind* (New York, 1937), pp. 187–91.

as generalized functional structure, but as a "generalized formal structure," with its "fixed essences," "fixed natures," and "fixed first principles"—the view Dewey criticises—a view, incidentally, *not* to be found in Aristotle himself. This view is most consistently worked out in Spinoza, in whose thought there is no distinction left between what things *do,* and what they *can* do; all "powers" have vanished, and everything is actuality. This is the consequence of leaving out all control, all "knowing how," all concern with mechanisms—just what Spinoza neglects in Book II of the *Ethics*. This denial of "powers" is found equally in traditional empiricism—in Berkeley, Hume, Mill, and Comte, and in all forms of observationalism and positivism. This is the counterpart of the "rationalism" or "formalism" of Spinoza, Leibniz, and Hegel. For both traditional views all that is, is "pure actuality." Both, that is, are non-functional positions; and as such, obviously inadequate.

We have escaped such a "scholastic science" in our own natural sciences, with their "experimentalism," which is always looking for new powers. We have not done so, to be sure, when we attempt to "formalize" them, to crystallize and fix what things have so far been found to do. This is the formal logician's view of science, as found in Carnap, for instance, which remains completely "scholastic." Science is actually not a way of stating and formulating what we have learned so far, but a way of asking questions; that is, it is not a formalized system or theory, but inquiry. Theory has an important function *within* the process of inquiry: it operates as an instrument for formulating questions more fruitfully. And within theory-construction, "formalization" plays a part, though its role is relatively minor. Logical consistency, that is, is only one factor in enabling theories to ask fruitful questions.

But in human and social matters we notoriously remain largely "scholastics." We assume that what human nature does, or what its institutionalized organizations do, is identical with what they *can* do. We take the limits we now find operating as *the* final limits, as in our very "scholastic" theories of "sin," of the limits of production, or of employment, or of capitalism, or of state control, or of democracy, etc. In such matters we remain with a purely formal knowledge. We don't "understand"—because we don't "know how" the complex mechanisms operate, whose cooperations are registered in the statistical pattern we can record. We have made some progress—but the major part is yet to achieve.

Thus Mind is not fully displayed, there can be no intelligibility discovered, without "knowing how," without discovering the means and mechanisms involved in the means-consequence relationship, through manipulation and experimentation. Now, we may want to "understand," to "know why," so that we can manipulate and control, in order that we can alter and reconstruct. Control, τέχνη, may be our motive in seeking "understanding." The achievement of intelligibility, of understanding why, may be for us a process, complex enough, that itself functions as a means in the larger context of art, or τέχνη. Understanding, knowledge, Mind, may well be *"for the sake of* action, of practice."

This has become, I think, socially and culturally true for the enterprise of science in our Western civilization, which has developed into a social institution with a definite "technical" function in our culture—the story is complex enough. Hence, for example, we judge an economic theory that goes off into a formal elaboration of a mathematical theory, and becomes a "pecuniary logic," or one that is content merely to describe the way in which our economic institutions are operating—the two major types of non-functional economic inquiry—without going on to function as an instrument of social control and manipulation, of "policy-making"—we judge such a theory to be not fully in accord with the aim and function of "genuine science," to be not doing what a genuine science of economics ought to be doing. This motive of control notoriously does not hold of many individual scientists, who pursue "understanding" and "intelligibility" with no thought of any further end or function for their "understanding"—"pure scientists," we call them. Indeed, the general irresponsibility of scientists toward the social—or anti-social—uses to which their hard-won "understanding" is put, poses its own problems, as even scientists have begun to realize recently.

But the important point is that all of these social and technical functions of "scientific understanding" are irrelevant to the fact that we *discover* intelligibility, functional structure, the means-end relationship, only *through* manipulation and control. Whether or not we may happen to want intelligibility as a means to a further practice of arts and techniques, we can *find* it only *by means of* the practice of the art and technique of manipulation and experimentation. We cannot secure "understanding why" without such "action" and "practice." This is something that hasn't dawned yet on poor Bertie Russell—and many others.

Intelligibility is achieved in knowing what things *can* do, not merely what they *are* doing, or *have done*. "Understanding" a man, for instance, involves a genuine difference between what a man *is*, and what a man *does*. This is a valid and important distinction. It is really the distinction between what a man *can do*, and what he actually *does*, and *has done*—between his powers and his operations. The instance serves to make clear why the distinction is so important. The distinction is probably greatest in the case of a man, with human personality. But it holds throughout.

A thing *is* its powers, not its actual operations. But powers are *known*, of course, only *through* their operations—though often, as in the case of a man we know well, analysis can reveal to us powers far beyond anything he has actually accomplished. Hence powers are never completely or exhaustively known. This is why knowledge can never be final and complete. The essence of the "scientific attitude," the "experimental temper," with its never-ending inquiry and discovery, is thus not limited to mere "fallibilism" or insistence on "corrigibility," but is grounded in the inexhaustible powers of things, which new contexts and new situations can bring to light.

It is often said, that science merely tells us "how" things behave, not "what" they are, or "why" they behave that way. It states, we are told, "how" electricity acts, "how" living things behave, "how" man acts, not "what electricity is," "what life is," "what the soul is," or "why" they all act in the amazing ways they do. Science, in a word, tells us "how"; but it gives no "understanding," no "intelligibility." The implication is, "understanding" must be sought elsewhere than in science; we must "go on" to some further kind of knowledge which will answer these questions.

Actually, the knowledge of "how" things behave, in the sense of what they do, is pre-scientific: it involves an empirical description of what they do, before we have analysed how they do it, in the sense of discovering the subordinate processes and mechanisms involved. To say that opium puts men to sleep is true and essential; but it is a pre-scientific statement. Science goes on to analyse the physiological mechanisms of the body, and the chemical mechanisms of opium, that cooperate to produce the state we call "sleep."

What things *can* do, is in a sense post-scientific, quite literally: science is a prerequisite to the discovery of as many powers as we may. "What things are," and "why they are as they are," is precisely a matter of the relation between what they *can* do—their powers—and the mechanisms *by means of which* they do it. "What a thing is" is a set of powers to cooperate in certain ways with other things by means of certain mechanisms. "Why a thing is as it is," is the relation between the functional structure of the operation of its powers, and the formal or internal structure of its mechanisms. In any other sense than this, the questions "what" a thing is and "why" it is that way, are meaningless. In other words, this *is* the meaning of "what things are" and "why they are as they are." It is the only intelligible meaning of intelligibility. And the power to find it is Mind.

CHAPTER 9

An Empirical and Naturalistic Theory of Signs, Signification, Universals, and Symbols

BY "EMPIRICAL" AND "NATURALISTIC" this account of signification and universality means what Dewey means in that chapter of his logic called "The Existential Matrix of Inquiry." A few quotations will illustrate this meaning.

> The primary postulate of a naturalistic theory of logic is continuity of the lower (less complex) and the higher (more complex) activities and forms. The idea of continuity is not self-explanatory. But its meaning excludes complete rupture on one side and mere repetition of identities on the other; it precludes reduction of the "higher" to the lower just as it precludes complete breaks and gaps. . . . What is excluded by the postulate of continuity is the appearance upon the scene of a totally new outside force as a cause of changes that occur. . . . If one denies the supernatural, then one has the intellectual responsibility of indicating how the logical may be connected with the biological in a process of continuous development.[1]

> Any thoroughgoing naturalist is . . . committed by the logic of his position to belief in continuity of development, with its corollary of continuity of factors in the respective patterns of logical and biological forms and procedures.[2]

This theory of signs and universals also takes for granted the basic position of Dewey in that chapter of his *Experience and Nature* entitled: "Nature, Communication and Meaning."

> When communication occurs, all natural events are subject to *reconsideration* and *revision;* they are re-adapted to meet the requirements of conver-

[1] John Dewey, *Logic: The Theory of Inquiry* (New York, 1938), pp. 23–25. Quotations used by permission of Henry Holt and Company, Inc.

[2] *Ibid.*, p. 41.

sation, whether it be public discourse or that preliminary discourse termed thinking. Events turn into objects, things with a meaning. . . . Events when once they are named lead an independent and double life. In addition to their original existence, they are subject to ideal experimentation: their meanings may be infinitely combined and rearranged in imagination, and the outcome of this inner experimentation—which is thought—may issue forth in interaction with crude or raw events. . . . [Language is] the natural bridge that joins the gap between existence and essence. . . . The quality of meaning thus introduced is extended and transferred, actually and potentially, from sounds, gestures and marks to all other things in nature. Natural events become messages to be enjoyed and administered, precisely as are song, fiction, oratory, the giving of advice and instruction. . . . When events have communicable meaning, . . . they are more than mere occurrences: they have implications. Hence inference and reasoning are possible; these operatings are reading the message of things, which things utter because they are involved in human associations.[3]

In other and more Aristotelian terms, it is λόγος, Language, Discourse, that is the "active intellect," as Aristotle clearly should have said.

This theory of signification and universality is not committed to any particular hypothesis as to the historical and evolutionary "origin" and development of language and thinking. I was not around myself while this important process was taking place, and I have never found any one who was, not even Dewey. But it is well to remember that any kind of naturalism is committed to the view, that language and thinking *did* have an historical and evolutionary "origin" and development, however great be our ignorance of the details.

But entirely apart from the support of Dewey, or of anyone else, I prefer to take an illustration which, curiously enough, has been often advanced *against* this naturalistic position—the illustration of music. It is indeed curious that this example has ever been advanced in opposition to a naturalistic position; for it is a basic contention of that position that language is *like* the other human arts. Like them all, it is a manipulation of selected natural materials, a reorganization of selected natural relations and structures to become the vehicle of a new structure, which then can and will perform new functions.

[3] John Dewey, *Experience and Nature* (New York, 1929), pp. 166, 167, 174. Quotation used by permission of W. W. Norton and Company, Inc.

Now music is an excellent illustration of just such a natural cooperation of processes. It is selective, of musical notes from mere noises, of the natural involvements of wave-lengths, etc.; and it is reorganizing—it makes them into the vehicles of new musical structures, which then proceed to operate in such a way as nothing without human manipulation does—that is, which proceed to function as "music," and to perform the work of music.

No one would dream of denying that music is a selection and a reorganization of natural materials, of sounds and their natural involvements. No one would dream of denying that music is "continuous," in precisely the sense maintained by Dewey, with natural sounds, or of maintaining that music is in some sense supernatural. There is, in fact, a clearer "rudimentary" and non-human form of music, in the form of the song of birds, than there is of anything non-human analogous to the language of men—much clearer, for example, than the gestures, vocal and otherwise, of the social animals. Music is thus an excellent illustration of precisely that type of naturalistic continuity which language also exhibits.

I

In the "universe of action" from which a universe of discourse arises, or in prelinguistic behavior, to function as a "sign" means, in the first place, to provoke the *same type of response* as something else. Conversely, to respond to something as a "sign" means to respond to that stimulus in the *same way* as to some other thing or things. A "sign" is thus a substitute or surrogate for those other things: for certain purposes it can function in their place. It can, therefore, be said to "signify" or "stand for" those other things for which it is a substitute. What other things it is a substitute for, that is, what things it can signify or stand for, is discoverable only in their functioning as stimuli; this depends, that is, on finding the range of things that can all alike provoke that common way of responding. Hence a sign's "range of signification"—or, logically speaking, its extension—is determined by the way of responding it provokes: that way selects the various things that can stimulate it, and thus selects that range of things the "sign" is a sign *of,* or signifies. Consequently, in the second place, in another and second sense of "signification," the sign can be said to "signify" or "point to" the common way of responding itself. There are thus two different *modes* of signification, "standing for" and "pointing to."

I shall call this second sense, the signifying of a common way of responding, "primary" or "proximate" signification: it is primary and proximate in the process of the functioning of the sign. I shall distinguish it from the first sense of signification, the signifying of the range of things for which the sign can serve as a substitute, calling the latter mode "secondary" or "derivative" signification. The distinction is important; the terminological designation is arbitrary. I find, however, that Dewey uses the same terms I had already selected: "Meaning is not indeed a psychic existence; it is *primarily* a property of behavior, and *secondarily* a property of objects."[4]

Thus primary or proximate signification is the relation of the various stimuli to the common response. Secondary or derivative signification is the relation of one stimulus to the whole range. In the diagram, primary signification is that expressed as s_1, s_2, s_3, s_4 R response. Secondary signification is that expressed in the relation: s_1 R (s_1 s_2 s_3 s_4).

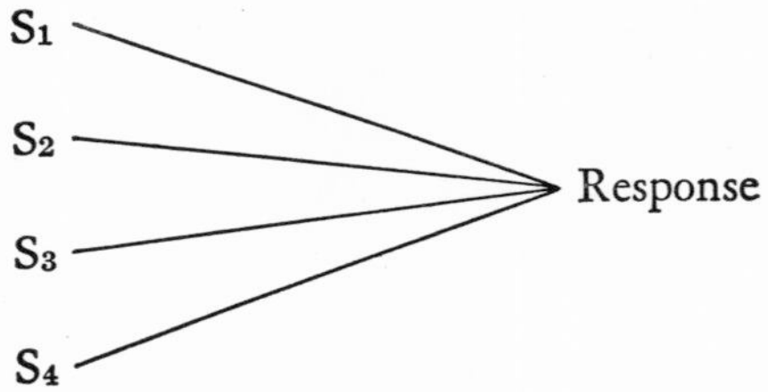

On the level of purely organic behavior, every stimulus is an "instance" or "illustration" of a whole "range of stimuli," all of which can provoke the same type of response—that is, it is one of a group of food-stimuli, or of sex-stimuli, or of danger-stimuli, etc. Each range or group provokes its own characteristic and common way of responding. These ranges of stimuli are thus discriminated into various "kinds," that is, into food, mate, danger, etc., by the organism's common way of responding to each range.

Every stimulus thus functions as a "sign," and thus can be said to

[4] *Ibid.*, p. 179. Italics mine.

"signify," in the primary mode of signification, a certain "way of responding" which the organism exhibits toward a whole range of stimuli. This range is in that respect "similar" *for* the organism: all its instances are sorted out from the stimuli of other responses and grouped into the "same kind," so that any one of them may serve as a substitute for any other in provoking that way, and may hence be said to "signify" all of them, in the secondary mode of signification. To respond to a stimulus thus means to react to something as a "sign"—on the human level, primarily of the expectation or suggestion it signifies or "means," and secondarily, of the whole range of stimuli which provoke on the organism's part that same way of acting, or that same disposition to act.

Dewey has an excellent statement of this on the human level:

Genuinely complete empirical philosophy requires that there be a determination *in terms of experience* of the relation that exists between physical subject-matter and the things of direct perception, use, and enjoyment. It would seem clear that historic empiricism, because of its commitment to sensationalism, failed to meet this need. The obvious way of meeting the requirement is through explicit acknowledgment that direct experience contains, as a highly important direct ingredient of itself, a wealth of *possible* objects. There is no inconsistency between the idea of direct experience and the idea of objects of that experience which are as yet unrealized. For these latter objects are directly experienced *as* possibilities. Every plan, every prediction, yes, every forecast and anticipation, is an experience in which some non-directly experienced object is directly experienced *as a possibility*. And, as previously suggested, modern experience is marked by the extent to which directly perceived, enjoyed and suffered objects are treated as signs, indications, of what has *not* been experienced in and of itself, or/and are treated as means for the realization of these things of possible experience. Because historic empirical philosophy failed to take cognizance of this fact, it was not able to account for one of the most striking features of scientific method and scientific conclusions—preoccupation with generality as such.[5]

Genetically, the organism does not react uniquely to each individual stimulus: it gives the "same" response to all within a certain range. All that can provoke the same response are of the same "kind." The organism hence reacts fundamentally to "kinds" of stimuli, to "kinds" of nat-

[5] John Dewey, "The Objectivism-Subjectivism of Modern Philosophy," in *Problems of Men* (New York, 1946), pp. 317–18.

ural action. To speak more precisely, each response of the organism is "individual" and "particular," but not "unique"—it is at the same time an instance of a typical way of responding. And each response is the response to a stimulus that is "individual" and "particular"—and that may even be, *as* a natural action or operation, ultimately "unique"—but which, *as* falling within a certain range of stimuli, and *as* stimulating a response in the organism, is an instance of a typical way of stimulating. Thus the organism responds in a typical "way" of responding to a typical "way" of stimulating.

Stimuli thus come to the organism already sorted by the organism's power of selective sensitivity; and sorted by their own power to initiate, under appropriate conditions, different ways of responding. The organism has a power of selective, discriminating sensitivity, which can be conditioned and refined indefinitely. The operation of this power is a cooperation with certain powers of the environment; that is, it is dependent not only on the internal structure of the organism, but also on the powers of the environment to stimulate such selective and conditioned response—powers themselves dependent on the structure of the environment itself.

To define "sensitivity to stimuli" as a "cooperation of 'powers' of the organism with 'powers' of the environment," means 1) "response to stimuli" is a genuine *interaction,* not an activity of the organism alone—it is what Dewey came, in the book written with A. F. Bentley, *Knowing and the Known,* to call a "transaction." It means 2) neither the organism alone, nor the environment apart from the organism, acts in that particular way: they act in that way only in cooperation. That way of acting is a way of acting of the organism, and it is a way of acting of the environment. But there are not two ways of acting, there is only *one way,* which is a way of cooperating, a way of interacting. That is, the structure, pattern, or way of functioning of the organism in responding to stimuli is identical with the structure, pattern, or way of functioning of the environment: it is the structure of an interaction or cooperation. There is only one way of interacting, but there are two sets of powers, the powers of the organism and the powers of the environment. Each set consists of powers to cooperate in a common interaction or "transaction."

The powers of the organism to respond are in fact found to be dependent on a certain physiological structure in the organism, a structure of receptor and motor organs. The powers of the environment to stimulate are likewise found to be dependent on a certain physical structure in the environment, a structure of determinate ranges of stimuli—that is, a structure of definite "similarities" and discriminable "differences." If everything in the environment were a pure particular, with no resemblance or similarity to anything else whatever—if nothing the organism ever interacted with were in any respect similar to anything previously encountered—then the organism could give no determinable responses: each of its innumerable responses would be unique. And if everything in the environment were so connected with everything else, that each response were really a response to the whole, then likewise the organism could give no determinate or selective responses: each of its responses would then be identical with every other response. The physical structure of the environment, like the physiological structure of the organism, is a matter to be discovered by inquiry: what kind of structure, in detail, does the environment actually exhibit, as the condition of selective response?

Now, things "are" what they *can do,* when they are cooperating with the activities of the organism just as well as when they are cooperating with any other natural activity. Hence, things are what they can do *to* the organism, in the same sense as they are what they can do to and with the other natural operations with which they can cooperate, and they are what the organism can do *with* them: they exhibit precisely those powers of interacting with the organism. This implies, as we have just seen, a structure of "kinds" of powers in the environment, of "kinds" of stimuli, or ways of cooperating: it is this structure of "kinds" that makes possible selective response.

Functioning as a "sign," or "signifying," is thus a way of operating of the Situation itself—of the organism *in* its environment. It is a co-operating of powers of the environment with powers of the organism. This behavioristic account of "signs" or "meanings" makes clear that such signs are not "created" by language, by linguistic behavior, but are traits of prelinguistic behavior that make language and communication possible. They are features of processes on the organic level, which in performing its own proper function language selects, reorganizes, and reconstructs. Hence "signifying," operating as a "sign" or "meaning," is not a mysterious addition to what we encounter, to natural interactions. Rather, functioning as a sign is found occurring at the lowest level of organic behavior, in any selective sensitivity to stimuli of the environment that is capable of being conditioned.

Determinate operations are thus "discriminated" in organic behavior, in terms of the organism's attitudes, and habitual and conditioned responses—though the possibility of any very precise determination is, as throughout, dependent on the formulation of the attitudes generated by experience, through the instrumentality of language, into *expectations* of specific future operatings of the factors in the situation, and *suggestions* of possible ways of acting and cooperating with them in detail. The field of action is hence not encountered *en bloc*—as a single, undifferentiated operation or activity—but rather as a cooperation of distinguishable operations or activities which are severally involved as factors in the situation. And these several operations are themselves not encountered as "merely" or "purely" particular and unique. They are encountered *together with* the possibilities they suggest, as Dewey puts it in the passage quoted on page 241. They are encountered *together with* our "expectation" that they will operate in characteristic ways, and as "suggesting" possible ways in which we can cooperate with them.

Dewey states this:

> There are organic activities upon the biological level which select and order existential conditions in a *de facto* way. If a lower organism were equipped with powers of symbolization [if it could talk] the result would be its ability to refer some things to certain gross generalizations or kinds—to sort them out, for example, as foods, as inedibles, and as poisons; and into things harmful and adverse and things helpful and favorable—foes and friends. The cultural matrix not only supplies, through the medium of language, means for explicit formulation of kinds but also extends vastly the variety and number of kinds. For culture institutes and consists of a vast number of ways of dealing with things. Moreover, certain ways of action are formulated as standard and normative rules of action and of judgment on the part of members of the cultural group. . . . Thus things and persons are sorted out into distinctive kinds on the ground of allowable and prohibited modes of acting toward and with them.[6]

The field of action is hence encountered as already sorted into a number of different operations as factors in it. And these several operations are encountered, not merely as the particular operation which each

[6] Dewey, *Logic,* pp. 264–65.

to be sure is, but also as "instances" or "examples" of characteristic "ways" of operating and cooperating with. Particular operations, that is, are encountered as "signs" of those ways of operating and being cooperated with: a stimulus is always an "instance" or a "sign" of a way things have of acting.

Thus operatings and their characteristic ways are encountered together in the field of action—behaviors and structures of behaving, "particulars" and "universals," "signs" and their "meanings." The "meaning" or universal is encountered in what Dewey calls "direct experience" as a *possible* way of acting. Genetically, the practical "discrimination" is encountered before the "distinction" is formulated—though the linguistic formulation is a potent means of further discrimination. What functions in the universe of action as an "operation encountered," and what functions as a stimulus to the expectation or suggestion of a possible way of acting—as a "sign" of that way—is thus a basic discrimination in all action, even on the organic level. It is reflected, formulated, and refined in and through language; but the distinction expressed *in* language is not created *by* language.

In the field of action—in "direct experience"—operations are actually encountered as signs signifying their mode of acting, or signifying possible ways in which we can act toward or deal with them. We encounter activities, we respond to the stimulus they provide by functioning as *signs* of possible ways of acting. That is, in cooperation with our activities, operations, though they are particular and individual, function as signs of universal ways of acting. It is to the "how," to the "way," to the "meaning signified," that we respond.

We have so far been considering the level of organic behavior, and have been employing a terminology developed to deal with such behavior. But such "universality" in operating is not limited to the cooperation of natural processes with acting organisms. It is not merely organisms that can be said to "respond to stimuli," that is, to respond to particulars as instances of ways rather than as mere particulars. There is a sense in which every interaction of processes can be said to be a reaction to the "stimulus" of an instance of a way of operating; and every interaction can be said to be an instance of a characteristic way of operating, capable of being provoked by a variety of "stimuli," all of which are instances of a common way of acting. It would of course be merely confusing to so extend the meaning of "signification" as to call this most general type of interaction the functioning of "signs." "Signification" is better confined to the organic level: the distinction is too valuable to lose.

Thus, the sun melts wax. So do fire, friction, electricity, and various other activities. The "melting" is a universal "way" of reacting, when the particular operation—of the sun, of fire, of frictional force, etc.—is functioning as an instance of a universal "way," "heating"—when, that is, it is exhibiting that "kind" of power or dispositional property, which is a universal. The particular action is functioning "universally" when it is functioning as an instance of that kind of operation that has been found to be a mechanism or condition involved in all cases of "heating," on which they are all dependent—namely, increased molecular activity. There is a continuity between the physical processes on which that specific eventuation, "melting," depends, and that eventuation: they are all instances of increased molecular action. The structure or pattern of "heating" and the structure of the eventuation, "melting," are identical: they are both the structure of increased molecular activity.

Thus selective "response" to "ways" of acting can be said to be found in every natural interaction: as powers or dispositional properties to act determinately, "ways" are exhibited by every means or mechanism. They can consequently all be said to function, in the broadest sense, as instances of "universals"—to function "universally." Universality, or response to "meanings," to "signs," is of course encountered by men in situations in which other processes are cooperating with the acting human organism—that is, we "experience" universals as stimuli to our own responses. But our responses to stimuli, that is, to operations functioning as signs, are merely special instances of a type of response found in every natural interaction. Hence the conditions of linguistic activity in the proper sense, the conditions of responding to a meaning, or to the signification of a sign, are not unconnected with the conditions of all physical response to a physical stimulus. Rather, linguistic activity—communication and thinking—makes use of and builds upon the structure involved in every natural interaction.

I am, of course, not proposing to call every natural interaction an instance of the functioning of a "sign." It is more proper, because it is more fruitful to preserve a valuable distinction, to say that strictly speaking only living organisms "respond to signs"; for only organisms are subject to conditioning, and can be said to "learn" relations of signification from experience. Our wax, for example, cannot be conditioned to a new stimulus. The response to a sign, in other words, is a special kind of response to the stimulus of a "way." But it is dependent on the response to the stimulus of ways exhibited in all natural interactions. No organism, that is, could respond to a sign, to a particular *as* standing for a universal way, if all natural interactions were not responses to the stimuli of ways. Further, linguistic response, or response to linguistic signs, which is peculiar to men, who are subject to social conditioning, is likewise dependent on the more general response to signs in organic behavior, and on the still more general response to the stimulus of ways, which is in turn dependent on a structure of "kinds."

We can now draw the threads of the argument together and summarize the analysis. We have so far distinguished three main levels of responding to the stimulus of a way, or of responding to an activity as an instance of a way:

1) Responding to *ways* in the broadest sense, in which every natural interaction can be said to be the response to an operation as an instance of a characteristic way of operating—that is, responding to something in the same way as to a range of other things. Such a type of response is found in every natural cooperation of processes: each can be said, in this broad sense, to be "functioning universally."

2) Responding to *signs,* that is, to a special kind of instances of a way, namely, those instances in which the organism has been conditioned to respond to the possible ways of acting suggested by past experience. Such responses to "signs" are found only on the organic level, where conditioning and "learning from experience" takes place. This type of response is "functioning universally" in the narrower sense, on the level of the process of "signification."

3) Responding to *linguistic signs,* that is, to a special kind of "signs," namely, those signs to which the conditioning of the organism is social. Such response is found on the linguistic level, that level on which the Situation can be said to be functioning "mentally," a level found only in human societies.

The response to linguistic signs is dependent upon the response to signs in general, and the response to signs is in turn dependent on the response to ways. There is, in addition, a fourth level:

4) Responding to *symbols,* that is, to a special kind of linguistic signs, namely, those that are artificially instituted and are freely manipulable. Such *symbolic systems,* or constellations of symbols, as are illustrated by mathematics, by logic, and by postulate systems in general, are dependent on the response to linguistic signs; and it is the somewhat questionable fashion today to speak of all postulate systems as "languages," and to treat them in terms appropriate to languages. Between "signs" and "symbols" there is a further basic distinction: "signs" can serve as logical evidence for what they "signify"; while "symbols" cannot serve as evidence.

II

This behavioristic account of signs and signification is also a behavioristic account of "universality." There is, it seems clear, no problem of *whether* we humans encounter "universality" or not. The problems concern rather the *locus* of "universality," and how pervasive a trait of our world it is. The evidence seems convincing that "universality" is as pervasive a trait of our experienced world as "particularity"; that the two are in fact "polar concepts," and form an ultimate metaphysical distinction, to be found in every existential subject-matter—though not in the subject-matter of the so-called "formal sciences," to which time is likewise irrelevant. That is why the distinction between ways and operatings, and that between kinds and powers, seems ultimate—that is, applicable to every existential subject-matter.[7]

I say there is no genuine problem of whether we encounter universality or not, but only of its locus, and its pervasiveness, because no responsible metaphysician—or critic of metaphysics—has ever denied that such universality is a power of our complex human systems of signs, like language and mathematics. It has always been recognized that we mortals can *talk* about many things—that in our discourse and

[7] I emphasize this pervasiveness of the metaphysical category of universality, because on the occasion of my reading this paper to the Eastern Division of the American Philosophical Association at the meeting held at Toronto in 1950, both my friendly critics, Mr. Charles A. Baylis and Mr. Nelson Goodman, called my position "nominalistic": and I know of no historic "nominalism" which has ever held that universality is an all-pervasive ontological trait.

our mathematics we can single out similar traits, relations, and patterns of acting. No one has ever denied this power of at least talking universally. Nor have there been many to deny that by manipulating linguistic and mathematical signs we can talk intelligibly about what has never been experienced, about things possible and impossible. Language does this by a variety of linguistic devices, by different kinds of linguistic signs, which function in our discourse in various ways, and thus single out quite different aspects of our experience of the world. The careful study to which these linguistic devices have been subjected of late by our philosophers of language emphasizes the need of more precise distinctions, especially among the different kinds of what have been traditionally called "universal terms." These different kinds of universal linguistic signs require distinguishing in terms of the ways they operate and what they actually do. There is clearly to be found in our human languages a great variety of distinctively different kinds of universal terms, which have been traditionally confused, and which have produced what our British colleagues like to call a "muddle" about "universals." Clarification through linguistic analysis is clearly needed here —especially of the distinction between terms that enable us to talk about "classes," and terms that enable us to talk "universally" about other traits of the world. These matters are all "problems" of universals, as universal terms are involved in linguistic communication and communicable knowledge—and the problems are surely complex and manifold. But these linguistic devices by which language is able to function universally, and to exhibit its power of speaking universally, of unifying the multiplicity we find in our world for the purpose of reorganizing, expressing, and communicating shared meanings and knowledge, have been well explored of late. Most philosophers of language today seem to be interested primarily in these devices of language for talking universally. I myself share that interest. Such technicians of language may well judge that I ought to be talking here about these devices of language—as I have elsewhere. They are probably right. But such "problems of universals" happen not to be the problems to which I am specifically addressing myself here.

The problems of universals I am here proposing to consider present a quite different set of difficulties. They are metaphysical rather than merely technical. What is language talking *about?* What do its many varieties of linguistic devices single out and grasp? Do all linguistic signs—all bits of discourse—signify something in themselves? Or do none? or do only "proper names"? Do universal terms signify something else, that can be called "universals"? Do some such terms, or do all of them? What is the ontological status of these hypostatizations?

To these questions as to the ultimate status of universals, history has given a wide variety of answers. It can be said with confidence, on the basis of such long experience, that no single one of them is "true," or "correct"—in the sense that it could possibly be warranted by any conceivable kind of evidence. Rather, like the nine-and-forty ways of singing tribal lays, every single one of them is right. That is, all of them are able to construe the fact of language and knowledge. All of them—within limits, of course: I mean, all that are responsibly maintained, and not merely imputed to opponents—all that locate universality somewhere at least, if only in language, and that conversely do not destroy the fact of particularity—all such construings are "right." They are all possible construings, because they are different ways of talking about the same fact of universality. Each, to be sure, has its own advantages and disadvantages; and each has far-reaching consequences of its own.

When we are confronted by the host of strange and diverse things that have recently been called "universals"—characteristics, possibilities, impossibilities, classes, properties, and what not—it is not hard to be persuaded it would conduce to clarification of what has become a good deal of a muddle, and would certainly simplify matters, were we to restrict the usage of the word "universal" as a noun to *terms,* to call only universal terms "universals," and to call by other and less ambiguous names all those fascinating entities to which universal terms seem so passionately attached.

Universal terms may be enough for the formal logicians, who prefer today to get along with as few ontological commitments as possible. But they are hardly enough for the student of language and communication, which after all is a natural process and not a supernatural heaven, like the abode of the formal logician. And they are clearly not enough for the philosopher, who is interested in exploring how things are connected in our world, in seeing farther, and not merely in the systematic exploitation of myopia.

For the fact of "universality" remains. How does language perform its universalizing function? What are its natural conditions? Is the power of language to unify the multiplicity of things wholly unique? Can there be said to be a universality in things, which language uses as its material and builds upon, going much farther in its many marvelous products, leading all the way to pure mathematics and logical postulate systems?

The answer here suggested is, yes. We do encounter a kind of universality in our experience of the world before we formulate it in our universal "terms," in our universalizing language. We come upon a rudimentary "universality," in the broadest sense, in all natural interactions. But this "universality" does not consist in discovering a host of "universals" cluttering up the metaphysical landscape. The functioning of language does not demand as a necessary condition innumerable ontological entities "hypostatized" to correspond to each of its universal terms. Rather, the power of language to universalize is built upon similar universalizing aspects of non-linguistic processes.

The necessary natural condition of the "universality" we clearly find in language is not a structure of "universals" in the world; it is rather the fact that things can function universally. Language does not copy or reproduce any ontological structure of "universals." But in a sense it imitates, and in a sense builds upon and carries farther, these "functionings universally" which men encounter in the universe of action, in the Situation. Properly speaking, therefore, "universality" is best taken as a way of functioning. And I am proposing to talk here about the fact of universality in these functional terms.

In the light of this analysis, it is now possible to give their due meed to both "nominalism" and "realism" as to the status of universals. This account can be said to be "nominalistic," in that it holds that there are no actual "ways" or "universals" unless a particular process is functioning as an instance of such a way. Stated on the level of the process of signification, there are no actual universals unless a particular process is functioning as a "sign," as a stimulus to an "expectation" of its future way of operating, or to a "suggestion" of a possible future way of dealing and cooperating with it. Stated on the broader level of natural interactions in general, there is no actual universality being exhibited, unless a particular process is functioning as the occasion for an instance of a way of operating, that can be occasioned by many other processes—as the occasion for a common way of operating—and is thus functioning as an instance of a common way of occasioning. There are no actual universals apart from a situation in which a particular is functioning *as* a universal, that is, as an instance of a universal way of responding, or "meaning."

Traditional "nominalism" has held, that that "term" is universal, which can be predicted of a number of particulars—i.e., a particular can be said to be an instance of a universal when it can provoke a universal *linguistic* response. It is here suggested, that a particular can be said to be an instance of a universal way of acting, when it can provoke an expectation or a suggestion of a possible characteristic or universal way of acting. "Universality" is thus not limited to the power to provoke a certain *linguistic* response, and it is exhibited not merely in discourse, but prior to discourse, in the universe of action. In a rudimentary form, it is exhibited "prior" to the level of organic activity, or the universe of action, on the still more general level of all natural interactions.

This account can also be said to be "realistic," in that it holds that it is not merely the response elicited that is "universal." The stimulus can be said to be universal also: stated on the level of the process of signification, a particular functioning as a stimulus to the expectation or suggestion of a possible universal way of action, can be said to be functioning "universally." Stated on the more general level of the process of natural cooperation, a particular functioning as the occasion for a universal way of cooperating, can be said to be functioning "universally." It can then be said to be operating in such a characteristic way, or to be "cooperatable with" in such a way. A particular process, in so functioning, is exhibiting the power of universality, of illustrating a way, and can be said to possess that power. As throughout, actual universality has its locus in and belongs to the functioning, to the whole cooperation of processes, to the situation as a whole. To be a universal is to function as a universal, to be operating universally. "Universality" is a way of functioning, and all "universals" are encountered as "ways."

I am emphasizing the fact that actual universality belongs *primarily* to the cooperation of processes: it is a way of functioning in that cooperation. It can be derivatively given a locus in the particular factors functioning as means or mechanisms in that cooperation. That is why I have been calling the response, or the way occasioned, "common" or "universal" in the *primary* sense, and the stimulus or the occasion, "common" or "universal" in a *derivative* sense. The latter is dependent on and derived from the former.

The whole position, of course, is dependent on a general "functional realism": any factor *is* and can be said to be its functioning; and the various functionings encountered *in* the cooperation of processes that is the active situation or universe of action can all be said to be "real"—they are clearly no less "real" than the factors taken in isolation apart from their functioning.[8] That is, a factor or process functioning universally can be said to be "universal"—in the language of medieval realism, it can be said to be "universal *in re*"—in the order of being.

The conversion of the "stimuli of ways" into "signs"—the institution of new stimuli for old ways of responding—is to be found in any organic conditioning of response, as in the classic case of Pavlov's dog. That is, it is found wherever conditioning or learning from experience takes place. Learning is thus a necessary condition for response to signs to occur. Conditioning is possible because the stimuli are naturally involved in a complex of operations and processes in a universe of action, as in the case of the bell and the food in Pavlov's experiment.

Now, in the case of response to the stimulus of a way, found in every natural interaction, the stimulus is an *instance* of a common way of stimulating, provoking a common response. In the case of the melting of the wax all the operations were instances of "heating," and provoked a "melting" of the wax. The instances were bound up together, and with the response, in a continuum of means and mechanisms, that of molecular activity. But they were selected as bound together as instances of a common type of stimulus, heating, only through the common response they are all capable of provoking.

In the case of response to signs, found only in organic cooperations, the stimulus is likewise capable of provoking the same common response as other stimuli. But it is bound up with those other stimuli, not because all are alike instances of a common way of acting—in the

[8] For a fuller statement of the "functional realism" here maintained, see pp. 192–93.

illustration of the wax, increased molecular activity—but because they are all naturally involved in a causally or serially connected complex of different processes. In the response to a "way" in general, the stimulus is an *instance* of a way; in the response to a sign, the stimulus is rather *one factor* involved with other different factors in a complex of processes.

This involvement and connection of different factors in a complex of operations and processes makes it possible for any one factor in the complex to serve as a stimulus of response to the whole situation, and to its objective for action. It makes it possible for any one factor to function as a *sign* of response to the whole situation—in the primary mode of signification; and hence to all the other factors involved, in the secondary mode of signification. Thus, smoke is a *sign* of fire: because smoke is causally involved with fire, the organism can be conditioned to respond to smoke as it reacts to the whole fire-situation. Again, clouds are a *sign* of rain: because the two are connected in a causal order, the organism can be conditioned, or can learn, to react to clouds as to an expectation of rain, or to a suggestion of how to deal with it.

Genetically, the problem is not how particular factors come to signify or "mean" responses primarily, and the other factors involved in the situation derivatively—as it would be if all the factors were pure particulars, with no involvement or relating structure, as is assumed in most nominalistic theories of signs. The response is rather to the entire situation or universe of action, in which the various factors are naturally involved; it is to their ways of acting and their kinds of stimulus, to the whole situation and its structurally involved factors, and not to particular factors as isolated particulars. The problem is not of instituting connections, or of generating "signification." It is rather of discriminating responses, of going from the "general" to the "specific," from universals to particular and appropriate responses—that is, of distinguishing different kinds of responses to signs carefully discriminated. It is a problem of *isolation,* which gives at once further discrimination, and greater freedom of response and manipulation. We "learn" to distinguish specific features of situations, specific powers or mechanisms or means; we "learn" to respond to expectations or suggestions of "proper powers" in a variety of contexts.

III

Linguistic signs are factors in the human social situation to which the members of a social group have been conditioned to respond linguistically in the same way, which can hence serve as group stimuli to responses to the language situation. Presumably, these factors were "originally" no different in character from the other factors in the human group situation, being gestures, cries, etc.

The conditioning in human group activities is "social," and linguistic or group signs are social and shared. "Signifying" in general does not seem to be in itself inherently social—I think G. H. Mead was mistaken on this point. Signifying occurs whenever conditioning of response has taken place. But linguistic signs and conditioning are obviously a group or social matter. This is clearly true genetically, in the case of children, or of learning a new language. And Mead may be right in his speculative anthropology, that language "arose" as "vocal gestures" in "the social act." I wasn't there, and know no one who was. And it is likewise clear that without linguistic signs and conditioning there can be no "social" behavior in any strict sense, no communication involving shared or group signs, or linguistic stimuli.

But if it cannot be said that it is social behavior that "generates" signification, and still less universality, such behavior does make necessary specific discriminations in response, and hence in the stimulating factors or signs. Language makes possible pointings to significant factors in the situation, factors "significant for" the appropriate group response. Thus we say, "Look out!" which serves as a stimulus to a general response to danger, a characteristic way of responding to a situation. "There's a bear!" leads to further discrimination in response, to the "bear response." "It's only Nicholas Murray" is the stimulus to the "tame bear response." Each linguistic stimulus is a sign of certain expectations, and of certain overt responses to those expectations. Each is a sign of "kinds of powers," which are themselves signs of certain ways of acting and of being responded to.

Linguistic signs are not isolated, but are members of a system or constellation of social signs, which taken together we call a "language." A language is a set of institutionalized habits of using social signs—it is a set of "usages." These habits or usages may be formulated approximately—there are always a host of exceptions—in a set of definitions, or "dictionary," of the various ways in which these habits operate in that group; and in a set of rules stating the ways in which they are related—the "grammar" or "syntax" of that particular language or institutionalized set of socially shared signs.

Linguistic signs have been traditionally distinguished as "artificial signs," in contrast to the "natural signs," like smoke as the sign of fire or clouds as the sign of rain. They have been said to be "arbitrary" and "chosen at will." Of course linguistic signs are no more "artificial" than any other institutionalized habits; and they are certainly not "chosen" at the will of any individual. They are, to be sure, involved in the situation in a different way from that in which "natural signs" are involved. They are not involved in the causal or functional structure of natural processes apart from human cooperation with those processes. But they are involved in the causal or functional structure of the human group cooperation with other natural processes: they are involved in *natural processes on a social level.* They are not involved on the purely organic level: they are *social signs.*

The usages—that is, the "dictionary" and "grammar" of "a language"—are "accidental" (this term is preferable to "conventional," which seems to be the heir to centuries of rationalistic analysis). The particular words employed, the particular grammatical structure embodied, are irrelevant to the functioning of a set of linguistic signs—that is, to their signifying of social responses in the process of communication. The grammatical rules and structure of "a language" are wholly irrelevant and accidental to the functioning of language in communication, to the situation, and to "nature." The group might have been conditioned to any other conceivable grammatical structure of its linguistic habits, just as it might have been conditioned to any other conceivable dictionary or set of words. This suggests that if logic be the science of the grammatical structures of languages, it is the science of the accidental, from the standpoint of communication.

But though the particular set and structure of a constellation of linguistic signs is accidental, and "conventional," it is not arbitrary. What words the group is conditioned to are accidental; but it must have some words to serve as stimuli to its socially necessary responses. What responses are socially necessary is subject to cultural and institutional determination or limiting. What grammatical structure the group is conditioned to is accidental; but it must have some scheme of linguistic usages. Whether this structure of usages is also subject to cultural and institutional determination is a matter for further inquiry. There is some evidence that all schemes of grammar are mutually translatable, in a sense in which vocabularies are not—that any grammatical structure can be employed for communication. But it is possible that changes effected by the institution of novel organized bodies of belief—in the past chiefly religious, but in our culture scientific—may lead to a new cultural conditioning of the grammatical structure of the language of groups with such bodies of belief. We may, for instance, discover that the natural involvements of things on a certain level of analysis—sub-atomic, for example—are so different from those of ordinary experience that the grammar of ordinary language is "misleading," that is, is not an effective instrument for organizing group responses to them. It is perhaps more likely that a new "language," with a more appropriate grammar, will be worked out for that purpose; and in fact mathematics has been employed in just such a fashion. It remains to ask, is ordinary grammar able to express present-day physical theory, for example? The attempts so to employ it are notoriously unsuccessful.

It is this element of accident, of "convention," in these systems of social signs that makes possible the further use of conscious "convention" in a stricter sense, the institution of genuinely "artificial signs" or symbols, signs that are freely manipulable, and the great systems of artificial symbols that men have devised, most notably in the case of mathematics. But these freely manipulable symbols take us to another level of responding to signs, which may well be beyond anything appropriately designated "linguistic."

IV

In the general scheme of levels of responding on pages 247–48, we distinguished the three levels of response to "ways," response to "signs," and response to "linguistic signs," and then suggested as a fourth level the response to "symbols." With both linguistic signs and symbols we are definitely dealing with subject-matter that falls under the metaphysical category of "Connectives" or "Conjunctions," the fifth way of functioning in Substance or the Situation distinguished originally on page 176. The ontological category of Connectives was briefly set forth on page 194. We must now explore somewhat further the nature and function of Connectives, distinguish the various main types —and this will lead us to the differences between signs and symbols, and to the various kinds of symbols—and at least raise and state the problems of the standards of the adequacy and validity of Connectives.

Connectives are extremely important. For they include not only such complex constellations of linguistic signs and symbols as the greatest Connective of all, language and discourse itself, and such elaborations of symbols as mathematics, logic, and theology. They include also all the hypotheses and theories of the several sciences, and all systems of spatial and temporal measurement; all legal systems and human moral and social ideals, all artistic symbols and religious symbols; and all myths, both historical and metaphysical. All such Connectives are symbols or manipulations of symbols and symbol systems.

What can be said about language after a careful metaphysical analysis of communication could be generalized to apply to all Connectives. And one could, indeed, generalize the notion of language itself, and call all these Connectives "languages" or instruments of language in a broad sense. I have myself been strongly tempted to follow this course; but it would do too much violence to our ordinary ways of speaking for even my hardy ears. Or, following a present fashion, one could generalize the notion of "myth," and call mathematics a "logical myth." But were I to do this, I would want to mean by "myth" thus generalized just what I would want to mean by "language" thus generalized. So I have preferred to use a less loaded term, "Connective."

Speaking most generally, Connectives are operations functioning in Substance or the Situation to connect or conjoin other factors, to institute relations between other operations and ways of operating. Connectives thus "lead us" from one operation to another, they "organize" or "order" operations, they "unify" them. They serve in general as instruments of relating. I am thus taking the process of "relating" as fundamental, rather than its outcome, the "relation"; the relation is itself an outcome, a past participle, "related." The power, or the instrument of relating, I am taking as the Connective proper.

I have grouped together these very different kinds of Connectives or Conjunctions, each with its own distinctive functions, serving its own distinctive values, to bring out what they all possess in common: their common ontological status and function in Substance. All Connectives display two distinguishing marks. Negatively, their formulation does not "signify" or "designate" anything, or any traits of things, apart from the Situation in which they are found functioning. Like language, or like myths, their formal structure is not isomorphic with the structure of the subject-matter on which they work—they are in no sense "representative." Positively, the functioning of Connectives involves a human cooperation with other operations: Connectives do not function without man's activities participating in Substance.

It is very difficult to state simply the common function of Connectives. To "connect," "conjoin," "relate," "organize," "order," "unify"—all these terms designate the most general function of Connectives; although the meaning of any one of them has to be stretched to include all the various ways of "connecting" encountered Situations exhibit. All Connectives select certain features of the Situation, and by connecting those features, manage to "reorganize" the Situation—just as in the specific functioning of linguistic Connectives that is "communication." The fact that this analysis of Connectives in general was developed out of the analysis of linguistic communication has obviously influenced the terminology employed.

As to the ontological status of Connectives in Substance, they are all functionally real, or real as functioning; and they are all "objective," like language or mathematics, because they institute objective relations that can be inquired into, just because they are determinately relative to other encountered operations in Substance. The operations of Connectives—what they do, and how they do it—are empirically encountered. Such Connectives are therefore not "fictions," not "imaginary." They may be "conventional," but they are not "arbitrary," as Ernest Nagel likes to put it. That is, their formal structure may be conventional, but their functioning, and the way they do it—their functional structure—is not arbitrary. They can be said to be grounded in the nature of things, in that the discovery of their functional structure is the discovery of the necessary conditions for performing the functions they do perform. As such, Connectives are as "natural" and as "objective" as any other way in which existence functions in Substance.

For instance, logical Connectives are formulations of the necessary conditions of successful inquiry, as Ernest Nagel has made clear in commenting on Dewey.[9] And what holds true of logical Connectives seems to hold of all Connectives. They are all formulations of the discovered relations of functional structure obtaining between other operations—of the necessary conditions of certain cooperations.

The operation of Connectives always involves human cooperation with other natural operations. Connectives do not function as Connectives in the absence of man's activities participating in Substance. Thus, without man's activities, there is no inquiry and there are no functioning logical connectives, there is no mathematical inference, there are no scientific theories or hypotheses, there is no measurement of time or space, there is no use of moral ideals, there is no religion, and so on—there are none of those various cooperations in which Substance functions by means of Connectives. Apart from man's cooperation, Connectives remain powers of Substance. In that cooperation, they are discovered, just like any other natural powers discovered in human art—just like the power of wood-pulp to be made into paper, for example.

But it is not man alone who can be properly said to "connect," nor is it human powers alone that are the necessary condition of the functioning of Connectives. It is existence cooperating with man that "connects," and the powers of existence to connect and be connected are essential to the functioning of any Connective. That is, man is a necessary but not a sufficient condition of the functioning of Connectives; the nature and powers of the world and its manifold processes are equally necessary.

Connectives are not "additions" to Substance, save in the sense that

[9] Ernest Nagel, "Dewey's Reconstruction of Logical Theory," in *The Philosopher of the Common Man,* ed. Sidney Ratner (New York, 1940), pp. 56–87. See esp. pp. 74, 75.

the operation of any power is an addition to the Situation in which it is not operating. Connectives are not "subjective," in the sense that they possess any different and unique ontological status from other powers of Substance. They are not merely human; they are certainly not "psychical," in the sense of being inaccessible and inherently private, and wholly closed to public inquiry. There is nothing "private" about such Connectives as mathematics, physical theory, or language.

Connectives are factors functioning in Substance, and as such are functionally real, real and objective in their cooperation with its complex of processes. This holds of "the Ideal" as well as of physical theory, of God as well as of mathematics. God and mathematics enjoy the same ontological status; it will be observed that in theology I am a good Augustinian. We can blow ourselves to Kingdom Come by the equations of physical theory, and probably will; but equally, we can save our souls by the grace of God, and probably won't. In each case, the process by which we can do it is complex, and requires analysis.

Negatively, the formulation of Connectives does not designate or signify any things or traits of things apart from the situations in which they are operating—it signifies no "things in themselves," in other or in all contexts. But in those situations in which Connectives do function, their formulation designates a process—of connecting and unifying by means of an instrument, the Connective proper. Positively, whatever may be the formal structure of Connectives—which is "conventional," in the sense that alternative formulations might be employed—that is, men can save their souls by many different ideas of God, they can save their skins by many different social ideals, they can lose both by many different mathematical formulations of physical theory, and they can celebrate the process in many different languages—Connectives *are* what they *do,* they *are* the way they operate: they are defined by their functional structure. They are cooperations of powers of the Situation—of powers of what is encountered and of the encountering. The operation of Connectives, like any art, is a cooperation of the powers of the materials and the powers of the instrument. This conception of the nature, function, and status of Connectives is advanced as a way of understanding symbolic systems, myths, religious symbols, and the rest.

Let us now distinguish various types of Connectives:

- A. Linguistic systems combining signs and symbols [10]
- B. Symbols:
  - 1. Cognitive Symbols:
    - a. Scientific hypotheses, scientific theories [11]
    - b. Constellations of Symbols:
      - i. Language symbols [10]
      - ii. Mathematics
      - iii. Logic
      - iv. Systems of measurement
  - 2. Non-cognitive Symbols:
    - a. Social Symbols
      - i. Ideals
      - ii. Legal systems
      - iii. Moral codes
    - b. Artistic Symbols
    - c. Religious Symbols
- C. Myths:
  - 1. Historical Myths
    - a. Origin Myths—Myths of Creation
    - b. Outcome Myths—Eschatological Myths
  - 2. Metaphysical Myths—Non-temporal Myths.[12]

[10] The complex constellation that is a language system includes both representative *signs* and non-representative *symbols,* both *cognitive* and *non-cognitive.* Language hence serves as a bridge from the level of "signification" to that of "symbolization." Language in this double function has been given a status by itself under A. B.1.b.i., "Language symbols," designates the non-representative cognitive linguistic symbols.

Of the four levels distinguished in this chapter, the third, that of language, aside from a few incidental comments, receives no treatment here. The chapter hence exhibits at least one notable gap. The author has tried to work out a metaphysical analysis of language, in the seminar referred to on p. 143, but is postponing publication at present, in the hope that Oxford in its wild gyrations will eventually and speedily come closer to his own functional and realistic approach.

[11] The reference here is to *non-representative* "scientific hypotheses" and "scientific theories," that is, to genuine scientific Connectives.

[12] In this attempt to elucidate a very complicated matter, I shall state some of the conclusions to which *I* have been led—if not always *he*—as a result of various seminars I have been privileged to conduct jointly with Paul Tillich. It has at times been my impression that while I was always conducting a seminar on Connectives, Mr. Tillich was usually leading one on Religious Symbols.

At the outset it is necessary to draw a sharp distinction between a "symbol" and a "sign." A "sign" we have defined as something which provokes the same human response as some other thing, for which it can stand as a kind of surrogate or substitute. A "sign" hence "stands for" or "represents" something other than itself: it is always the "sign of" something else, and can hence serve as evidence for that other thing. In contrast, a "symbol" is in no sense representative: it never stands for or takes the place of anything other than itself. Rather, a "symbol" *does* something in its own right: it operates in its own characteristic way. On this point the terminology is as yet hardly settled; but though the particular way of expressing it is in the present state of usage arbitrary, the distinction is fundamental. It is important to realize that social, artistic, and religious symbols are not "signs"; they are all non-representative symbols which function in various ways in both intellectual and practical life.

Symbols fall into two main classes, cognitive and non-cognitive, which have quite different specific functions, and quite distinctive ways of operating—so distinctive that the two classes might well be called by different names. Both classes of symbols agree, however, in 1) performing the general functions of all Connectives: they serve to relate and connect and organize; in 2) having the ontological status of Connectives: their reality is functional, and consists in what they do; in 3) being built upon the functioning of linguistic signs, of language, though each of the two classes is made possible by different traits of language.

Cognitive symbols function in various ways in the knowing-process, in inquiry. They include mathematical and logical symbols, which, in Dewey's words, are "artificially instituted and freely manipulable." Such cognitive symbols operate in activities that are themselves cognitive and that eventuate in knowledge and truth. The body of scientific concepts, hypotheses, and theories is full of such non-representative but cognitive symbols. An instance is the notion of "velocity at an instant."

In contrast, non-cognitive symbols, including those that play a role in social processes, in art, and in religion, do not have as their function to participate in activities that eventuate in knowledge and truth. Their function is to lead to other kinds of consequences than knowledge. Such non-cognitive symbols can be said to "symbolize" not some external thing that can be indicated apart from their operation—they are not evidence—but rather what they themselves *do,* their proper functions. Social symbols include legal systems, moral codes, and ideals. Artistic symbols are symbols functioning in the artistic situation, in the Situation functioning artistically. Such artistic symbols are often drawn from other fields: thus religious symbols, or social symbols, can on occasion function artistically. Religious symbols are symbols functioning in a distinctive way as instruments or means in the religious situation.

The third major type of Connectives is made up of myths. One established usage of the term makes "myth" synonymous with Connectives in general, and I should personally find no objection to thus generalizing the concept. If "myth" be more narrowly restricted, it might be well to keep it to its original meaning of μῦθος, or story, as in Plato, for example. This would make "myth" an especially appropriate term for the instruments of historical unification, historical myths. These include origin or creation myths, like the myth of a Golden Age, or of a primitive Communism: and also outcome or eschatological myths, like the Stoic final conflagration, or like the myth of a classless society. Such an historical myth would be defined as a "story," the historical accuracy or inaccuracy of which is irrelevant to its functioning as a myth, that is, as an instrument of historical unification. The term "historical myth" should not be limited to mean an "historically false story." Evolution, for instance, is a unifying "myth," whether or not our theories and knowledge of the process can be warranted.

There is a second, non-temporal kind of intellectual unification which might well be called metaphysical myths—close to what Kant called "regulative ideas." These instruments of unification would include the metaphysical myths of the "Unmoved Mover," the "Unconditioned," the "Universe as a Whole," the "Ultimate Context," the "Principle of Concretion," and such other generalizations and unifications of factors found by metaphysical analysis in every particular process. Metaphysical myths of unification of this sort are widely used by rational or philosophical theology, which could hardly dispense with them. Occasionally they even manage to function religiously as well. And in the Western religions, like Judaism, Christianity, or Communism, historical myths have always played a central role.

I should like to conclude with a few observations as to the functions and the standards of adequacy of non-representative, non-cognitive symbols, social, artistic, and religious. Just what is it that such non-cognitive symbols do? In the first place, all of them, including religious symbols, provoke in men an emotional response, and stimulate appropriate human activities. In traditional terms, they act on the will rather than on the intellect. They act as motives, they lead to action on the part of the men who are influenced by them. They do not, like signs, merely lead the mind to other things: they produce results in conduct.

Secondly, they provoke in a group of men—the community for whom they serve as symbols—a common or shared response. They stimulate joint or cooperative activity. This response can become individualized; but even then its individualized form is derivative from what is fundamentally a social or group response. The response is common or shared, although the "meaning" of the symbol—that is, its relation to other elements of men's experience—would receive a different intellectual interpretation from different members of the symbol-community. Thus a physical "social symbol," like the flag, or an intellectual "social symbol," like "the state," or "liberty," would be fitted in quite differently with other ideas by different men, though all would be stimulated to patriotic emotions and activities, or to libertarian feelings and attitudes.

Thirdly, non-cognitive symbols are able to communicate qualitative or "shared" experience, experience that it is difficult to put into precise words or statements, and may well be "ineffable." This is particularly clear with artistic symbols: they act powerfully in men's experience, but it is notoriously almost impossible to state exactly what they "mean." Needless to say, such artistic "symbols" must be carefully distinguished from what are often indeed *called* "symbols" in works of art, but what are in fact really representative "signs"—signs of something else. It is just that element in a poetic metaphor that is lost through translation into common prose that distinguishes the "symbol" that is at work from the element of mere "sign."

Religious symbols share with other non-cognitive symbols these three characteristics. But in addition, and fourthly, religious symbols in particular can be said to "disclose" or "reveal" something about the world in which they function. Religious symbols thus have a very intimate relation to what is usually called religious "knowledge," one that is peculiarly close in the case of those intellectual religious symbols that are religious beliefs or ideas.

Religious symbols are commonly said to "reveal" some "Truth" about experience. But it is clear that this "Truth" is not what we should call in the ordinary sense "knowledge." This revelation can be called "knowledge" or "truth" only in a sense that is equivocal or metaphorical. It is more like direct acquaintance than like descriptive knowledge: it resembles what we call "insight" or "vision." Such religious symbols do not "tell" us anything that is verifiably so; they rather make us "see" something about our human experience in the world.[13]

Non-cognitive symbols resemble linguistic signs in many ways. Like linguistic signs, they are factors in the human social situation to which the members of a group have been conditioned to respond. Like them also, they seem to have their foundation in the process of signification on the lower, organic level. This resemblance is so striking, indeed, that these symbols are often dealt with in terms of "language." By a certain extension men have talked as though they constituted a distinctive "language" of their own, and have tried to explore them in terms of the "language of art" or of the different arts, or of "the language of religion." They have approached these symbols as though their function could be easily identified with certain of the functions of language, like expression and communication. Such symbols, it has been assumed, must "express" and "communicate" something. What is it that they express and communicate? Such questions have led to theories of "artistic truth," and to a new version of the ancient "religious truth."

It is very doubtful whether the extension of "language" to cover the functioning of non-cognitive symbols, for all its suggestiveness, and for all the illumination it brings, does not also introduce so much confusion as to make the game not worth the candle. To be sure, the very same question can be raised about treating cognitive symbols—all postulate systems of "artificial signs"—likewise on the analogy of

[13] For a fuller development of religious symbols, and what they can make us "see," see the author's *The Role of Knowledge in the Western Religious Tradition* (Boston, now in press), Chapter 4: "Knowledge, Intelligence, and Religious Symbols."

language. The ensuing confusions, though very different, are probably just as great. Each of these extensions of the notion of language complements the other. Each seizes upon certain functions of language in the narrower sense, while disregarding other functions. Hence, in terms of this general analysis, it might be better to say, that while both such systems of artificial and manipulable signs on the one hand, and such non-cognitive symbols and their functioning on the other, are founded upon and made possible by different traits of language, it would be clarifying to distinguish both of them from the functioning of language in any strict sense.

A symbol, we have made clear, signifies not something else that might function in its place, but rather it signifies what it does, the response it provokes, in the primary mode of signification. It points to what it does, not to anything else that can do the same thing. Now this is certainly one of the functions which the use of language performs, one of the directions in which the functioning of language tends. It has been said that language oscillates between mathematics and music. It might also be said that language oscillates between performing the function of mathematics and performing the function of "symbols." The former is the exact and precise statement of and expression of certain relations; the latter is the poetic or artistic use of language. In much recent literature, the use of language to convey information in precise and exact statements has been contrasted with its use to "express emotions"—its so-called "emotive" use. This way of stating a significant contrast seems to go at the matter from the wrong end. One use of language is certainly to make exact statements—to "express" certain relations. But the poetic or artistic use of language is hardly "expression" as contrasted with "statement"—it is rather "impression"—its use to create certain "impressions." Many individual words are "impressive" in this way: that is, they can function as *symbols* to provoke a response, without standing for anything as *signs*. Santayana has remarked on the "awful" impression which can be made in English by the word "God." But it is generally certain combinations of words—certain unforgettable phrases or lines—which thus function as symbols.

It is just at this point that we go wrong, when we extend the notion of language to deal with the arts. We go wrong, if we conceive that the arts share with language the function of expressing and communicating in exact statement some proposition or truth—or some dubious "artistic truth"—in the case of the art of religion, some "religious truth"—that might be—perhaps better, at any rate more clearly—stated in words. The arts, including religion, do not significantly employ "signs" of anything else. Their resemblance to language lies not in their "expressive" function; it lies in their "impressive" function. They resemble language to the extent that it employs *symbols,* not to the extent that it uses *signs.* They are not, except incidentally, "significant," in the secondary mode of signification, of anything else for which they stand. They are "significant" in the primary mode—like all symbols, they point to what they do. Those who emphasize the autonomy of the arts, including religion, and regard as incidental the "expression" of culture, social conflicts or trends, ideas, or what have you, seem clearly to be right. A "Bible in stone" like the cathedral of Chartres, overladen as it is with innumerable *signs* of the Christian faith, becomes, according to Paul Tillich, for that reason at least, no more "significant" than, to use his favorite example, a teacup by Cézanne. With all due deference to Paul Tillich, this is an obvious prejudice. It is a prejudice which, very regretfully, I must confess, I share with him completely. Of course, the cathedral of Chartres itself, being the work of inspired artists, is also an artistic symbol—like the teacups of Cézanne.

The various arts differ greatly in the extent to which they do employ signs. Some types of poetry and literature, some kinds of plastic art, use signification in the secondary mode for a large part of their material. On the other hand, it has always been exceedingly difficult to treat music in such terms. The point I am suggesting here is this: no matter how extensive its employment of signs, that belongs to the materials and techniques, to the procedures of the art—that is not the art's primary function, which is to create "impressive" symbols. One of the main problems in the analysis of the arts is to inquire in detail just how they manage to transform the signs they use into symbols. I have elsewhere examined in some detail how in the art of religion religious symbols function as instruments of imaginative "revelation" —which is something quite different from what the signs of theology may possibly "signify" as truth.

If non-cognitive symbols function, not to produce knowledge and truth, but something else, and their products cannot therefore be judged by their truth or falsity, what are the standards of the adequacy and the validity of such non-cognitive symbols—moral, social, artistic, and religious? All Connectives are used to *do* certain definite things, to perform certain determinate functions. Their "adequacy" and "validity" can only be judged and appraised by *how well* they perform their respective functions. A functional test is alone possible, and such a test will of course vary with the specific function. Moreover, the appraisal of the validity of Connectives must always be *comparative*—in comparison with how well another Connective performs the same function—as in the case of theories or organizing hypotheses in the sciences.

Can the standard of the functioning of non-cognitive symbols be properly said to be "truth"? It is well to remember that Connectives, even cognitive symbols, though they play a part in all knowledge, are not themselves "true." Though they are used in formulating "true statements," neither language nor systems of measurement are "true" themselves. Ideals, like Democracy or Liberty, are hardly "true." Mathematics is formally "valid," and strictly speaking should not be called "true." Scientific theories and hypotheses are not "true," in contemporary philosophies of science, but rather "warranted" or "tested."

This is especially important in the case of religious symbols, of which so many are "intellectual" symbols, that is, religious "beliefs" and "doctrines." Stated very briefly, it can be said that the *religious* function of religious beliefs is to strengthen religious faith and commitment—it is not to give "knowledge" but rather "salvation"—it is to express, strengthen, enhance, and clarify a practical commitment, to one's "ultimate concern," in Tillich's phrase, or to "faith in God," the more traditional intellectual religious symbol. The "truth" of religious beliefs is quite irrelevant to their performing their *religious* function. They can do it just as well if they are not "literally" true; and they do it no better if they are. This may be disconcerting to the "rationalist," but it seems to be a fact of life.

Intellectual consistency between "scientific" and "religious" beliefs—if the latter are taken as giving an intellectual explanation of anything

—is a very great value. But it is an intellectual and philosophical value, not a "religious" value. From a living religion, most men continue to want other things more than they want intellectual consistency and clarity. The appeal of intellectual consistency between religious and philosophic beliefs seems to be limited to those whose religious interests are severely intellectual and philosophical. In any event, there is a basic distinction between religious beliefs that are "fundamental," and perform a religious function—that are religious symbols—and those that give intellectual understanding, that construe and interpret religious insight in terms of some particular philosophy, and adjust it to the rest of a man's knowledge and experience. The latter beliefs are the basis of a "rational" or "philosophical" theology. Their function is very important, and not to be lightly discarded. But it is a philosophical, not a religious, function, though certain terms in such a philosophical theology can *become* religious symbols in time, like the Logos, or the Trinity.

But these interesting questions I have dealt with more fully elsewhere.

CHAPTER 10

Qualities, Qualification, and the Aesthetic Transaction

THIS ANALYSIS has so far been led to distinguish five fundamental ways in which factors can function in Substance, or the Situation, taken as a cooperation of processes. These are ontological distinctions: since to function is to be, five different ways of functioning are five different "ways of being." They might indeed be called five "types of being," did this not suggest that there are five different kinds of thing, and did this not in turn seem to say that any one thing is determinately and always that particular kind of thing and no other. But the five ways are rather five different ways in which the *same* thing or "factor" can function. There is nothing that can function in only one way, or that is always of the same type. Moreover, since these are five ways in which factors can be *said* to function, or *said* to be, they might be called five "predicables" or categories. But since the ways of functioning are prior to the ways of stating them, they are *ontological* categories.

These five ways of functioning or ontological categories have been called: Operations and Ways of Operating, Powers and Kinds of Power, and Connectives. For convenience, they can also be designated: Verbs and Adverbs, Nouns and Adjectives, and Conjunctions—though in so doing these terms are being used in the same *ontological* sense as the other set.

I

So far, this analysis has managed to get along without "qualities" as a metaphysical concept, in any technical sense; it has not yet been forced to come to terms with them. The question is, is "Quality" a sixth fundamental way of functioning in Substance, that must be added to the other five? If not, just what is the ontological status of qualities?

Many analyses, especially recent analyses, make them metaphysically ultimate—ultimate features or traits of "being," say the philosophies of being; ultimate traits or features of "experience," say the philosophies of experience. There is Charles Peirce and his "Firstness." [1] There is W. R. Dennes, who distinguishes three categories, "Events," "Relations," and "Qualities." [2] There are the emergent evolutionists, like Samuel Alexander, who identifies "emergence" with the appearance of a new "Quality," [3] to say nothing of Hegel and the Marxians, with their "transformation of Quantity into Quality." There is the whole tradition of empiricism, for which atomic "sense qualities" are fundamental. And there is the whole recent criticism of that particular analysis of "experience," which in appealing to so-called "immediate experience" has brought to light a host of other less precise "qualities" of experienced Substance—in Bradley, Bergson, James, Whitehead, and Dewey, to name only a few—as well as in the elaborate phenomenological and existentialist analyses, like Heidegger's. And of course there is Aristotle, whose chemistry or theory of elements is qualitative, and who makes "qualitative change" one of the basic types of process. It is clear that any responsible metaphysical analysis has got to do something about "quality."

I am here at last attempting to face up to this obligation. In what follows I am trying primarily to explore the question in preliminary fashion, trying to see how qualities can be fitted into this general ontological analysis—following the lead, as Woodbridge liked to put it, of the subject-matter itself. This paper might well bear as subtitle the traditional classification of certain of the more Socratic of the Platonic dialogues, πειραστικός. To use a more recently fashionable term, it is definitely "work in progress." Its primary concern is not to defend this tentative exploration against objections, however richly deserved—above all, not to defend the whole enterprise against those whose

[1] Charles S. Peirce, *Collected Papers,* Vol. VI (Cambridge, Mass., 1935), paragraph 32.

[2] William R. Dennes, "The Categories of Naturalism," in *Naturalism and the Human Spirit,* ed. Y. H. Krikorian (New York, 1944).

[3] Samuel Alexander, *Space, Time and Deity* (London, 1920), esp. Vol. II, Book III.

philosophical interests flow in other channels—the Isis, perhaps, or the Cam. My own follow the Miljada and the Winooski—though some may judge that it is rather the Caÿster.[4] What I should most appreciate is suggestion and help.

Now I am of course very far from denying the existence or the "reality" of qualities as encountered in Substance. Qualities are certainly encountered. And they are encountered, as we say, "immediately." They are clearly a pervasive aspect of experience, as the many sensitive "phenomenological" descriptions well attest. This is not the question I am raising. What I am asking is, rather, Is "Quality" an ultimate and unanalysable metaphysical category? Or is it more illuminating to treat qualities as falling under one of the more general "ways of functioning"? Is "immediacy" an inherent character of at least certain types of quality? Or is it rather to be taken as a distinctive "way of operating?" Just what is the ontological status of qualities, and how are they to be best construed?

In recognizing qualities as encountered, I mean to include not only "sensed" qualities—the so-called "secondary qualities" of Locke—but also all those interesting further qualities which many perceptive analyses of experience have revealed, which are usually said to be "felt" rather than "sensed," and are today often called—though not by Locke —"tertiary qualities." These are the qualities explored by what Santayana calls "literary psychology": they pretty completely elude laboratory psychology. They seem to be best revealed by the poet or the novelist, by a Proust. Indeed, many such qualities seem to be literally "ineffable": they cannot be stated or expressed directly, but they can be communicated, and thus "shared," only by suggestion. Such indirect communication of what cannot be directly stated is one of the most important functions of language, and of the other arts— the "poetic" function of language, we often call it.

I should certainly emphasize also what used to be called the "affective" side of experience, which was one of a trinity of sides, the other members being the "cognitive" and the "conative." The separation was of course preposterous. The elements of this "affective aspect" were called "feelings." Indeed, "quality" is the term in the language

[4] Of these philosophical rivers, Stagira lies on the Miljada, Burlington on the Winooski, and Ephesus on the Caÿster.

of the philosophies of being for what in the language of the philosophies of experience is called "feeling." When quality and feeling are separated—when experience is held to be *of* being, rather than, as it should be viewed, *in* being—then qualities are said to be "felt," and feelings are said to be feelings *of* qualities.

This seems to be a misleading reduplication. "Quality" and "feeling" are rather two ways of looking at the same factor: they are the same interaction, the same "transaction," looked at from opposite ends, as it were. It is another case of Aristotle's road from Athens to Thebes being the same road as the road from Thebes to Athens. Such qualities can more properly be said to "belong" to the Situation, to Substance, and to have their "locus" in the interaction or cooperation of processes that goes to make it up. Tertiary qualities certainly do not belong to the Situation apart from human participation in it; but neither are they mere "feelings" in a "feeler."[5]

Thus, in the familiar—and controversial—illustration from Dewey, of the "situation of inquiry," it is the situation that is "doubtful" or "indeterminate," and not merely the inquirer who doubts and is uncertain, or the context before the inquirer comes into it. There are plenty of situations in which we participate that are "indeterminate" in just this sense—the outcome is genuinely "doubtful," as in the reader's response to the contentions of this paper. It is not merely *we* who are uncertain about the outcome, in the sense that we do not yet know what the outcome is going to be. The outcome itself is not yet determined, and is hence not merely unknown to us, but is as yet unknowable—save perhaps to God, who never tells, and possibly to the Marxians, who do not possess that virtue, but like the rest of us often guess wrong.

But this example does illustrate my difficulty as to the metaphysical ultimacy of "quality": what is to be gained by calling this "inde-

[5] "If we designate this permeating qualitative unity in psychological terms, we say it is felt rather than thought. Then, if we hypostatize it, we call it *a* feeling. But to term it a feeling is to reverse the actual state of affairs. The existence of unifying qualitativeness in the subject-matter defines the meaning of 'feeling.' The notion that 'a feeling' designates a ready-made independent psychical entity is a product of a reflection which presupposes the direct presence of quality as such. 'Feeling' and 'felt' are names for a *relation* of quality." John Dewey, "Qualitative Thought," in *Philosophy and Civilization* (New York, 1931), p. 99. Quotations used by permission of G. P. Putnam's Sons.

terminacy" a "quality"? A "situation of inquiry" that is "indeterminate" is a situation in which a process of inquiry is taking place in a certain way; it is one in which certain processes are functioning "indeterminately." The "indeterminacy" is clearly what I have called a "way of operating," an adverb. Again, the situation is not "indeterminate" before the process of inquiry begins—the "outcome" is not uncertain before there is a process directed toward an "outcome." When there has arisen a process operating "indeterminately," we can then say, the situation becomes "qualified" with "indeterminacy"; but this, too, clearly points to a "way of operating." However "directly" this "qualification" of indeterminacy may be *felt*, it is clearly not ultimate and unanalysable, and does not demand a distinctive ontological category.

So I am quite willing to recognize all the qualities encountered in Substance—provided only that the category of "quality" be not taken as "ultimate." We do indeed live in a qualitative world, and all the adjectives that men like Dewey or Whitehead or Heidegger or the rest hurl at the Situation in their impressive catalogues are justified and deserved. Substance is "shot through and through" with qualities. Only—I want to ask, "What's all the shooting about?" How does this process of "qualification" take place? What is its ontological status?

But though I am thus far from denying the existence of qualities as encountered, I do think the category of "Quality" is today suffering from a metaphysical inflation. To begin with, it is an extremely confused concept. As our British friends like to say, it is a good deal of a muddle. The term is used to cover many different types of factor in Substance that seem to possess very little in common. In a sense, this is true of any generalized metaphysical category: such a category brings together a wide variety of things. But to be fruitful, the various factors such a category designates must all have the same ontological status—they must all perform the same function. But the various factors that have all been recently called "qualities" do not have the same ontological status or function—such diverse things as traits, characters, properties, sensed qualities, tertiary qualities, "pervasive" qualities, immediate values, aesthetic values, and the rest. Thus by no means all these diverse types of so-called "qualities" fall very clearly under the heading of "kinds" or "sorts," the traditional Aristotelian category of Quality, *τὸ ποιόν*. Whitehead, indeed, seems to have been sound in rejecting the term "quality" and in trying to invent a more precise terminology.

Then again, "Quality" is clearly not an ultimate, irreducible, and unanalysable metaphysical category. All the diverse types of quality just listed fall under other categories, and can be more fruitfully dealt with in their terms. This, to be sure, would require illustration in detail—an illustration briefly suggested in Section IV. The concept of "quality," I take it, implies unanalysability—except, perhaps, into component qualities. In particular, the "simple, unique" qualities are not only unanalysable; they are also wholly inaccessible: they are either "seen" or "felt," or not. If you don't see or feel them, you are, as Santayana puts it, "merely blind," or "merely numb." Such a non-operational conception certainly stops all further inquiry.

It seems much more fruitful and suggestive to approach "quality" operationally. A quality, like everything else, would then not be a unique "way of being," but rather, it would *be* what it *does*. It would be what I call a "power"—a power to operate in a determinate and discoverable way. And, like every power, it could be grasped and defined through its way of operating—even if it should turn out that all we could discover about what it does is that it serves to "immediatize" experience, to "qualify" the human or "private" pole of the transaction with "immediacy."

Hence, since Quality seems to be a stopping-point beyond which exploration cannot go, it seems best not to start with Quality, but rather to introduce it only when we are forced to. In this respect Quality appears to resemble the "Unity" treated in Chapter 7. Since it is clearly impossible to get from Unity to Plurality, while it is very easy to get from Plurality to a variety of "unifications," it is always best to start from Plurality as encountered, and then to trace the various "unifications" to which we are led in our exploration. Equally, since we can clearly get nowhere *from* Quality, it seems best to approach Quality through the process of "qualification."

One of the reasons for distrusting a metaphysical emphasis on qualities, and certainly one of the sources of the difficulties in dealing with quality in the recent literature, is the central place it occupies in various dubious theories of experience. I am thinking not only of "sense data" theories, but still more of theories of so-called "immediate experience." Quality has been appealed to by all those who have been trying to get away from the exclusive emphasis on relations or structure—by F. H. Bradley in criticising T. H. Green, and by the phenomenologists in Germany in criticising the German Neo-Kantians. The emphasis on quality in British and American analyses of experience has been due primarily to Bradley's insistence that "feeling" is more ultimate than "thought"—more "real," Bradley would put it. This emphasis has been carried over even in thinkers like Whitehead and Dewey. Dewey, indeed, who like Bradley was reacting strongly against T. H. Green's structuralism—Green's reduction of all "feelings" or particulars, or "qualities," to "relations" or universals—often sounds just like Bradley—like a *pluralistic* Bradley, to be sure, with not one but many "qualitative wholes of feeling." Dewey's "pervasive and integrating qualities" [6] have puzzled many an inexperienced reader unaware of their background in the reaction against Green, in which both Dewey and Bradley shared.

In Bradley, "Quality" is identified with "Reality," as over against the "Appearance" that is created by "Thought," which by its analysis breaks up qualitative wholes, seizing upon particular structures, and plucking them out of such qualitative continua. This is another version of the old complaint of the idealists, that in using "understanding," or science, "we murder to dissect." And what we "murder" always turns out to be Quality. Hence Quality is what has to be added to relations or structure to get back to "Reality," for all good Hegelians, however unorthodox, like Bradley or Dewey.

Quality is indeed bound up with all theories of "immediate experience" as experience "unmediated" by thought, undistorted by analysis and interpretation, experience that is thus a kind of direct contact with what is. To find what is, therefore, we must get *back* to Quality, *back* to the starting-point, *back* to the undistorted datum. Bradley, being after all British, is a true follower of Locke's dubious principle, that the "original" of knowledge is the criterion of its "extent" and "certainty."

Now this seems to be a perverse view of the status of qualities in existence. Accepting the position that qualities are a fundamental and

[6] *Ibid.*, pp. 93–117.

important aspect of what is, of Substance, sound metaphysical advice would seem to suggest, rather, *Get on* to qualities! Qualities, that is, are bound up, not with starting-points, with "data," but with outcomes and eventuations, with the result of the cooperations of activities and powers, with the completion of transactions. In the complex cooperation of operations that is Substance, the Situation can be said to *achieve* "qualification," to *become* "qualified." All process has an aspect of "qualification," and "quality" is most fruitfully viewed as the outcome of this process of "qualification." The primary meaning of "quality" is thus to be seen as "qualified," the past participle of a "verb" or process.

Thus Whitehead seems to have been on the right track, in maintaining that qualities belong, not to "subjects"—that is, not to starting-points—but to eventuations—to what he calls "superjects" of "informed value." Dewey put it more narrowly, that in inquiry, qualities belong, not to the objects inquired into—what he calls "antecedent subject-matter"—but to the objective of inquiry, objects known—the "consummation" of the process of inquiry.

In stating this position, I do not mean—as Whitehead and Dewey certainly do not mean—that nothing in the Situation can be said to "have" any qualities to begin with. Clearly, all the factors involved do. But their qualities are the outcome of previous processes of "qualification": they are already "past participles."

II

This view that "quality" is the outcome of a process, that it is a way of being "qualified," holds with the simplest "qualities," like color. What the "color" of anything actually is, is the outcome of a very complicated process. "Colors," far from being "given," just "as they are," as is sometimes said, especially by British epistemologists, are first encountered as distinguishing marks, or stimuli to selective and "discriminating" response. The precise "color"—that is, the actual "quality"—is not only the outcome of a complicated set of natural mechanisms—the nature of the surface, of the particular light rays, of the receptor organ, etc.—but also of long processes of attention, analysis, comparison, etc., on the part of the visualizer. It notoriously takes a very high degree of training, in a sophisticated painter, educated to "observe" the actual colors of things, to "qualify" the situation, on his canvas, with those actual colors. Even a so-called "simple quality," like the particular color of a particular surface, is thus not "immediately given," but is "mediated" by a long experience, certainly, and probably also by reflection or thought—by what may even be called "inquiry" —though not necessarily—and certainly not exclusively—by "linguistic" reflection and inquiry. Such a simple quality, in other words, is the outcome of such processes of "qualification."

Hence, if we want to call the direct encountering, or enjoyment, of so-called sensed qualities, "immediate experience," then "immediate experience" is always "mediated," and always comes as the outcome of complicated processes. A more precise term might well be, an "immediatizing" of experience. "Direct experience," "immediacy," is always the outcome of such a process of "immediatizing."

If we now ask, what is the ontological status of such qualities as color? we are led to an analysis of the "visual situation," or the "visual transaction," in which this process of qualification takes place. "Seeing" is a complex cooperation of Powers, involving various mechanisms as its necessary conditions. The "seeing," we can say, "belongs to," is a "function of," "takes place in," the "visual situation." It does not "take place" in the sense-organ, the eye, or in the brain, or in the object seen—though all these mechanisms are involved as necessary conditions of the functioning of the "visual situation"—or of "Substance functioning visually." We do not see *in* our eyes, but *with* our eyes; we do not see *in* our brain, but *with* our brain, etc. More properly, we see *in* the "seeing situation," in the "visible world."

The so-called sensed qualities, like color, can likewise be said to "belong to," to be a "function of," to "operate in," the seeing situation. In the visual transaction, grass functions or operates as "green," it is there properly said to *be* green. And it can also properly be said to have that "power" of cooperating in that particular way, even when it is not being seen. But that power does not operate in the absence of any of the necessary conditions of that cooperation—i.e., it does not operate in the absence of light of the right intensity and the right character, in the absence of radiation of the right wave-lengths reflected, or in the absence of a normal eye, not color-blind, etc.

The situation of color, a "quality," is precisely analogous to that of the seeing of structural relations. In the visual transaction, the railway track converges in perspective, when the seeing eye—or the camera—is at a certain location. The track "looks" or "shows itself" that way. The "looking," the "showing," belong to the specific cooperation of Powers. Neither the color of the grass, a "quality," nor the converging of the track, a "structure," can be said in any intelligible sense to be "in" the eye, or "in" the brain; i.e., neither is in any intelligible sense "subjective," or "mental": both are clearly in the "visible world." Nor are they in any intelligible sense "in" the grass, or "in" the track, taken by themselves, in isolation from the visual situation. When thus taken in isolation, ἁπλῶς, *simpliciter,* we can say that grass has the "power" to interact with other necessary factors in the visual situation *as* "green," the track has the "power" to interact *as* "converging." But these powers could of course never have been discovered apart from their cooperation with other powers of other factors—that is, they are all "relational" in character, they are powers to interact, to cooperate. They are not "intrinsic," "inherent," or "absolute." They are "dependent on" the constitution or make-up of the grass, or of the track. But they are not inferrible from that constitution alone, because these powers are dependent on the constitution of a number of other factors as well.

I have been speaking of "the visual situation"—and of its characteristic powers, the generalized powers of the grass or of the track to function as "green" or as "converging." These are the "properties" or ways of interacting and cooperating, displayed by factors in all visual situations. But ultimately, each visual situation is unique—it is a concrete individual "Substance." It involves, that is, the unique past experience which each "seer" brings to the seeing, determining his sensitivity and his selective attention, the unique character of *his* active cooperation in the visual transaction. Thus the process of seeing which qualifies the visual situation with color is in each case ultimately unique.

For seeing, like all perceiving, is not the operation of a passive power of being acted upon by what is perceived: our psychologies force us to break with Aristotle on this fundamental point. Seeing is an interaction, a cooperation, a transaction, in which both the perceived and the perceiver are "active," as well as many other factors. I well remember how puzzled G. E. Moore was that we should so improperly speak of an "act" of perception, since perceiving for him so clearly involved no action at all. He was almost as horrified at the idea that the perceiver *does* something, as at the complementary idea that the grass does something when it "looks" or "shows itself" green. But perceiving, like all types of experiencing, involves activity on the part of the experiencer—it is a "doing," ultimately an "art," that selects, manipulates, and reconstructs. This is true of even that type of experience usually thought of as most nearly "passive," the perceiving or feeling of a simple quality like color.

In most cases, of course, this *unique* character of every visual transaction, of every process of qualification, and hence of every quality of color seen, can be disregarded; and it is so disregarded in any scientific formulation of what is seen or observed. There are, to be sure, striking differences among men in the qualifications they can effect, and hence in the qualities they can see, like that between strong visualists and weak—William Pepperell Montague once startled a class by confessing that he did most of his thinking flat on his back seeing things. And the funded past experience men bring to perception is clearly culturally conditioned: if an illiterate savage cannot "see" a printed page, neither can a degenerate urban soul "see" a patch of woods or a water-hole.[7] But there is much agreement also: surely the main features of the world must "look" pretty much the same to all cultures, and perception of structural relations must be almost universal, especially of all those so insistent for practice. The differences seem to be not so much structural and pragmatic, as aesthetic, and to lie precisely in these qualities we are exploring.

The aesthetically sensitive painter or poet can "notice" further features, in the seeing of grass, for instance, than the mere "green" that suffices for most practical purposes. He brings to the visual transaction an experience, a skill, a trained art of perceiving, that enables him to qualify it in new ways; and he can "communicate" these new "qualities" in his particular "language" or medium. He can thus reveal unsus-

[7] Compare the extraordinary results obtained at the experimental laboratories at Princeton by Harvey Cantrill and his colleagues, with their "Rooms of Illusion"—making clear that the simplest "perception" is culturally conditioned. These experimental results should occasion surprise in some of our more epistemological British colleagues.

pected powers of being seen, unsuspected "qualities," in grass. Chinese and Japanese painters are notoriously good at this; so, in very different ways, are the Impressionists and Van Gogh.

This is the source of the enormous fertility of painting or poetry, in revealing new visual, new perceptual powers in things—in "enhancing the significance," as we say, of the visible world, in "disclosing new meanings and consummatory experiences," as Dewey puts it. The painter can "qualify," not merely his canvas, and not merely our experience, but the visible world itself with new qualities hitherto unsuspected. That is why we feel that his work is "educating" us, even "teaching" us something; and why we are tempted, despite all the difficulties and paradoxes to which that leads, to say that he is increasing our "knowledge" and teaching us "truth"—"artistic truth," we call it. Painting, poetry, music, religion, all the arts in fact, do indeed "teach" us something. They may not teach us *that* anything is so—that is as it may be, and I myself think it isn't. But they certainly teach us *how to do* something better. The painter shows us *how to see* the visible world better—how to see grass. Even so the prophet and the saint show us *how to see* the Divine better—*how to see* God.

This "knowledge" is not the kind of thing that can be put into words and statements, and formulated in neat manuals of "How to Look at the Visible World," or "How to See the Divine." It is not the aesthetician with his books, but the painter who by his *painting* teaches us how to "see" the world, just as it is not the theologian with his words, but the prophet and the saint who by their *quality of "holiness"*—I heartily detest this apparently established term—teach us how to "see" the Divine. But surely we Americans, with our devotion to technical intelligence, are willing to call this "knowledge." Artistic "truth," religious "truth," if we are to use the terms at all, must be taken, not as the truth of the propositions of a science, but as what we Americans have come to call a "know-how." It is a knowing *how* to qualify the world with the qualities appropriate to each art.

And such processes of qualification are, I take it, just what we mean by "revelation" or "disclosing."[8] For the qualities that are their out-

[8] Compare Ernst Cassirer, *An Essay on Man* (New Haven, 1944), Chapter IX, "Art": "Language and science are abbreviations of reality; art is an intensification of reality. Language and science depend upon one and the same process of abstraction; art may be described as a continuous process of concretion. . . .

comes are qualities of the world, and what the painter or the prophet has done can properly be said to be to "reveal" new powers in things. Just as in the visual situation the grass is qualified by "green," and *is* green, so in the aesthetic situation it is qualified by aesthetic qualities, and *is* beautiful; and just so in the religious situation, the world is qualified by the Divine, and *is* Divine. What is revealed in each case is the power of such a qualification—a power both of seeing and of being seen.

Indeed, as a discoverer, the painter has much in common with the scientist. What he does with, and makes out of, what he sees—selecting it, manipulating it, reorganizing and reconstructing it, by means of the instrument of his distinctive art, his "language" or medium—is very much like the "experimentation" of the scientist. Both the scientist and the artist, by revealing new powers and pushing back the limits in things, enlarge our horizons, increase our knowledge, and extend our power. This suggests that to perform his function successfully, the artist, like the scientist, should be accorded by right the freest possible experimentation and manipulation of his materials, and that he should likewise recognize the obligation to bring to his experimentation the widest possible past experience and store of resources—both are essential to the artistic transaction. And dare I add that the activities of the prophet and the saint also resemble the "experimentation" of the scientist, and are subject to the same conditions? [9]

If the position I am trying to explore, that qualities are the outcome of a process of qualification, holds of such "simple qualities" as color,

---

Leonardo da Vinci spoke of the purpose of painting and sculpture in the words: 'Saper vedere'. . . . The great painters show us the forms of outward things; the great dramatists show us the forms of our inner life. Dramatic art *discloses* a new breadth and depth of life. It conveys an awareness of human things and human destinies, of human greatness and misery, in comparison to which our ordinary existence appears poor and trivial. All of us feel, vaguely and dimly, the infinite potentialities of life, which silently await the moment when they are to be called forth from dormancy into the clear and intense light of consciousness. It is not the degree of infection but the degree of intensification and illumination which is the measure of the excellence of art" (pp. 143, 144, 147–48).

[9] For a further development of this conception of religious "knowledge" as a "know-how" and a "revelation" of possibilities through this process of qualification, see the author's *The Role of Knowledge in the Western Religious Tradition* (Boston, now in press), Chapter IV, "Knowledge, Intelligence, and Religious Symbols."

how much more clearly does it hold of more complicated qualities like those we call "aesthetic qualities!" These are "more complicated" in that they depend on a much more complicated set of mechanisms, and are the outcome of much more complex processes, the whole complex of the "aesthetic transaction."

In the "aesthetic situation," or "transaction," in which various factors are functioning and cooperating "aesthetically"—that is, in hearing music, in seeing a painting, in listening to a poem, in being impressed by a building, etc.—the situation is becoming "aesthetically qualified." Such "aesthetic qualification" is an aspect, a part, of what Dewey calls the *"work* of art." It is a part of what art *does* aesthetically—though not the only thing, of course. Employing a term of Dewey's, we can say, "Aesthetic qualities accrue to the situation that is functioning aesthetically." That is, the aesthetic qualities that function in the aesthetic transaction are not given at the outset, if the situation is really functioning aesthetically. They are certainly not given in the so-called "artistic object." In that object, we can say, there are exhibited "artistic qualities," which are themselves the outcome of the complex processes by which the artist succeeded in giving an "artistic qualification" to his product.

In the "artistic situation," or "transaction," the situation functioning "artistically"—that is, in the painting of a picture, the making of a poem, the composing of music—the situation becomes "qualified artistically"—that is, "artistic qualities" can be said to "accrue" to it. Many such artistic qualities are "embodied" in the artistic product, in the painting, the poem, or the composition. These "artistic qualities" can hence be said to have achieved a locus in the artistic object.

Into this complex "artistic transaction" there enter, to be sure, a number of "aesthetic transactions." The painter or the composer at the outset certainly qualifies his materials or his theme aesthetically. The Chinese painter has qualified his grass aesthetically through his sensitive perception before he begins to select and manipulate with his brush. Beethoven surely qualified aesthetically the opening theme of the second movement of his 7th symphony—that inexorable march of fate slowly revealing itself, a veritable Oedipus of sound—before he let his imagination develop it. And at every stage of the artistic transaction the artist finds himself also in an aesthetic situation—he is qualifying what he is doing aesthetically, and these aesthetic qualities are important, even controlling factors in his artistic activity. Any adequate analysis of the "artistic transaction"—of creating a work of art—must explore these intimate relations with the many aesthetic transactions involved.

But in the end these processes of creation eventuate in the embodiment of *artistic* qualities in the finished product. When that product enters in turn into the aesthetic situation of the "seer," the "hearer," the "reader," these artistic qualities serve as "powers"—powers to function *aesthetically*. The artistic qualities of the painting, poem, or musical composition serve as powers to qualify the situation aesthetically, in cooperation with the many other powers of the aesthetic observer. They serve also as powers to function aesthetically in various other ways. "Qualifying," producing aesthetic qualities, is far from being the only way in which things can function aesthetically.

Of course, to say that "aesthetic qualities" are the outcome of a complex "aesthetic transaction," is not to say that such qualities need be themselves in every sense "complex." In themselves, they can easily be "simple," "pervasive," and "wholes." We all know what these terms point to—though I am none too sure that this is a good way of stating it. They mean, that these qualities are "immediately experienced," "directly felt." They point to the power such qualities possess of *doing* something to us—to the power they exhibit of cooperating with our own powers in a certain way. They do not mean what would be clearly false, that such qualities are actually and inherently "simple," "immediate," "direct," etc. That is, "simplicity," "immediacy," "directness," are ways of functioning rather than inherent characters. In any event, it is clear that, complex or "simple," aesthetic qualities, like the simple qualities of color, are the outcome of a process of qualification.

III

At this point it would be appropriate to include an analysis of the "aesthetic situation" or "transaction." But this is work, if not in "progress," at least still in "movement." It is possible here only to make a few preliminary suggestions as to how to approach this complex and difficult matter. Let us begin by distinguishing the "aesthetic transaction" in terms of "functioning aesthetically," and then try to follow the lead of this leading principle. Let us take "aesthetic" as primarily an "adverb," as a distinctive way of operating, and only derivatively as an adjective characterizing a noun. But, as always, this adverb is translatable, and the distinctively "aesthetic" has been, and of course can be, construed in terms of each of these categories, of each of the metaphysical types of functioning. It has been defined in terms of man's relation to a noun, as an experience or "sense" of some unique object, traditionally held to be "beauty" or aesthetic "form." It has been taken as an adjective, "aesthetic," as designating certain kinds of materials, like the objects of so-called "fine art." It has been viewed as a verb, "aesthetic experience," assumed to be a specific and distinctive "experience" or activity. And, most fruitfully, it has been taken as an adverb, as a way of interacting—"functioning aesthetically."

Now as in the case of all similar general types of "situation" or "transaction"—the visual situation, the linguistic situation, the evaluative situation, the moral situation, the religious situation, and the rest—all these construings are possible, and each is "right": there is a sense in which the aesthetic situation can be construed in each of these ways, and certain important aspects of it thus brought to light, especially if the others be not denied. But in line with this general metaphysical analysis, it is proposed that we try to explore where we get when we define "the aesthetic situation" as the situation—or Substance—that is functioning "aesthetically," in which various factors and powers are cooperating aesthetically to produce a distinctive aesthetic outcome or consequence. This is to define "the aesthetic transaction" in terms of its outcome or eventuation, as a complex of processes of aesthetic "qualification," in which various factors in the situation become aesthetically qualified in different ways.

This approach has several important negative implications. It means, first, that the aesthetic situation is not to be defined in terms of any particular factors or materials involved in the cooperation—in terms of any distinctively "aesthetic materials," of any "aesthetic" qualities, forms, organizations, structures, devices, mechanisms, or the like. All such factors and materials and devices *become* "aesthetic" if and only if they enable the situation to function aesthetically, if they produce a distinctively "aesthetic" outcome, if they contribute to the process of "aesthetic qualification." Only then do they become powers to function "aesthetically," only then do they become factors or powers qualified as "aesthetic."

Secondly, this approach means that "aesthetic experience" is not to be taken as a unique kind of experience, distinct from all other kinds of experience, and possessing no continuity with them. In fact, all experience exhibits an aspect of "functioning aesthetically": this way of functioning is discriminable in every situation, though it is not always, or even usually, so discriminated. This way is merely selected, accentuated, intensified, and concentrated in what we are calling the "aesthetic situation." It can then in turn enter into other ways of functioning: it can become a power in the cooperation that goes to make them up.

Thirdly, "aesthetic experience" is not unique in being directed to a unique object, in being the experience or "sense" of some unique "aesthetic object," like "beauty," or "aesthetic form," or "aesthetic qualities" —however this aesthetic object may be construed. All such so-called "objects" of aesthetic experience can, to be sure, on occasion function aesthetically—they can play a part in the aesthetic transaction. But they are "objects" of a genuinely aesthetic experience only if they do so play a part in functioning aesthetically.

In other words, the functional approach here proposed precludes taking "aesthetic" as inherently either an "adjective," a "verb," or a "noun."

Any set of factors can be involved in functioning aesthetically, and can serve as powers to cooperate aesthetically. There is no one type of material that alone possesses aesthetic powers, or qualities. There is no one type of experience that alone possesses aesthetic powers. The powers of materials and experiences, as throughout, cannot be determined before they cooperate in functioning aesthetically. Only the experimental manipulation of materials and experiences can discover the powers—and the limits—they can display, and enlarge their range. This suggests, as has been already noted, the freest possible experimentation and manipulation of materials and experiences, and the widest possible past experience, to be brought to the aesthetic situation.

No attempt is made here to define, or even to try to explore, what it means to "function aesthetically." This is notoriously an exceedingly complex and difficult matter. The definitions always turn out to be far too narrow: they have neglected something. And to set some line of demarcation around "functioning aesthetically" is an empirical inquiry. It involves starting with a function vaguely and imprecisely denoted, then exploring the great variety of effects different "works of art," or more precisely, different artistic qualities, can produce in conjunction with different human participants in the aesthetic transaction; and on the basis of a certain number of these diverse functions, trying to draw some kind of a line. Since clearly all the functions that all artistic qualities perform for all men are not performed by any one type of artistic quality, it seems unlikely that "functioning aesthetically" can be identified with any common core. The aesthetic function of "art" or of artistic qualities seems to be actually a complex group of functions, any selection from which can be properly said to be "functioning aesthetically" in some fashion. The problem and the situation seem to be precisely analogous to what is involved in trying to define what it means to "function religiously."

Still, to give some indication of the formal conditions of a preliminary denotation of what is involved in "functioning aesthetically," it might be said:

1) Something happens to the individual participant in the aesthetic transaction. His "experience" is reconstructed, and thus "educated," as Dewey puts it. That is, his experience becomes aesthetically qualified, as the outcome of a process of aesthetic qualification. Aesthetic qualities "accrue" to his experience.

2) Something happens to the situation as a whole, and to the non-human as well as to the human pole of it, that is, to the artistic objects as well as to the aesthetic beholder. Something "accrues" to the situation: both it and the artistic object become qualified with new and "aesthetic" qualities.

3) This process of qualification of the situation as a whole, of the artistic object, and of the beholder's experience, is effected through the practice of "aesthetic arts and skills," which employ certain activities and techniques, including the mechanism of artistic connectives. These arts, skills, and techniques become themselves "aesthetic"—they are qualified "aesthetically"—in the measure that they succeed in effecting

such aesthetic qualification of the situation, the artistic object, and the beholder's experience.

These three functions, the function for the individual participant, the function for the situation and the artistic object, and the employment of the aesthetic arts, seem to be necessary conditions of any case of what could be properly called "functioning aesthetically."

I emphasize the employment of "aesthetic arts," for the aesthetic transaction involves the active cooperation of the human participant, the beholder, the "appreciator" or "valuer." Seeing a painting, hearing music, listening to a poem, and the rest, are, like perceiving in general, not the operation of a passive power of being acted upon, but rather an interaction, a cooperation, a transaction, in which both the painting and the participant are active, as well as various other factors in the situation. And this transaction can itself be viewed as an "art": that is, like every art, it involves a selection from the artistic qualities of the painting, and a manipulation and reorganization of what is selected, in order to effect the aesthetic qualification. It is a) a making something—aesthetic qualities, b) out of something—artistic qualities, c) by certain means, techniques, and connectives, d) for some end—which in the aesthetic arts is immediately or proximately the qualification itself, and more ultimately, something like what the artist can say of his own artistic end: as Dylan Thomas put it, quoting an earlier artist, "I work for the glory of God and to please myself."

Finally, what is the function of the aesthetic transaction itself? What do the various aesthetic qualities with which the aesthetic arts can qualify the situation, the experience of the participant, and the artistic object, themselves do in turn? We have already suggested that this function is to "teach" something, to "re-educate" us, as Dewey puts it—to teach us a know-how, to reveal or disclose something to us. What do these aesthetic qualities teach us?

The aesthetic qualities we make out of the painter's artistic qualities clearly teach us how to see selected aspects of the world more adequately than we could without their assistance. Sometimes they teach us how to see the face of nature, or of the works of man; sometimes they teach us how to see another human being better. At bottom, they teach us how to see color and form, their relations and qualities. They reveal powers and possibilities we had not noticed before. They enable us to see what can be done with lines, masses, colors, with the features of nature, with the gestures and attitudes of men, with the symbols in terms of which men lead their emotional lives. The aesthetic qualities we make out of the composer's musical qualities teach us how to hear sounds better, how they can be put together, how they can illustrate a pattern of musical logic and dialectic, how they can create a world of pure and unalloyed form. They teach us how emotion can be expressed, communicated, and resolved through a purge of pity and terror. What aesthetic qualities we make out of the poet's poetic qualities teach us the music and the logic of words and language, the feel of words, and the tang of life as lived. They teach us the emotional intensity of thought. They teach us the sweetness and the glory of being a rational animal, and the abysses to which reason misused can lead. They teach us the possibilities of human nature, for weal or woe.

The aesthetic qualities we make out of the work of the painter, the composer, the poet, teach us how to use our eyes, our ears, our minds, and our feelings with greater power and skill. They make us more keenly aware both of what is and of what might be, in the world that offers itself to our sensitive receptivity. They point to unsuspected qualities in the world encountered. Still more, they point to the new qualities with which that world, in cooperation with the spirit of man, can clothe itself. For artistic qualities and the aesthetic qualities they can in turn produce are the product of an enterprise in which the world and man are genuinely cooperative, and in which the working together of natural materials, of human techniques, both artistic and aesthetic, and of human vision is most clearly creative of new qualities and powers.

Every aesthetic transaction seems to be ultimately unique. Not only, since it involves human cooperation, does it involve naturally all the powers and limits of the individual participant—not only is it "determined" by his own particular culture, his particular traditions, his unique experience and training. In addition, the process of aesthetic qualification "immediatizes" the situation, clothes the human pole of the transaction with the quality of "immediacy" which many have called "private consciousness," and which Santayana names "spirit"—"the flame of spirit."

Here if anywhere is to be found the locus of ultimate "privacy"—and not in toothaches, that favorite example of the conventional "subjectivist." Toothaches are really very public affairs, as anyone who has ever had one in the family knows. And likewise "intelligence," taken as the cognitive power, the power to know, is exceedingly public—as Averroes, Spinoza, Dewey, and Mead have long maintained. It depends upon language, which is scarcely a private possession, and its fruits can be communicated through words and public statements. There is a genuine "unity of the active intelligence," a genuine "social intelligence."

In contrast, let us call the power to participate in the aesthetic transaction, "imagination." (I am by no means sure that this is the best name for this power; if we do adopt it, it must be called something like "aesthetic imagination," to distinguish it from the "intellectual imagination" that is dependent on the power of language.) Then this "aesthetic imagination," defined as "the power to participate in the aesthetic transaction," seems to be ultimately private, and its fruits appear capable of being only very imperfectly communicated and "shared" with others, and then only by symbolic devices. There seems to be thus no "unity of the active imagination," no genuinely "social imagination," as there is clearly a "social intelligence"—unless indeed "social imagination" be merely another name for religion. But in the religious transaction, it is clearly those religious arts and skills that employ unifying connectives—the religious symbols that can provoke a common and shared response—that make religion essentially and primarily a social matter. There seems to be little that is analogous to these public connectives in the aesthetic arts, and what there is seems incidental and not primary. Indeed, it is not in religion, where Whitehead perversely found it,[10] but in aesthetic qualification, that we begin to approach "what the individual does with his own solitariness."

Hence if in general "quality" be the principle of individuation, "aesthetic quality" may well be central to the principle of personalization. In the transaction of perceiving perceptual qualities, man comes to consciousness. In the aesthetic transaction, it may well be, man at last finds his inmost self. Quality is indeed a mighty power.

[10] A. N. Whitehead, *Religion in the Making* (New York, 1926), p. 16.

IV

It remains only to return to the initial contention, that important as Quality is for man's experience of the world, there seems no need to make it an ultimate metaphysical category, or way of functioning. It can be construed in terms of our other five; we do not need "Quality" as a sixth independent way. But to illustrate this in detail demands distinguishing at least some of the many different types of entity, with differing ontological status, that have been confusedly lumped together in the grab-bag of "quality."

1) There is first the traditional meaning, stemming from Aristotle, that takes quality as the answer to the question, *ποιόν*; *Qualis?* of what sort or kind? The Aristotelian "category" of quality is one kind of *predicate,* that indicating the *class* into which the subject falls. This kind of "quality" is what, in the scheme of ontological categories here being explored, is called a "kind" of power, an "adjective." As such, it is translatable into a "way of operating." It is what Dewey calls a "general of the form of kinds," or classes. Such a quality is not only not "unique," it is not even particular; it is the predicate in a "generic proposition," one type of what has been traditionally called a "universal."

2) Quality is also used as a particular, as one instance of a sort or kind, that is, as a power of a determinate kind. Again, there is clearly no need to introduce "quality" for such natural powers, properties, and kinds. Normally, quality in this sense is encountered in reflective experience, mediated by language, not in "immediate" experience. Such qualities, even when taken as particulars and not as kinds, are neither themselves "immediatized," nor do they serve to "immediatize" anything else.

3) Again, there are the ordinary sense-qualities, which are clearly "ways of operating," and as such translatable into "kinds of power." The grass "looks" green—it "is seen" to be green—we "see" it green. Sense qualities are ways of operating of the visual or more broadly the perceptual situation—they are "adverbs." Again, I remember how G. E. Moore, whose capacity for being horror-stricken is notoriously phenom-

enal, was horrified at the notion that in the "seeing" of grass, the grass is *doing* something.[11]

4) Again, there are the so-called "tertiary qualities"—in Santayana's sense, not Locke's. They are already past participles, outcomes of a process in which the situation has become qualified with them. In turn, they themselves serve as powers to operate and function in various ways. Both artistic and aesthetic qualities would fall under such tertiary qualities.

5) Finally, there are those peculiar Bradleyan, Deweyan, Heideggerian "pervasive" qualities, which "bind together into a whole" a work of art, a person, or an historic event. Such "underlying and pervasive qualities" are indeed for Dewey what makes a situation a single situation and a "whole":

> A situation is a whole in virtue of its immediately pervasive quality. When we describe it from the psychological side, we have to say that a situation as a qualitative whole is sensed or *felt*. . . . The pervasively qualitative is not only that which binds all constituents into a whole but it is also unique; it constitutes in each situation an *individual* situation, indivisible and unduplicable.[12]

[11] Compare Dewey: "A certain quality is experienced. When it is inquired into or thought (judged), it differentiates into 'that thing' on the one hand, and 'sweet' on the other. Both 'that thing' and 'sweet' are analytic of the quality, but are additive, synthetic, ampliative, with respect to each other. The copula 'is' marks just the effect of this distinction upon the correlative terms. . . . To say that 'that thing is sweet' means 'that thing' will *sweeten* some other object, say coffee, or a batter of milk and eggs. The intent of sweetening something formed the ground for converting a dumb quality into an articulate object of thought.

"The logical force of the copula is always that of an active verb. It is merely a linguistic peculiarity, not a logical fact, that we say 'that is red' instead of 'that reddens,' either in the sense of growing, becoming, red, or in the sense of making something else red. Even linguistically our 'is' is a weakened form of an active verb signifying 'stays' or 'stands.' But the nature of any act (designated by the true verbal form) is best apprehended in its effect and issue; we say 'is sweet' rather than 'sweetens,' 'is red' rather than 'reddens' because we define the active change by its anticipated or attained outcome. To say 'the dog is ugly' is a way of setting forth what he is likely to *do,* namely to snarl and bite. 'Man is mortal' indicates what man does or what actively is done to him, calling attention to a consequence. If we convert its verbal form into 'men die,' we realize the transitive and additive force of predication and escape the self-made difficulties of the attributive theory." "Qualitative Thought," in *Philosophy and Civilization,* pp. 105–6.

[12] John Dewey, *Logic* (New York, 1938), p. 68.

Dewey goes on to explain:

There is a difficulty in grasping the meaning of what has been said. It concerns the use of the word "quality." The word is usually associated with something specific, like *red, hard, sweet;* that is, with distinctions made within a total experience. The intended contrasting meaning may be suggested, although not adequately exemplified, by considering such qualities as are designated by the terms distressing, perplexing, cheerful, disconsolate. For these words do not designate specific qualities in the way in which hard, say, designates a particular quality of a rock. For such qualities permeate and color *all* the objects and events that are involved in an experience. The phrase "tertiary qualities," happily introduced by Santayana, does not refer to a third quality like in kind to the "primary" and "secondary" qualities of Locke and merely happening to differ in content. For a tertiary quality qualifies *all* the constituents to which it applies in thoroughgoing fashion.[13]

Dewey insists that such "a pervasive and internally integrating quality . . . regulates and controls the terms of thought."[14]

When it is said that I have a feeling, or impression, or "hunch," that things are thus and so, what is actually designated is primarily the presence of a dominating quality in a situation as a whole, not just the existence of a feeling as a psychical or psychological fact. . . . The "given," that is to say, the existent, is precisely an undetermined and dominant complex quality.[15]

All these statements could, I think, be paralleled in Heidegger—in rather different language, to be sure. And as phenomenological descriptions of human experience, the reports of both acute observers are surely accurate. Dewey's objectless "doubt," and Heidegger's objectless "dread"—*Angst*—seem to be qualities genuinely felt in experience. It

[13] *Ibid.,* p. 69. It may be doubted whether Dewey and Santayana were speaking of the same type of "quality." In "Qualitative Thought" Dewey puts it: "All thought in every subject begins with just such an unanalyzed whole. . . . Something presents itself as problematic before there is recognition of *what* the problem is. The problem is had or experienced before it can be stated or set forth; but it is had as an immediate quality of the whole situation. The sense of something problematic, of something perplexing and to be resolved, marks the presence of something pervading all elements and considerations." *Philosophy and Civilization,* p. 100.

[14] Dewey, *Philosophy and Civilization,* p. 98.

[15] *Ibid.,* pp. 100, 105.

might be said that "doubt" is the form "anxiety" takes in Dewey—and equally, that "anxiety" is the form "doubt" takes in Heidegger. It is hardly necessary here to enter into the suggestiveness or the validity of the further ontological implications these representatives of two very different cultural situations find in their respective phenomenological descriptions. It is enough to recognize that there do seem to be such "pervasive and internally integrating qualities."

But for our problem, it is enough to see that since these curious "qualities" obviously *do* something—they "bind things together into a whole," and then they go on to "regulate and control thought"—they are obviously complex powers, which are encountered as ways of operating of the Situation; and they can be easily treated and dealt with as such, without our being forced to institute a sixth ultimate metaphysical category of "Quality." Dewey clearly calls them "qualities" because they are "felt" or "intuited" in pre-reflective and pre-linguistic experience and activity—they are the object of "hunches." And for him whatever is thus "felt" non-reflectively is "quality": "'Feeling' and 'felt' are names for a *relation* of quality."[16] The background of this controlling assumption of Dewey's in Bradley and ultimately in Hegel is to the historically-minded obvious.

In conclusion, therefore, we can say: It is quite unnecessary to institute a sixth ultimate ontological category, or way of functioning, "Quality." All types of quality can be treated adequately under some one of the five categories or "ways" we have distinguished.

[16] *Ibid.,* p. 99.

EPILOGUE

Unifications of Knowledge: What Is the World to Be Unified?

AS REFLECTED in the microcosm of the modern university, the world of knowledge has today become radically plural. It is a world of many different knowledges, pursued in varied ways to diverse ends. These many inquiries are normally carried on with little thought for their relations to each other. The student of John Donne's poetry, the student of the learning curve, the student of Soviet economy, the student of the structure of the atom—each gives little enough attention to what the others are doing, and none at all to any total picture of anything. Each has his own goals, his own methods, his own language for talking about what he is doing and what he has discovered. Each seems happiest when left to his own devices, glad indeed if he can keep the others from treading on his toes. Each is convinced that what he himself is doing is worth while. But none has too much respect for the others, though he is willing enough to tolerate them. They all have little understanding of each other's pursuits—what they are trying to do, how they are doing it, and what they really mean when they talk about it. And lacking understanding, and the very possibility of communication, neither they, nor, it would seem, anyone else, is in a position to appraise the respective importance of what each is doing.

Its importance for what? The question gives us pause. For it seems to take us beyond all these manifold pursuits of special knowledges. Man, being what he is, finds it good to seek knowledges. And the mod-

---

This paper was originally prepared for the Fifth Bicentennial Conference of Columbia University, and was delivered at Arden House on October 28, 1954. It is printed in *The Unity of Knowledge,* ed. Lewis Leary (New York, 1955), pp. 63–78.

ern university, reflecting our intellectual world, seems committed to the view that it is good to seek almost any kind of knowledge. But if we stop to ask, what is the respective importance of this or that inquiry, we seem to be suggesting that they all form part of a common enterprise of learning, in which each has a role of its own to play. Without such a common enterprise, the question of importance seems to possess no significant meaning. Do all our sciences and humanities and arts in some sense belong to, or contribute to, such a common enterprise of inquiry? This is the central question raised by the diversity of our eager pursuits; and it bids fair to remain with us to the end. If we are lucky, we can hope to throw some light on what sense it is in which this is the case—in what sense our many knowledges have a place in some "unity" of knowledge.

But before we seriously embark upon this question, it is well to ask a prior question. If there indeed be in our present-day intellectual world any such sense, what wisdom could we hope to gain from such a common enterprise? What might we expect it to tell us? It would tell us something about man, surely. It would tell us how man understands. Even though the answer might be, that man understands in various ways to different ends, it would tell us that these many ways are not totally irreconcilable with each other. It might even tell us how all man's distinctively human pursuits—all those into which intelligence enters, all those that involve knowledge—are related to each other. It would contribute to our knowledge of man, and at best it might carry us toward "a whole view of man." At the very least, it would make plain to us how man's urge to know can grow into the desire to see his world whole, and not merely as the discrete parts and aspects which his separate sciences and arts select and pursue.

But is this all a common enterprise of learning would tell us—how man sees and understands his world? Would it take us beyond *his* world to *the* world—the world in which all these pursuits and activities take place, and in which whatever common enterprise they might all contribute to is carried on? For all our preoccupation today with the relativities of human knowledges and human perspectives, it is difficult to avoid the conviction that these are all perspectives on the same world. We may well ask whether our many knowledges can lead to any unified and coherent view, but it makes little sense to question whether such a view would be a view of *the* world. The world *of* knowledge may remain many; the world *for* knowledge, we assume, is one.

Is this assumption justified? Expressing what is surely the prevailing modern temper, authoritative spokesmen of two major intellectual disciplines have seriously questioned it, if they have not denied it outright. Speaking for revealed theology, Étienne Gilson [1] has shown that a world taken to be the free creation of an infinite being has ceased to be the intelligible cosmos of the classic tradition, and has become instead a world in which exploration can go on endlessly without ever becoming more complete. It is our familiar world of many adventurous pursuits and knowledges. But in it *the* world for knowledge has ceased even to exist as a problem; it is left to God alone. Speaking for physical theory, Niels Bohr [2] has generalized his complementary principle, that what we observe depends on how we set up our experiment, and pushed it into the equally valid but equally arbitrary knowledges of other cultures. Different experimental arrangements depending on the free subjective choice of the observer lead to different but equally important aspects of knowledge; the historically conditioned traditions of different cultures enable each to exhibit within its own limitations aspects of the richness and variety of human life. Thus both theology and science, which used to be the bulwarks of the faith that we are living in an intelligible universe, proclaim today that the world for knowledge is at best a pluriverse, in which many intelligibilities may indeed be sought and found, but in which the question of any unified intelligibility does not arise.

It is such a world *for* knowledge that seems to confront us. Is this all we can say of it? This much at least we must say. In truth, "the world for knowledge" seems to be a collective name for quite a mess of miscellaneous stuff. The world in which we all live and carry on our pursuits and measurably achieve our ends—poets and physicists, prophets and psychologists, saints and statesmen, musicians and anthropologists, and all the rest—assuredly displays an inexhaustible variety, ordered by no tidy housekeeping. Our many knowledges, sciences, and arts seize on their respective fields, their subject-matters, their aspects, their per-

[1] Étienne Gilson, "Theology and the Unity of Knowledge," *ibid.*, pp. 35–46.
[2] Niels Bohr, "Science and the Unity of Knowledge," *ibid.*, pp. 47–62.

spectives, and explore them in isolation. The fact that they can all do it so successfully shows that those fields and aspects and perspectives are all there, and that no one is so bound up with the rest that it can not be selected, detached, and explored in its own terms.

However far men in their craving for "unity" may try to overlook or minimize it, this thoroughgoing diversity or plurality of the world is a fundamental fact. It augurs well for the progress of philosophical inquiry in our day that some form of pluralism has come to be accepted by most responsible philosophers. Only the philosophical "nothing-butter"—the brusque apostle of the method of reductive analysis—has ever managed to get all the world's immense variety of miscellaneous stuff unified into a neat system following from a few "first principles," or dependent logically on a single "first cause." That can be done only if we happily forget everything that refuses to fit snugly into the Procrustean bed of our tidy framework. And even when we succeed in bringing forth a unified system that will somehow embrace all we know of the world, that is no proof that the world is really "one," but only that we have found a system. The wise man cannot forget that in its time the world has patiently tolerated a host of others, and that in due course it will doubtless bring forth countless more.

It is a fundamental fact that the world is radically and ineradicably plural. But equally basic is the fact that the world can be unified in human vision. Again and again the wit of man has been able to turn the trick. Now surely such works of unification are a tremendous achievement. They need not, however, be the product of great intellectual sophistication. The unknown poets responsible for the creation myths of the most "primitive" cultures—like those men of genius whose inspired thought is preserved in the opening of Genesis—were the first to see the world whole. And we dare to hope that the world can be likewise unified in the vision that is knowledge and science, even as it has so often been unified in the vision that is myth and symbol. It has been the dream of physics, which its history has surely gone far to encourage, that men might some day discover a single unified formula of calculation and prediction. Fortunately, the practice of physics has not had to await the consummation of that hope. But physics has exhibited a significant trend toward unification, and scientists have been able to institute progressively more general ideas or principles, in terms of which the available facts do fall into a systematic and intelligible order.

But the fact that the world can be unified in vision through myth and symbol, even the fact that it has been slowly approaching unification in knowledge and science, is no proof that the world constitutes in sober truth a "unity." It is proof only that the world *can become* unified in vision, and more doubtfully in knowledge. No one—not even a Creator—could generate the world, with all its infinite and inexhaustible variety, out of physical theory. Physics certainly did not create the world. The world rather gave birth to physics and physicists. And if our best established unified knowledge cannot be said to have created the world, still less can our many other unified visions and systems be credited with the responsibility for what is. Such unification is a human achievement, man's bringing of the world to a focus.

The world provokes man to many and diverse systems of unification in terms of his varied pursuits and knowledges. This clearly tells us much about man, and about what is distinctively human in his nature. It tells us so much that Ernst Cassirer could see in these systems the major clue to that nature—in the way man achieves his unifications through his methods, his languages, and his symbols. In following up this insight, we are really concerned with a single theme—the nature of man. For the nature of man is what he does that is human, and how he does it, by means of his symbolic instruments of unification.

But we are also concerned with the world. For what man does, in all his sciences and arts, is to explore the world in which he finds himself, and to express and communicate his experience of and in that world. His ways of exploring and expressing and communicating tell us what he is—but they also tell us what he finds. That the world provokes man to so many different unifications through knowledge and vision tells us much about man. But it also tells us much about the world, which so obviously lends itself to those unifications. If we are to see the world whole and entire, indeed, if we are to see *the* world at all, and not just this or that aspect, we must see it as having a place for them all.

For our knowledge of the world and our knowledge of man clearly go together. Our knowledge of man is not merely of the intricate and curious way he is put together—it is a knowledge of all the many things he can do in and with the world. And our knowledge of the world is not merely a knowledge of what a world would be like without any men in it—it is a knowledge of all man can find in and make out of the world. Making poems and building mathematical systems, creating symphonies and a science of physics, working out a biology and finding and praying to God—human experience in this concrete and evident sense is the source of all our knowledge of the world, and equally of all our knowledge of man. Through all these arts man discovers the world, and discovers himself. Our knowledge of the world and our knowledge of man go together.

And if these many arts that man practices in a sustaining world seem at times irrelevant to each other, and indeed often difficult to reconcile—if the biology man has constructed leads to a knowledge of his biological make-up and behavior that sheds no light on his vision of a God who condemns his unrighteousness—this is a failure equally to see how man's pursuits fit together, and how the aspects of the world that generate them fit together. If we have achieved no coherent view of the world, it is because we have no whole view of man. And if we have no coherent view of man, it is because we have no whole view of the world. Our knowledge of the world and our knowledge of man still go together, even in our ignorance. Both are involved in any unification of knowledge. The pursuit of such unification forces us to consider the problems of both.

What are the implications of the fact that we must know man and the world together, and cannot know either apart? The world for knowledge, it is clear, must be a world with man in it. It cannot be taken as a world from which man and all his works have been carefully eliminated. Not only would a world without man not be man's world. Such a world would not even be a world for knowledge; it would be a world in which there was no knowledge, and in which nothing could be known. We can indeed conceive the world before man appeared in it, but we cannot conceive the world without the possibility that man would there appear, to find in it all he does find. For strive as we may, we can never forget what was to come. All our theories of evolution are inescapably theories of how a world with man in it came to be.

Nor is the world for knowledge a world to be known and understood without reference to man. We cannot first work out a scheme for understanding the world to which everything human is irrelevant, and then claim to understand man in terms of that scheme—or man's world. For a world with man in it is a different world from a world defined regardless of man. It is a world in which many things occur and are made and found that would not occur without man. And the world in which they occur cannot be understood as being what it is without their occurrence. Man's world—the world for knowledge—cannot be reduced to a world without man—even if we then note man's presence, as something that introduces confusion and threatens to spoil it all, and so try to fit man and all his pursuits into the scheme in which we see the world. We shall not that way see the world. We shall see only those features which everything in the world possesses in common—stars and rocks and amoebae and men—atoms, perhaps, and what we used to call laws. That is not a portrait of the world, that is only a blueprint. Man's finding of those common features, in himself as elsewhere, has been of momentous importance, and surely his making of blueprints is one of his most significant arts. But those blueprints leave out all the features of the world that have been disclosed by man's presence in it —all the possibilities revealed by his many other arts.

For all that man does, from birth to death, from waking to thinking, is a genuine co-working with the world. In realizing the world's possibilities, it is a revelation of what those possibilities are. Man's life in all its manifold productions makes clear what the intricate engines his blueprints describe can do, with man to direct them. The world is surely all that man can do in and with it and make out of it; it cannot be less. His doing and his making are a genuine discovery about the world. They are a finding of what the world contains.

A world with man in it contains the richness of human experience. It holds terror and love and thinking and imagination, good and evil and the wrestling with them, knowledge and ignorance and the search for truth, failure, frustration, defeat, beauty and vision and tragedy and comedy, the abyss of despair and the love of God. It has the reflective commentary of the spirit of man on all these wonders, the imaginative expression of what man has felt and suffered and thought and judged, the concentration of it all in words and paint and stone and sound. It has the pursuit of the ideal and the vision of the Divine.

All these things are found in a world with man in it. This is the world for knowledge, the world that challenges us to tell how they are found and just how they are there. To be sure, it takes men to find them, even as it takes men to find the equations of physics. Without man's aid a star might well find other things, and understand the world differently—or an angel. Stars, however, seem neither to find nor to understand anything; and angels, admirable creatures though they be, have left us no reports of their philosophic achievements. But surely there is no inference that because only men find anything, what they find is not found. The finding is a finding in the world, in cooperation with the world's possibilities. The fact that we must see, and, hopefully, understand the world from a human focus, is not only a fact about human vision and understanding—and since human vision and understanding are the only ones we know of, a fact about all vision and understanding. It is also a fact about the world. The world is seen whole and brought to a selective unification only in a focus the world has itself generated in revealing its possibilities to man.

If all these things be in the world, if they must be seen there to see the world, if a view of *the* world for knowledge must see them all—then the enterprises that see what the world does with man in it are fully as important for seeing the world as the enterprises that inquire into how the world is put together and works its wonders to perform. What we call the humanities and the arts are equally necessary with what we call the natural sciences for seeing the world in all its variety and richness. Indeed, they may well claim to be more important, for they reveal what the world can do, its possibilities, far more adequately than does a knowledge of the devices by which the world does it. Even that knowledge itself is more significant as a revelation of possibility—the possibility of endless inquiry—than as inquiry consummated and achieved. Science is more revealing as a pursuit, as a humanity, as an art, than as a body of knowledge arrested and completed, soon stale as last week's newspaper. It is the humanities and the arts, and the sciences as human arts, that present to us most fully the world for knowledge. Their visions of the world are what must be seen if we are to see the world and all that in it lies, if we are to acknowledge what is and to discern what might be.

This is the world of vision—of the seeing of what man finds in the world. But it is only the world *for* knowledge, the world that is a challenge to be known, and, if possible, to be understood. It is not yet the world *of* knowledge. For vision is not understood by vision itself. What man finds and sees, in all its variety, is a subject-matter to be understood; the finding and the seeing are not ways of understanding. The poet's vision of man's life in the world is not an understanding of that life; the saint's vision of God is not an understanding of what the Divine is—though what the poet or the saint sees is surely there—if may be, to be understood.

But what can we mean by understanding what men have found and seen, out of all that is and all that might be, of the world and its possibilities? We can, it seems, mean at least three different things: understanding what the vision is, understanding what it means, and understanding how what is seen and the seeing are brought about. Broadly, we can say that the arts give the first understanding, the humanities the second, and the sciences the third. What the vision *is* can only be understood by sharing it; and the many languages of the many arts, including the art of religion, are devices for communicating and sharing what has been found and seen. What the vision *means* can only be understood by relating it to other things; this is the function of interpretation, clarification, and criticism, which belongs to the humanities as disciplines; and here I would place both theology and philosophy. How the vision, the seeing and what is seen, is brought about, the devices by which the world has produced it, belong to the sciences, of nature and of man. But this is far too simple a divison of labor. For all three are arts, in finding and revealing what is and what might be, though they are not all sciences; and all are humanities, in clarifying and criticising meanings. It is functions rather than disciplines that are here distinguished.

We have, then, three major ways of understanding the world of vision—of understanding what man finds in the world. Are we to call what each of the three gives us, equally "knowledge"? The question seems idle, and any answer gratuitous. Would we deny knowledge to Plato and Dante, to Shakespeare and Goethe, because they are poets and not scientists? Surely they have seen the world. And who would deny knowledge to Kant and to Thomas, yes, to Dewey and to Niebuhr, who, being poets who have seen the world, are also critics and interpreters who have explored the meanings and the relations of what they have seen?

Do we have then three kinds of "knowledge"—vision, interpretation and criticism, and science? If we take knowledge broadly, so it can be said. But in what sense can these three kinds of knowledge hope to find a "unity"? How are they related? Surely they are not rivals—their aims, their ways of understanding are too different for them to compete. And surely they do not just lie side by side, supplementing each other, though they all alike exist and are sought in a world with man in it. Their cooperation seems more intimate than that. The knowledge that is vision of what a world with man in it contains has a kind of primacy—it presents to the others the subject-matter to be understood, what men have found there. The specific knowledge of the artist—the man who finds—is an understanding how to make us see and find what he has seen and found. The knowledge that is science tries to discover the conditions of the being and the finding of what is found, the devices that make both possible, on which they depend. The knowledge that is interpretation and criticism seems to require both the others. In seeking the meaning of what is found, in relating it to other findings and other meanings, it must know both what a world with man in it can do, and how it does it. It must seek to relate possibilities to their conditions, outcomes and eventuations to the devices by which they are achieved. This third kind of knowledge seems thus to call for a fuller understanding than either of the others alone.

What sort of "unity" may we hope to find within each of these three kinds of knowledge? In the knowledge that is vision and finding, the outlook is not promising. Many radically different things have been found, and so long as the world has man in it, many more will be. Every new poem, every new prophet's vision, will reveal new possibilities in the world, and these possibilities are in no significant sense "one." Visions are many, and many are the unified visions to which they can be pushed; but there is no unity of visions. The very idea is unintelligible and repellent. If, then, there be no unity in what is found, save that it is all found in the same world, is there a discoverable unity in the way of finding? This is the problem the experts on method must wrestle with—do all the various arts, with their various media and symbolic devices, pursue any common way in coming to see what they see? Is there indeed a common way in a single art even, like poetry or music or religion? Or are there rather many ways of making poems and songs and finding the Divine? Is there a common language in which all the arts tell us what they have found? Or if the tongues remain many, are they in any sense mutually translatable?

In the knowledge that is science, great claims have been made for unity. Science has indeed been unified in terms of a single scientific method—again and again, for the particular method for which the claim has been advanced has never proved able to embrace all fields and all subject-matters, and men have had to try once more, with a method more adequate. The claim is perhaps idle, for different fields notoriously demand differing procedures, and the unity of method can always be maintained by excluding from the single method these varying procedures. More recently, science has been unified in terms of a single language of science, though again the common language clearly requires different vocabularies in the various sciences, and the attempt to formulate a language of "basic science" is still an ideal.

These "unities" of science remain as yet human unifications of the world of science, more interesting to the interpreter, the philosopher, than to the scientists themselves. But the world does still reveal, if not a unity, at least a continuity of the conditions by which it does all it does—a continuity of those devices by which all its processes are brought about. However distinctive their outcomes—whether they eventuate in a star, a dog, or a poem—they seem bound up together in a network of common interactions without which they would not be. And this network can be followed out indefinitely—there is no field into which it does not lead us. It can be, and has been, pursued into man and all his works. The conditions and devices found elsewhere are found also in the life of man. Nothing has proved more futile than the repeated attempts to set barriers to the tracing out of this network. Our successive dualisms, claiming that man, or at least something in man, is not like all else caught up in it, have always broken down. The world for science knows no limits—it is coextensive with the world of vision, with everything man finds in the world. Tracing this network of causes and conditions may not tell us all we want to know, about the world, or about man; but it always tells us something, and what it tells is truly told. There can be no gainsaying the story. It encounters many complications at many points—when it comes to tell us about living things, or when it comes to man; and new chapters are required. But there is no fresh start. The world for science may not be a unity. But it is at least a continuity of processes and conditions, making possible a continuity of inquiry, a continuity of analysis, a continuity of scientific method.

This continuity of processes found has suggested to many an eventual unification of the causes and conditions of things into a single system—an eventual unity of the knowledge that is science. This seems a not unreasonable hope. It clearly possesses great value as an ideal of science—as what Kant called a regulative idea. Surely here if anywhere in our knowledges we may hope to look for system, coherence, even "unity." Doubtless it will always remain what it has been heretofore, a process of unification. But the notion of an ideal limit to be approached seems not wholly inappropriate.

But the world approaching unification through science is not identical with *the* world for knowledge. That world contains much else besides. It contains also everything these processes and conditions are able to accomplish, all the manifold eventuations and outcomes found in a world with man in it. And here is not even continuity, in any sense that would obliterate encountered distinctions of importance, of value, of meaning. Uniqueness and individuality are characteristic of the products and outcomes that man finds. Here are many dimensions and many levels, new beginnings and fresh starts. And it is just here that the knowledge that is interpretation and criticism operates, trying to relate the many things a world with man in it does, to each other, and to the way it does them—trying to relate possibilities to each other and to their conditions, trying to find what they mean.

The knowledge that is criticism and interpretation, since it is trying to establish relations, is itself a never-ending process of unification. When pushed, it becomes, in the philosopher, the attempt to understand *the* world in the light of the totality of its possibilities and of their conditions. But the world's possibilities have no discoverable totality—man is forever finding out more. Even their conditions are not unified in any existent science. Hence the unifications of meaning are many, and must so remain. We can understand the world whole in many ways—find many meanings in terms of which to unify it. Here is no unity. But here is the opportunity for more and more comprehensive unifications—as men learn more of the world's possibilities, and come to understand more of the other meanings that other men and cultures have found.

Do our three ways of understanding, then, commit us to three kinds of truth? I think and hope not; it seems more confusing than clarifying so to speak. The knowledge that is vision is what it is. We can ask of the poet or the painter or the saint or the prophet only if his vision be genuine or authentic. The only test is whether he knows how to make us see what he sees, and find what he has found. The knowledge that is interpretation and criticism is better called an understanding of significance or meaning than of truth. "Adequacy" seems the best name for its test. It is well to keep "truth" for the knowledge that is science, with all its complex procedures and criteria for verifying propositions that can be stated. We should then be left with vision, truth, and meaning.

But perhaps the scientists themselves are abandoning "truth" as the name for their knowledge, for some other property like "confirmability" or "warranted assertibility." And in calling the understanding of meaning something to be judged by its "adequacy," I remember the old definition of truth as "adequation of thing and understanding." Perhaps after all we have come the full circle, and it is now the unifications of the world in the light of some meaning understood that we are permitted to call "true." If so, this "truth" of meaning is not to be confused with the knowledge that is science. It is rather the Truth of which it was said of old, "Ye shall know the truth, and the truth shall make you free."

And so we come back to our central question: is there a common enterprise of inquiry to which all our arts and sciences and humanities contribute? Have we found it? It is not the enterprise of the artist—the poet, the musician, the saint. His contribution is essential, but his own enterprise is not to contribute: it is to make what he makes and find what he finds, though his makings and findings tell us what we have to understand. It is not the enterprise of the scientist, though that too is essential to it: his enterprise is to explore the processes and conditions he sets out to explore. He can indeed hope for a unification of his own, a unification of the sciences in terms of their method, their language, their continuity of processes. But the unity of science achieved would not be the unification of the world. No, our common enterprise seems to be the enterprise of the critic and interpreter, of the humanist and philosopher, of the searcher after more adequate meaning. Drawing on both the others, he can hope to unify the world for knowledge through a meaning found. He must indeed see the world from a selective focus, but he can hope to see it steadily and whole. In asking our question, for a coherent and adequate view of the world, whatever our special knowledges, we are all in the end humanists and philosophers. The answers will be ours, and we shall not agree. But the question is not ours alone. It is the question the world poses to the searcher after more adequate meaning. What is the world, that man is mindful of it? What is man, that he is mindful of the world? These questions—no, this single question, in all its ramifications—is what the world for knowledge asks of him who seeks to know the world. The answers are many; the question at least is one.

INDEX